Computer Incident Response and Forensics Team Management

Computer Incident Response and Forensics Team Management

Conducting a Successful Incident Response

Leighton R. Johnson III

Mike Kessler, Technical Editor

AMSTERDAM • BOSTON • HEIDELBERG • LONDON
NEW YORK • OXFORD • PARIS • SAN DIEGO
SAN FRANCISCO • SINGAPORE • SYDNEY • TOKYO
Syngress is an imprint of Elsevier

Acquiring Editor: *Chris Katsaropoulos*
Editorial Project Manager: *Benjamin Rearick*
Project Manager: *Punithavathy Govindaradjane*
Designer: *Matthew Limbert*

Syngress is an imprint of Elsevier
225 Wyman Street, Waltham, MA 02451, USA

Notices
Knowledge and best practice in this field are constantly changing. As new research and experience broaden our understanding, changes in research methods or professional practices, may become necessary. Practitioners and researchers must always rely on their own experience and knowledge in evaluating and using any information or methods described herein. In using such information or methods they should be mindful of their own safety and the safety of others, including parties for whom they have a professional responsibility.

To the fullest extent of the law, neither the Publisher nor the authors, contributors, or editors, assume any liability for any injury and/or damage to persons or property as a matter of products liability, negligence or otherwise, or from any use or operation of any methods, products, instructions, or ideas contained in the material herein.

Library of Congress Cataloging-in-Publication Data
Johnson, Leighton.
  Computer incident response and forensics team management: conducting a successful incident response/Leighton Johnson.
    pages cm
  Includes bibliographical references and index.
  ISBN 978-1-59749-996-5 (alk. paper)
  1. Computer crimes--Investigation. 2. Evidence, Criminal. 3. Forensic sciences. I. Title.
  HV8079.C65J637 2014
  658.4'78--dc23

                                                                                              2013035259

British Library Cataloguing-in-Publication Data
A catalogue record for this book is available from the British Library

ISBN: 978-1-59749-996-5

Printed and bound in the United States of America
14 15 16 17 18 10 9 8 7 6 5 4 3 2 1

For information on all Syngress publications,
visit our website at *store.elsevier.com/Syngress*

Working together
to grow libraries in
developing countries

www.elsevier.com • www.bookaid.org

Dedication

I dedicate this book to RKS who has supported me throughout
the writing and editing of this book.

Contents

Contents

About the Author

Leighton Johnson, the CTO of ISFMT (Information Security Forensics Management Team), a provider of computer security, forensics consulting, and certification training, has presented computer security, cyber security and forensics classes, training and seminars all across the United States and Europe. He has over 35 years of experience in Computer Security, Cyber Security, Forensics and Incident Response, Software Development, and Communications Equipment Operations and Maintenance.

Introduction

When I started as the corporate Computer Security Manager for a large retail organization 15 years ago, there was no response team, no computer security awareness among the IT staff or senior management, and no driving need to implement any security activities, structures, or requirements for the corporate workers. Everyone from the CEO down thought the computer security situation was someone else's problem and concern—the classic "not my problem" syndrome.

The first task I embarked on as the Computer Security Manager was to educate the senior executives in the need for corporate computer security and the ability to respond to potential threats to the work environment. It took almost a year, but the corporate leadership did finally accept and fund the development of an incident response capability which was that industry's first team specifically designed to handle and manage incidents which affected the day-to-day operations of the organization and its "bottom line."

Security Incident Response and Forensics Response Teams (SIR&FT) are needed more today than ever before during the Computer and Internet Era which has developed over the last 40 years. Today, with most security response organizations and vendors reporting an incredible 30,000–70,000 pieces of new malware being introduced each day, the need for responders and investigators is at an all-time high. Every major corporation, all governmental agencies, and most organizations operating on the Internet, using e-mail, or transacting business online require the ability to respond to an unexpected or malicious attack on their networks and infrastructure just to stay in business, let alone perform their daily tasks safely and securely.

All incidents threaten the business or government organization as a whole. The organization's primary business process, all its other processes and reputation—they are all in jeopardy when these incidents strike. Security incident response and management seek to prevent such incidents from happening. And when they inevitably happen, to contain and resolve them, and use the response lessons learned for the next time. Therefore, security incident

1

response and management serve both the primary response process and the organization as a whole.

Since the proliferation of malware is rampant today where the adversary eventually breaches some aspect of a corporation's protective measures, along with the high impact of insider threat issues as evidence by recent Corporate, Intelligence and Defense incidents, the primary focus for the SIR&FT is simple but profound:

1. detect compromise as efficiently as possible;
2. respond to incidents as quickly as possible; and
3. investigate using digital forensics as effectively as possible.

The Incident Response team will become one of your most important development activities as the manager in the first days as you start up the management and oversight of the security incident response team (SIRT) and the Forensics investigation team. The team member makeup, the team charter, the corporate executive officer support, the response criteria, all make the SIRT one of the more important team-building activities you will be responsible for at the start.

These SIR&FT have very specialized management needs in order to accomplish their goals in today's work and response environments. The SIR&FT need to be constructed with general skills and specialties; however, during the response activity, the skills needed maybe other than originally planned and the Team Manager must change the team members and the skills rapidly to meet the threat and necessary response.

This book introduces the special management needs and requirements for Incident Response and Forensics Teams, how these teams are constructed and developed, the team members and support staff, and the basic framework for managing response and forensics teams. Ensuring that proven policies and procedures are established and followed are manager level responsibilities, along with personnel certifications and levels of expertise. These will be discussed along with Incident Response Team Makeup and Management.

SIR&FT management personnel have many areas of focus to address and requirements to meet. They include:

A. *First, ensuring team members are properly hired, trained, and certified.* The criticality of the response always will require the best of the best to respond.
B. *Second, ensuring the Incident Response Team has the proper unencumbered senior executive level support, authority, and responsibility.* Full exposure and support at the top of the corporate leader is needed and required these days in the business world with Sarbanes-Oxley Law (SOX) reporting requirements, industrial espionage threats, and the competitive nature of each industry.

C. Third, proper case management activities are performed, which include:

- *Investigator time and schedule management.* Each case requires detailed oversight and management to ensure full accountability and proper actions during the investigation.
- *Quality assurance processes.* Ensuring the accuracy of every investigation is often the key to an investigation.
- *Chain of custody procedures.* Following the proper methods for evidence collection and analysis is important to the proper prosecution of any case.
- *Change management.* Making sure the software, hardware, and tools used during the case activities is vital to providing the legal framework of the case.
- *Final review of all case work.* Full review of all of the case details is commonly where the manager can provide the best return on expertise and viability of the case.

D. Fourth, provide the proper response at the proper level for the currently active incident while simultaneously making sure the incident is contained, controlled, repaired, and reported on correctly and in accordance with corporate or organizational policies and guidance.

E. Fifth, ensuring all legal, regulatory, statutory, organizational, and governmental guidance for incident handling and reporting is met within the appropriate time frames.

This book is intended to provide to the SIR&FT manager the answers to the following questions to insure their activities are acceptable, legal, and complete:

a. Have the team members met their objectives?
The objectives may include incident fixed or removed, report been delivered and accepted, security posture improved as result of lessons learned about attack; and many others.

b. Is the incident contained and eradicated?
The basic requirement for the security group is to "secure the data," so now the data should be protected and controlled, the issue which prompted the SIRT response completed and the corporate equipment which was "compromised" has been either cleaned or removed from operations.

c. Have the users returned to normal business operations?
The operational need for the SIRT is to get the normal business operations back in place and functioning, so always place that as one of the goals for any response.

d. Have all activities been completed in a reasonable amount of time?
Each team member will have a set of tasks to accomplish during the response, so quick completion of these will allow faster response and return to normal operations for the organization and the personnel.

e. Did the team respond quickly and efficiently?
    Ensuring the timing requirements for business recovery needs to be quickly assessed during the initial stages of the response, so all actions by the response team need to be expeditious and complete.

f. Was there any time where response actions could have been performed earlier?
    Looking at the response effort, the team leader needs to assess if any of the required actions could have been accomplished earlier in the actions, or if any pre-deployed tools would have assisted in the response effort.

g. Were the team member's skills applicable to incident?
    One of the SIRT manager's jobs is to assess the team in reference to the response and see if any additional skills, techniques, or knowledge would have contributed to a quicker and possibly safer resolution to the incident.

h. Have team members followed the documented procedures?
    Reviewing the generated reports and documentation allows the SIRT manager to verify the proper procedures and techniques were followed during the response.

i. Were all activities reported and written down?
    All incident response actions need to be documented for after action reports, improvement of skills and abilities, and to place the organization in a strong position to handle any external or potential legal action.

j. Are team members turning in quality and defendable documentation?
    Always making sure all documentation is detailed, direct, and technically strong is a criterion for all SIRT members. Does the report make sense and does it follow the events are both questions to be answered by the SIRT manager.

k. Is the documentation being produced in correct format?
    The SIRT manager has to have a documentation guide for each team member that they must follow during and after an event is responded to by the team.

l. Is all the document content in the report?
    The full and complete "picture" of all of the events making up the incident response need to be recorded and delineated within the final incident report.

m. Are team members performing in an efficient and effective manner?
    Utilizing the skills and knowledge each has, the team members have to be evaluated to ensure they performed correctly in the response.

n. Are the incident/forensics artifacts controlled through the proper chain of evidence?
    The "chain of custody" for the gathered and retrieved artifacts must be maintained during and after the event for proper handling and so they do not become contaminated during subsequent activities.

o. Are the team members properly certified?
All team members should be professionally certified in their areas of expertise, as well as in the incident handling procedures they use during the response activity.

p. What are the lessons learned from each incident?
Conducting a "lessons learned" meeting after the completion of the response always brings new areas for training and skill development for the SIRT which will improve their abilities for the next incident response.

We will discuss all these areas and more as we explore the SIR&FT Management arena in today's "wild west" operational environment in three parts:

1. Part 1 will cover the management of Incident Response teams, starting with an explanation of what incident response is and the two standard methods for incident response. Then we will discuss the requirements for team members. The incident evidence gathering process is next, along with what IR tools are available for use. The IR policies, procedures, and legal considerations are then defined, discussed, and explained for the IR Team Manager. We close out Part 1 with a review of the various governmental statutory and regulatory requirements for Incident Response.

2. Part 2 covers managing and directing the Forensics Teams. The Forensics process is explained and the Team Member requirements are defined. The Management Policies and procedures are then discussed and my personal experience has shown this area is usually not well defined in an organization. The management of forensics evidence is then discussed along with chain of custody requirements and the tools which can be used during the forensics investigation. The legalities of forensics investigations in various parts of the world are then explored, along with some general forensics team management oversight observations.

3. Part 3 defines some general team management criteria, corporate relationships for the team and team manager. It closes with the Relationship Management needs with all of the outside entities the Teams will interface with during their activities, such as Law Enforcement, The IT Staff, the various lines of business units within the organization, outside consultants and subject matter experts, etc.

We close with a summary and appendixes of tools, references, and research sources.

Definitions

This section provides definitions and descriptions of the various terms, jobs, roles and responsibilities, and positions within the response and forensics teams.

First, we will list a couple of primary definitions, and then the definitions in alphabetical order:

Event: An "event" is any observable occurrence in a system and/or network. An event can indicate that an incident is occurring. Examples include:

- Entries in system boot logs (eventlog/syslog)
- System crash
- Network performance slowdown
- 500 new e-mail messages in last 5 min
- Modified checksum on login.exe.

Incident: An adverse event in an information system, and/or network, or the threat of the occurrence of such an event. Incident implies impact and harm or the attempt to harm. Also defined as an assessed occurrence that actually or potentially jeopardizes the confidentiality, integrity, or availability of an information system; or the information the system processes, stores, or transmits; or that constitutes a violation or imminent threat of violation of security policies, security procedures, or acceptable use policies. Examples include:

- Malicious code attacks
- Probes and network mapping
- Unauthorized access
- Unauthorized utilization of services
- Denial of service (DOS)
- Misuse
- Espionage
- Hoaxes
- Virus
- Intrusions.

Accountability: The security goal that generates the requirement for actions of an entity to be traced uniquely to that entity. This supports nonrepudiation, deterrence, fault isolation, intrusion detection and prevention, and after-action recovery and legal action.

Adware: Software typically installed that displays advertisements (such as browser pop-ups). Often in today's computing environment, adware is loaded and tracked without the user's knowledge or consent.

Artifact: A recoverable object created by actions of humans; especially an object remaining from a particular action, period, or time frame.

Attack Cycle: The process of malicious activity that attempts to collect, disrupt, deny, degrade, or destroy information system resources or the information itself. This is often expressed as the four Ps of Attack: Penetrate, Pilfer, Persist, and Proliferate.

Attacker: Person or entity performing any kind of malicious activity that attempts to collect, disrupt, deny, degrade, or destroy information system resources or the information itself.

Attribution: The process of ascribing origin to an object, artifact, incident, or event.

Authenticity: The property of being genuine and being able to be verified and trusted; confidence in the validity of a transmission, a message, or message originator. This process allows one to know for sure the origin of the information and the originator of the data.

Availability: The property of being accessible and usable upon demand by an authorized entity. Ensuring timely and reliable access to and use of information, or in other words, being able to get what you want when you want it.

Botnet: Shorted term for Robot Network, this is a network of compromised computers and servers that are remotely controlled by unauthorized personnel where the compromised devices are performing activities not under the control of the main user.

Chain of Custody: A process that shows the current and all past retention of a piece of evidence and all activities which relate to that piece of evidence during the course of investigative action.

Chain of Evidence: A process and record that shows who obtained the evidence; where and when the evidence was obtained; who secured the evidence; and who had control or possession of the evidence. The "sequencing" of the chain of evidence follows this order: collection and identification; analysis; storage; preservation; presentation in court; return to owner.

Computer Forensics: The practice of gathering, retaining, and analyzing computer-related data for investigative purposes in a manner that maintains the integrity of the data.

Computer Trespass: It consists of, with malicious intent, copying, altering, or erasing data from a computer, causing a computer to malfunction, causing an electronic funds transfer, etc., unauthorized installation and use of software Keyloggers.

Confidentiality: The property that information is not disclosed to system entities (users, processes, devices) unless they have been authorized to access the information. Preserving authorized restrictions on information access and disclosure, including means for protecting personal privacy and proprietary information. This is the process that allows you to get what you are allowed to get and nothing more.

Court of Jurisdiction: The practical authority granted to a formally constituted legal body or to a political leader to deal with and make pronouncements on legal matters and, by implication, to administer justice within a defined area of responsibility.

Cracking: Breaking into or circumventing a computer system (such as copy protection).

Cybercrime: These crimes are usually offenses that are committed against individuals or groups of individuals with a criminal motive to intentionally harm the reputation of the victim or cause physical or mental harm to the victim directly or indirectly, using modern telecommunication networks such as Internet and mobile phones. This category of crime tends to include crimes on or through a computer; generally, however, it may be divided into two categories: (1) crimes that target computers directly and (2) crimes facilitated by computer networks or devices, the primary target of which is independent of the computer network or device.

Crimes that primarily target computer networks or devices include:

- Computer viruses
- DOS attacks
- Malware (malicious code).

Crimes that use computer networks or devices to advance other ends include:

- Cyberstalking
- Fraud and identity theft
- Information warfare
- Phishing scams.

Cyberterrorism: The intentional use of computer, networks, and public Internet to cause destruction and harm for personal objectives which may be political or ideological. The use of Internet-based attacks in terrorist activities, including acts of deliberate, large-scale disruption of computer networks, especially of personal computers attached to the Internet, by the means of tools such as computer viruses. This can include use of information technology to organize and execute attacks against networks, computer systems and telecommunications infrastructures, or for exchanging information or making threats electronically. Examples are hacking into computer systems, introducing viruses to vulnerable networks, website defacing, DOS attacks, or terroristic threats made via electronic communication.

Digital Signature: A digital signature is a mathematical encryption mechanism for proving the authenticity of a digital message or document. A valid digital signature gives a recipient reason to believe that the message was created by a known sender, such that the sender cannot deny having sent the message (authentication and nonrepudiation) and that the message was not altered in transit (integrity). Digital signatures are commonly used for software distribution, financial transactions, and in other cases where it is important to detect forgery or tampering.

Encryption: This is the basic process of encoding messages (or information) in such a way that eavesdroppers or hackers cannot read it, but that authorized parties can read it. Encryption is the sending side of the scrambling of the data to make it unintelligible. Decryption is the receiving side of the data scrambling.

Examiner: The assigned person who conducts the detailed review and analysis of the evidence and artifacts gathered for the potential case.

Exclusivity: The process which ensures that only the intended recipients can use the information as it is being presented or delivered; shutting out all others from a part of or sharing the information.

File Attributes: File attributes are metadata associated with computer files that define file system behavior. Each attribute can have one of two states: set and cleared. Attributes are considered distinct from other metadata, such as dates and times, filename extensions or file system permissions. In addition to files, folders, volumes, and other file system objects may have attributes.

File Protection: Aggregate of processes and procedures designed to inhibit unauthorized access, contamination, elimination, modification, or destruction of a file or any of its contents.

Forensics Copy: An accurate bit-for-bit reproduction of the information contained on an electronic device or associated media, whose validity and integrity has been verified using an accepted algorithm. Also known as a "Bit-Stream Image" copy.

Hacker: Unauthorized user who attempts to or gains access to an information system.

Hashing: The process of using a mathematical algorithm against data to produce a numeric value that is representative of that data; these hash algorithms which map arbitrarily long inputs into a fixed-size output such that it is very difficult (computationally infeasible) to find two different hash inputs that produce the same output. Such algorithms are an essential part of the process of producing fixed-size digital signatures that can both authenticate the signer and provide for data integrity checking (detection of input modification after signature).

Identification: An act or process that presents an identifier to a system so that the system can recognize a system entity (e.g., user, process, or device) and distinguish that entity from all others.

Impact Level: The magnitude of harm that can be expected to result from the consequences of unauthorized disclosure of information, unauthorized modification of information, unauthorized destruction of information, or loss of information or information system availability.

Incident Handling: The one service that involves all the processes or tasks associated with handling events and incidents. It involves multiple functions:

- Detection and reporting: The ability to receive and review event information, incident reports, and alerts.
- Triage: The action taken to categorize, prioritize, and assign events and incidents.
- Analysis: The attempt to determine what has happened, what is the impact and threat, what damage has resulted, and what recovery or mitigation steps should be followed.
- Incident response: The action taken to resolve or mitigate an incident, coordinates and disseminates information, and implements follow-up strategies to prevent recurring incidents.

Incident Response: Security Incident Response involves the monitoring and detection of security events on a computer or computer network, and the execution of proper responses to those events. Computer security incident response is a specialized form of incident management, the primary purpose of which is the development of a well understood and predictable response to damaging events and computer intrusions.

Integrity: The property whereby an entity has not been modified in an unauthorized manner. Guarding against improper information modification or destruction to ensure that information stays the way it was intended to be.

Intent: The intent to commit a crime: malice, as evidenced by a criminal act; intent to deprive or defraud the true owner of his property. A person *intends* a consequence they *foresee* that it will happen if the given series of acts or omissions continue, and *desires* it to happen.

Intrusion: The unauthorized act of bypassing the security mechanisms of a system for the purposes of causing an incident.

Intrusion Detection System: A device or software application that monitors network or system activities for malicious activities or policy violations and produces reports to a management station. Intrusion Detection Systems are used for identifying possible incidents, logging information about them, and reporting attempts, identifying problems with security policies, documenting existing threats and deterring individuals from violating security policies.

Investigator: The assigned person who conducts the initial capture of forensics data and initiates the chain of custody for the investigative evidence for the potential case.

Key Logger: Software or hardware device which performs the action of recording (or logging) the keys struck on a keyboard, typically in a covert manner so that the person using the keyboard is unaware that their actions are being monitored.

LEO: Law Enforcement Officer, usually from, but not limited to, the local or regional law enforcement agency which will response to request for support during an incident or investigation.

Logic Bomb: A piece of code intentionally inserted into a software system that will set off a malicious function when specified conditions are met.

Malware: Malicious software which is designed to damage or disable computers with the intent to steal information or gain control of the device. Software or firmware intended to perform an unauthorized process that will have adverse impact on the confidentiality, integrity, or availability of an information system. Examples include virus, worm, Trojan horse, or other code-based entity that infects a host. Spyware and some forms of adware are also examples of malicious code.

Man-in-the-Middle attack: A form of active wiretapping attack in which the attacker intercepts and selectively modifies communicated data to masquerade as one or more of the entities involved in a communication association.

Network: Information system(s) implemented with a collection of interconnected components. Such components may include routers, hubs, cabling, telecommunications controllers, key distribution centers, and technical control devices.

Nonrepudiation: Assurance that the sender of information is provided with proof of delivery and the recipient is provided with proof of the sender's identity, so neither can later deny having processed the information. This protection against an individual falsely denying having performed a particular action provides the capability to determine whether a given individual took a particular action such as creating information, sending a message, approving information, and receiving a message.

Obfuscation: Concealing the meaning of something by making it harder to read.

Obligation: The requirement for an investigator or examiner to guarantee that due diligence requirements are fulfilled during the process of incident handling and/or forensics investigation.

Packet Sniffing: The act of intercepting others' network packets and reading them, allowing a person to read another's e-mail, view the same websites, read conversations, among other activities.

Penetration Test: A test methodology in which assessors, typically working under specific constraints, attempt to circumvent or defeat the security features of an information system.

Personally Identifiable Information (PII): Information which can be used to distinguish or trace an individual's identity, such as their name, social security number, biometric records, etc. Alone, or when combined with other personal or identifying information which is linked or linkable to a specific individual, such as date and place of birth, mother's maiden name, etc.

Phishing: Deceiving individuals into disclosing sensitive personal information through deceptive computer-based means.

Piracy: Illegally reproducing copyrighted work. Music, photographs, movies, and software are all potentially copyrighted and can be pirated.

Privacy: The act of guaranteeing that the interests of persons and organizations are protected and secluded from outside disclosure.

Prosecutor: The prosecutor is the chief legal representative of the prosecution in countries with either the common law adversarial system or the civil law inquisitorial system. The prosecution is the legal party responsible for presenting the case in a criminal trial against an individual accused of breaking the law.

Public Key Infrastructure (PKI): The framework and services that provide for the generation, production, distribution, control, accounting, and destruction of public key certificates. Components include the personnel, policies, processes, server platforms, software, and workstations used for the purpose of administering certificates and public–private key pairs, including the ability to issue, maintain, recover, and revoke public key certificates.

Responder: The initial person or team that is first on scene and conducts the starting response actions for the event or incident.

Risk: A measure of the extent to which an entity is threatened by a potential circumstance or event, and typically a function of

1. the adverse impacts that would arise if the circumstance or event occurs and
2. the likelihood of occurrence.

Root Kit: A set of tools used by an attacker after gaining root-level access to a host to conceal the attacker's activities on the host and permit the attacker to maintain root-level access to the host through covert means.

Security Point of Contact (SPOC): This is the primary person who serves as the contact for any security issue resolution with internal or external parties, organizations or people.

SIRT: Group of individuals usually consisting of Security Analysts organized to develop, recommend, and coordinate immediate mitigation actions for containment, eradication, and recovery resulting from computer security incidents. An SIRT can also be called a Computer Security Incident Response Team (CSIRT) or a CIRC (Computer Incident Response Center/Computer Incident Response Capability) or CIRT (Cyber Incident Response Team).

Situational Awareness: Within a volume of time and space, the perception of an enterprise's security posture and its threat environment; the comprehension/meaning of both taken together (risk); and the projection of their status into the near future.

Spam: Electronic junk mail or the abuse of electronic messaging systems to indiscriminately send unsolicited bulk messages.

Spear phishing: A targeted phishing attack on a select group of victims, usually executives.

Spoofing: There are two meanings to spoofing in our context:

1. Either faking the sending address of a transmission to gain illegal entry into a secure system or
2. the deliberate inducement of a user or resource to take incorrect action.

Note: Impersonating, masquerading, piggybacking, and mimicking are forms of spoofing.

Spyware: Software that is secretly or surreptitiously installed into an information system to gather information on individuals or organizations without their knowledge; a type of malicious code.

System Assets: The hardware, software, or information which is usually the target of malicious attacks or the vehicle for the attack.

Subject Matter Expert: The individual or resource which has the necessary and detailed expertise in a particular area of focus during the response, incident investigation, or court proceedings.

Team Leader: Individual who is responsible for the conduct of the response or forensics team, i.e., its conduct and activities.

Team Member: Individual who has assigned responsibilities and a role on the response or forensics team.

Trace Evidence: Trace evidence is created when objects contact. The classic Locard's Principle states that the perpetrator of a crime will bring something into the crime scene and leave with something from it. Use of trace evidence is to reconstruct crimes and to describe the people, places, and things involved in them.

User: The primary reporting person for any issue when discovered; the person who discovers the issue or problem while performing normal operations.

Virus: Malware with the ability to self-replicate, but it generally cannot self-propagate to other computers. Usually, a user must assist it by sharing infected files or media.

Worm: Malware with the ability to self-replicate and self-propagate through a network and attack other computers (e.g., by sending a copy of itself to everyone in a user's address book).

Zombie: An infected computer that floods another computer with packets in an attempt to infect or crash it without the consent or knowledge of the infected computer's owner.

Further definitions are available in the "Glossary of Key Information Security Terms" recently published (May 2013) by National Institute of Standards and Technology (NIST) as NIST IR 7298 rev. 2 on the http://csrc.nist.gov website and in the "National Information Assurance Glossary," CNSS 4009 document (June 2006) from the US Department of Defense (DOD) Committee on National Security Systems available in the attached documents to this book.

Incident Response Team

This part provides a framework for directing and managing an Incident Response Team for your organization or agency. As the ITSG's COBIT standard states:

"Management should establish a computer security incident handling capability to address security incidents by providing a centralized platform with sufficient expertise and equipped with rapid and secure communication facilities. Incident management responsibilities and procedures should be established to ensure an appropriate, effective and timely response to security incidents."

The purpose of security incident response is to bring needed resources together in an organized manner to deal with an adverse event known as an "incident" that is related to the safety and or security of the information system. The security incident response process is centered on the preparation, detection and analysis, containment, investigation, eradication, recovery, and post incident activity surrounding such an incident. The objectives of security incident response activities are to:

A. Limit the immediate incident impact to customers and business partners.
Always keeping in mind the first objective of any security activity is to secure the data.

B. Recover from the incident.
Recovery and returning to normal operations is critical for every business or agency.

C. Determine how the incident occurred.
Detailed evaluation and analysis to find out how an incident occurs is a best business practice.

D. Find out how to avoid further exploitation of the same vulnerability.
Prudent security practices show need for mitigation of identified risks.

E. Avoid escalation of further incident.
Containment is one of the important steps to any incident-handling action.

F. Assess the impact and damage in terms of financial impact, loss of data, loss of processing, data breaches, reputation, etc.
Risk and impact assessments post incident provide more focus and attention to actual issues for security and operations in any organization.

G. Update corporate security policies and procedures as necessary.
Developing lessons learned for incidents gives organizations ways to improve security posture and procedures for both actual security and compliance-reporting efforts.

Some of the primary factors for security incident response on a corporate/agency level are:

- Incorporate and formalize a specialized Security Incident Response Team (SIRT). This specialized SIRT consists of a senior team leader, multiple team members, corporate legal counsel representative, and potentially other staff members based upon the extent and depth of the incident.
    - The SIRT is directly responsible for the entire incident investigation and response and has the authority to override all other corporate staff decisions and activities with respect to the incident.
    - The SIRT receives its authority directly from the highest levels of the organization—either the Board of Directors or the Corporate Office/Senior Executive/Senior Management.
- Clearly defined corporate incident response policies and procedures are important to ensure proper data and information handling during incident response and potentially any legal actions resulting from such an incident.

- SIRT roles and responsibilities, especially with respect to the other corporate staff, during the response efforts and subsequent investigations.
- Corporate guidance and oversight especially focused on the financial and continued operations of the corporation/department/agency as a result of the incident.
- External Statutory, Regulatory, and Legal standards and requirements in such cases. There are many areas to be considered in this one arena alone.

Each of these areas are defined and discussed in the following chapters as we develop and manage the activities of our SIRT.

The Stages of Incident Response

There are multiple stages for incident response. Each stage should be performed in sequence with the integrity of the system in mind. From ensuring the company/organization is properly prepared for the inevitable incident to the complete and successful prosecution of a malicious insider or external "hacker," all incident response stages are necessary to be followed and completed. We are going to present two different methods for Incident Response, which are used in the industry to provide the services and response needed when providing the Incident Handling and Response activities.

METHODOLOGY #1

There are seven stages for incident response. Each stage should be performed in sequence with the integrity of the system in mind. From ensuring the company/organization is properly prepared for the inevitable incident to the complete and successful prosecution of a malicious insider or external "hacker," all incident response stages are necessary to be followed and completed.

Preparation

Preparation is critical to the successful identification, handling, and recovery for any computer incident. Preparation includes identifying the start of the incident, identifying how to recover from the incident, and how to get back to normal business operations sooner. This preparation includes the creation and approval of well-established corporate security policies, including warning banners, user privacy expectations, established incident notification process, the development of an incident containment policy, creation of incident handling checklists, insuring the corporate disaster recovery plan is up to date, and making sure the security risk assessment process is functioning and active.

Another important part of preparation is training: training for the incident responders (SIRT team members) and training for the organization's system administrators. Types of training include operating system support, specialized investigative techniques, incident response tools usage, and corporate environmental procedure requirements. An additional focus of specialized training includes decision-making efforts to determine if and when local law enforcement authorities should be contacted during investigations.

Third area important to preparation is having predeployed incident handling assets. These assets include:

A. Sensors, probes, and monitors on critical systems—these automated mechanisms allow monitoring of:
   1. System applications with a service and network monitoring program;
   2. CPU utilization, disk space, processes, and other pertinent metrics and investigating any unusual activity;
   3. Access to the application (allows and denies).
B. Tracking data bases on core systems based upon minimum security baselines (snapshots of the systems or networks during normal operations) and the corporate Configuration Management Data Base (CMDB) and
C. Active audit logs for all server and network components—where the logs are retained, how often the logs are updated, who controls them, etc.

It is best to have automated mechanisms employed to increase the availability of support features to users as well as to signal the need for a possible criminal investigation.

One final thing to understand about preparation is a few questions you always need to present to your users so they know what is expected.

- What action are they to take or not take at identification of incident?
- Who do they call?
- When do they call?
- What information do they provide when calling?
- Who should they notify or not notify about the possible incident?

Providing a basic response template for users to fill in when reporting an event or incident is a good way to ensure the right information is provided in a timely manner.

Identification

The second stage of Incident Response is proper Identification of the incident. Is the event simply an unusual activity, or can you identify it as suspicious? If so, what are the surrounding activities? Are there multiple reports of issues on the network, or is it confined to one machine or location? Some of the areas to check include:

1. *Suspicious Entries in System or Network Accounting*
   The accounting logs for each location should provide indicators of unusual actions in the system or network activities.

2. *Excessive Unsuccessful Login Attempts (>3 per user)*
   Usual security controls are designed to deny access once three unsuccessful logins are attempted in a row. This is an indicator of potentially malicious attackers trying to access systems or networks without having compromised credentials.

3. *Unexplained New User Accounts*
   Compromised administrative accounts often will indicate the creation of new accounts for the purposes of creating malicious user access to systems and networks.

4. *Unexplained New Files*
   New files are often added to the system directories expecting users not to be aware of the normal file set within these directories.

5. *Unfamiliar File Names*
   The modern malware event today often loads files onto a system hard drive with files which are not normally found in a modern operating system. These files can be identified and evaluated quickly once discovered.

6. *Modifications to file names and/or dates, especially in system executable files*
   "Hackers" often rename malicious executable files with names of normal files and then place them into the expected directories of the operating system.

7. *Intrusion Detection System (IDS) Alerts or Alarms*
   Network- and host-based Intrusion Detection Systems can often provide the responder indications of potential malicious or harmful activity so they should be reviewed and examined during initial response efforts to gain a possible path of attack and/or access of the malicious incident.

8. *External notifications (either outside users, customers, or emergency personnel)*
   Often the first indication of a problem comes from external sources, such as the local Computer Emergency Response Team (CERT) or outside users indicating they have received a strange or unusual indicator.

9. *E-mail flood from unsuspecting helper*
   E-mail flooding, often an indicator of a worm event, can provide a responder with indications of access methods and techniques used to gain a method of ingress into the network and should be used to instigate a response.

All of these potential incident indicators can allow you to determine if this event really is an incident or just an unusual event.

Who notices a suspicious or unusual event and when did they notice it?

What has happened or has changed?

These are couple of questions asked when an incident occurs which helps identify the event or potentially the incident. The reporting person, the end user or the system administrator, should fill out a standardized computer incident report. This report should contain multiple fields wherein the reporting person identifies the time and date of occurrence, location of occurrence, machine/system/network involved and activity active when the event occurred. This form provides valuable initial identification data for ensuring the proper handling of the event. For example if system/computer has an apparent identifiable virus/malware then this could be reflected on the reporting form by the type of end-user interaction and response reported.

The point of incident response and gathering of all the facts and data is to evaluate the extent of the unauthorized disclosure and/or distribution; determine its origin; identify the account(s) involved (if applicable); identify the potential agencies, information systems, and/or network(s) affected (if applicable); identify the type(s) of file formats involved in the incident (e.g., e-mail, Web posting, and database); document all actions taken; and gather any evidence processed.

NOTE: The primary and paramount step, in initial identification of the event or incident, is the absolute requirement that all investigative activities, all initial inspections, and all initial responses are performed AFTER a complete bit-stream image copy is created on the system under investigation, the system under question. This process can be completed quickly with the proper tools and support equipment; therefore, it is imperative to have these available at the start of the identification stage of incident response process—not later on during the containment or eradication steps. The logs to be evaluated should also be digitally copied off the suspect system(s) as well as the e-mails or other supporting data. This is the most important requirement to ensure proper and successful prosecution of any resultant civil or criminal case.

Some of the other activities that assist in identification are correlation of events through system logs, network logs, firewall logs, and application logs. Attention to detail is the primary attribute here when looking for potential malicious code, such as a "key-logger" or "rootkit," backdoors and trapdoors placed into a system by a "hacker" or even an insider, or some other malicious mobile code. Other areas to look at:

- Are there other indications of problem or an issue, such as IDS alerts and alarms, third-party e-mail recipients complaining about excessive e-mail from your domain, which would indicate a worm is running on your network?
- Excessive unsuccessful login attempts per user, unexplained new accounts or files, modification of system executable files, etc.

The basic requirement for incident response is the identification of the type of incident that has or is occurring at the time of response. The six levels for classifications of incidents are provided here. This list originated with the US-CERT and National Institute of Standards and Technology (NIST) organizations for use with governmental systems but has been modified to encompass both public and private organizations. This list includes the generally accepted security practices reporting requirements for each type of incident (Table 3.1).

Table 3.1 Incident Categories by Type of Incident

Category	Name	Incident Description
Level 1	Unauthorized access	In this category an individual gains logical or physical access without permission to a department/agency/corporate network, system, application, data, or other resource (e.g., physical documents). This category includes any breach of Personal Identifiable Information (PII) or Privacy data. This type of incident should be reported to the responsible corporate or organizational office as soon as the incident is identified.
Level 2	Denial of service (DoS)	An attack that successfully prevents or impairs the normal authorized functionality of networks, systems, or applications by exhausting resources. This activity includes being the victim of or participating in the DoS. The DoS attack is focused on not allowing users to access the needed computing resources to accomplish their tasks. Most current router devices have mitigation techniques built-in to their operating systems, so this type of incident is either based against older equipment, or focused on large-scale attacks from multiple sources.
Level 3	Malicious code	Successful installation of malicious software (e.g., virus, worm, Trojan horse, or other code-based malicious entity) that infects an operating system or application. This level is, today, by far and away has the largest number of incidents reported. Most all of the antivirus and malware security vendors are reporting large increases in the number and deployment of malware across the entire Internet. Departments and Companies are NOT usually required to report malicious logic that has been successfully quarantined by antivirus software.
Level 4	Improper usage	A person violates acceptable computing use policies. This is the typical classification for an insider threat or disgruntled employee incident within the organization. This type of incident typically causes large-scale losses but is often isolated to one network or location and carries the potential to harm an information system or enterprise through destruction, disclosure, modification of data, and/or denial of service... There are potentially major activities which require incident handling with this type of incident.
Level 5	Scans/probes/ attempted access	This category includes any activity that seeks to access or identify a corporation or department computer, open ports, protocols, service, or any combination for later exploit. This activity does not directly result in a compromise or denial of service. This type of incident can be caused by vulnerability scanning tools, network mapping tools, as well as penetration testing tools. This incident level can be related to expected or unexpected scans, tests, automated equipment evaluations, as well as outside reconnaissance of networks and machines.
Level 6	Investigation incident	This category covers unconfirmed incidents that are potentially malicious or anomalous activity deemed by organization/corporation to warrant further review. Once this incident is determined to require additional investigation, this level remains in effect during the entire investigation. This is the level for all levels of investigations, criminal, civil, and administrative, as well as forensics investigations.

Containment

Limiting the scope and magnitude of the incident is of paramount interest. There are two primary areas of coverage here: Protect and keep available critical computing recourses where possible, and determine the operational status of the infected computer, system or network. Protecting resources includes immediately changing administrative passwords, reevaluating and determining trust relationships between systems and networks, and, if you are a governmental agency, contacting your local computer emergency response team to check the scope of the incident. Once again, the initial record of all logs for review, examination, and investigation needs to be bit-stream "hash-encrypted" copies of the originals, not the originals themselves, for the purposes of legalities and potential future criminal or civil litigations.

To determine the operational status of your infected system and or network, you have three options, based upon immediate appearances when incident is discovered and on what type of processing device is the occurring event based:

A. Disconnect system from the network and allow it to continue stand-alone operations—i.e., if a workstation is contaminated, responders should disconnect the workstation from the network immediately by removing the physical connection (e.g., RJ-45 cable and fiber) and the workstation will remain in operational mode.
B. Shut down everything immediately—i.e., if the server or workstation shows immediate activity on monitor of active file deletions when responder arrives at scene, an immediate assessment is performed to see if files are required, important or could provide evidence in response efforts—if so, then turn off workstation or server to preserve remaining files before deletion activities are completed—this provides some remaining system integrity before total deletion of all files.
C. Continue to allow the system to run on the network and monitor the activities.

All three options are available at the beginning of an incident response and should be determined as quickly as possible to allow movement to the next stage, which is investigation of the incident.

Investigation

(Break-off point for Forensics)

This step is the initial investigative step necessary to determine the breadth and scope of the incident. Once all the bit-stream copies of the drives, external storage, real-time system memory, network devices logs, system logs, application logs, and other supporting data is assembled, then systematic review of each piece of evidence is conducted. Yes, at this time, these components and drives are considered evidence at least until it has been evaluated and determined not to be relevant or germane to the incident investigation. Some of the areas for investigation include:

- How much? Where it went? How widespread?—Determining extent of infection or penetration.
- Was it a network- or host based, i.e., computer/user system access?
- What data was accessed?
- Where did the suspect/malicious activity go?
- What happened to this device/component?
- When did it occur?
- In what log was it used or found?
- Who did it?
- Was it an inside threat or outside attack?
- What do the log reviews reveal?

Document each step of the investigation, especially since external threats may require law enforcement involvement. This is often the point of separation between the return to normal operations actions from a business perspective and the detailed investigation action to be performed by the forensics and potentially even law enforcement personnel if the incident warrants legal actions.

Eradication

Eradication is getting rid of the problem. Once the investigation shows there are no further external or internal actions necessary to complete the containment or investigations, then the Eradication step is initiated. Two important parts are cleanup and notification. Cleanup usually consists of running your antivirus software, deinstallation of infected software, rebuilding the entire operating system or replacement of the entire hard drive and reconstituting the network communications and equipment.

Notification always includes relevant personnel, both above and below the SIRT manager in the reporting chain. By getting the system back into operation, the next stage, Recovery, is activated.

Recovery

Recovery is returning the system/network/component to normal business operations. There are always two steps to any recovery effort. First part of recovery involves service restoration, based upon implementation of corporate contingency plans; second part of recovery involves system and/or network validation, testing, and certifying the system as operational. Each system or component which has been determined to have been compromised must be recertified to be both operational and secure so as to not reintroduce the problem into the operating environment of the organization after initial recovery.

Follow-Up

After the incident is completed, there are questions for the incident response team and the corporation to answer. These include:

A. Was there sufficient preparation?
B. Did detection occur promptly?
C. Were communications adequate?
D. What was the financial or informational cost of the incident?
E. How can we prevent it from happening again?

In this stage the follow-on review is done as an objective evaluation, for computer security mistakes are our best hope for improvement because progress is measured by making new mistakes, instead of the same ones over and over again.

METHODOLOGY #2

Incident Response was devised by the US Government's NIST organization and is straightforward and simple in its design, but detailed in implementation.

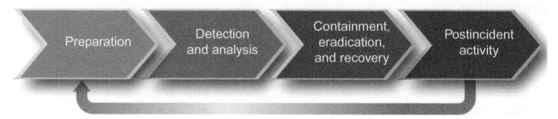

NIST incident response life cycle.

Preparation

The first step in this methodology is the Preparation Stage. The purpose of this stage is twofold: to create an incident response mechanism within the organization and to install a minimum security baseline in the IT and network infrastructure of the organization so as to set criteria to help prevent incidents from occurring in the first place. This first part includes security engineering activities for the network, systems, and the various applications running on the systems and networks. Reviews of security products, services, and systems before installation are considered important which can establish the base level of security in the multiple areas of administrative, technical, and operational security controls. The incident response team level of security experience and subject matter expertise is vital to this effort.

Detection and Analysis

The second stage of this Incident Response Methodology is the Detection and Analysis Stage. This is the phase where the actual detection of an incident occurs. There are many methods available today which allow for the automated detection of possible events and incidents. Software- and hardware-based devices and components can detect changes in network traffic patterns, change in file directory structures and sizes of the files themselves, or even the behavior of files on the servers or network. However, still in today's interconnected world, the most common way to receive notification of a problem is from the users themselves. They will know when a program is running exceptionally slow, or when a directory is unavailable which should be open, etc. There are many incident indicators which will need to be reviewed, prioritized, and evaluated each day in a large commercially active organization. So it does become important to have the right people with the right skills at the right location and time who are able to provide the needed actions in response to each incident.

These skilled responders will read the "signs" of an activity or event to see if it indicates an incident needing review. Some of these "signs" can indicate a potential area of concern—something to watch for in the near future and some can indicate an active activity which needs immediate attention. The skill of the responders in their methods of identification of incidents is critical in this stage to ensure the correct incident events are responded to and the false-positive ones are identified and properly evaluated.

Containment, Eradication, and Recovery

Containment of the incident is usually the next major step necessary during the response after identifying what the incident really is that is taking place. As a part of this containment, the team leader's decision-making becomes paramount to allow the right resources be applied to the effort, to properly gain management support during the response. And, to "secure the data" which, of course, is the primary goal of any response action. Various questions need to be answered during this stage by the responders and their managers, such as:

a. Should we shut the system off?
b. Should we disconnect the network from the machine?
c. Should we disable certain ports, protocols, or services first?

Depending upon what kind of incident it is, some other considerations are then considered for eradication during the response. The type of incident will, in itself, provide these areas. These considerations include:

- Potential damage to and theft of resources.
- Need for evidence preservation.
- Service availability (e.g., network connectivity, services provided to external parties).
- Time and resources needed to implement the strategy.
- Effectiveness of the strategy (e.g., partially/fully contains the incident).
- Duration of the solution (e.g., emergency workaround to be removed in 4 h, temporary workaround to be removed in 2 weeks, permanent solution).

Full eradication of the cause of the incident is the next goal within this framework for response. Eradication actions could include deletion of the malicious software or code snippet, disabling certain accounts on the system, closing the applicable firewall ports, etc. Remember, based on the type of incident, full eradication may not be needed and could actually cause further damage, so the method of eradication is also an important consideration during this stage.

Recovery back to full business operations is the ultimate goal of this stage. Recovery activities will include restoring the system affected from full, uninfected backups, rebuilding systems from scratch, hardening systems to prevent further occurrence of incident, adding new or expanded security parameters on boundary devices, changing administrative passwords, increasing the logging of events immediately after the incident to ensure full recovery, and increased monitoring of the network and system since the incident often has follow-up event and attacks applied in its aftermath.

POST-INCIDENT ACTIVITY

In the full arena of incident response, one of the most important activities is after the event learning action. The results of the response are ideally always improving and this postincident effort is the key to ensuring the learning process is taking place. Each team and team member should review the effort, the techniques used, the timing of the response, the threat realized, and the support actions taken with the eye on improving the response then next time. Each incident response team should evolve to reflect new threats, improved technology and lessons learned. These lessons learned actions can dramatically improve the security of the organization, as well as improve the incident handling and response mechanisms within the response team.

The National Institute of Justice has produced a document entitled *Electronic Crime Scene Investigation: A Guide for First Responders*,[1] which discusses the techniques taught to law enforcement personnel when responding to incident scenes. Their basic steps are four as described in this document. They are:

Secure and Evaluate the Scene

- When securing and evaluating the scene, the first responder should:
    - Follow departmental policy for securing crime scenes.
    - Immediately secure all electronic devices, including personal or portable devices.
    - Ensure that no unauthorized person has access to any electronic devices at the crime scene.
    - Refuse offers of help or technical assistance from any unauthorized persons.
    - Remove all persons from the crime scene or the immediate area from which evidence is to be collected.
    - Ensure that the condition of any electronic device is not altered.
    - Leave a computer or electronic device off if it is already turned off.

Document the Scene

Documentation of a crime scene creates a record for the investigation. It is important to accurately record the location of the scene; the scene itself; the state, power status, and condition of computers, storage media, wireless network devices, mobile phones, smart phones, PDAs, and other data storage devices; Internet and network access; and other electronic devices. The first responder should be aware that not all digital evidence may be in close proximity to the computer or other devices.

The initial documentation of the scene should include a detailed record using video, photography, and notes and sketches to help recreate or convey the details of the scene later. All activity and processes on display screens should be fully documented.

Documentation of the scene should include the entire location, including the type, location, and position of computers, their components and peripheral equipment, and other electronic devices. The scene may expand to multiple locations; first responders should document all physical connections to and from the computers and other devices.

---

[1] Electronic crime scene investigation: a guide for first responders. 2nd ed. National Institute of Justice; April 2008 [NCJ 219941].

Record any network and wireless access points that may be present and capable of linking computers and other devices to each other and the Internet. The existence of network and wireless access points may indicate that additional evidence exists beyond the initial scene.

Perform Evidence Collection

The first responder must have proper authority—such as plain view observation, consent, or a court order—to search for and collect evidence at an electronic crime scene. The first responder must be able to identify the authority under which he or she may seize evidence and should follow agency guidelines, consult a superior, or contact a prosecutor if a question of appropriate authority arises.

Digital evidence must be handled carefully to preserve the integrity of the physical device as well as the data it contains. Some digital evidence requires special collection, packaging, and transportation techniques. Data can be damaged or altered by electromagnetic fields such as those generated by static electricity, magnets, radio transmitters, and other devices. Communication devices, such as mobile phones, smart phones, PDAs, and pagers should be secured and prevented from receiving or transmitting data once they are identified and collected as evidence.

Business environments frequently have complicated configurations of multiple computers networked to each other, to a common server, to network devices, or a combination of these. Securing a scene and collecting digital evidence in these environments may pose challenges to the first responder. Improperly shutting down a system may result in lost data, lost evidence, and potential civil liability.

The first responder may find a similar environment in residential locations, particularly when a business is operated from the home in some instances; the first responder may encounter unfamiliar operating systems or unique hardware and software configurations that require specific shutdown procedures.

Package, Transport, and Store the Collected Digital Evidence

Digital evidence—and the computers and electronic devices on which it is stored—is fragile and sensitive to extreme temperatures, humidity, physical shock, static electricity, and magnetic fields.

The first responder should take precautions when documenting, photographing, packaging, transporting, and storing digital evidence to avoid altering, damaging, or destroying the data.

Packaging Procedures

All actions related to the identification, collection, packaging, transportation, and storage of digital evidence should be thoroughly documented. When packing digital evidence for transportation, the first responder should:

- Ensure that all digital evidence collected is properly documented, labeled, marked, photographed, video recorded or sketched, and inventoried before it is packaged. All connections and connected devices should be labeled for easy reconfiguration of the system later.
- Remember that digital evidence may also contain latent, trace, or biological evidence and take the appropriate steps to preserve it. Digital evidence imaging should be done before latent, trace, or biological evidence processes are conducted on the evidence.
- Pack all digital evidence in antistatic packaging. Only paper bags and envelopes, cardboard boxes, and antistatic containers should be used for packaging digital evidence. Plastic materials should not be used when collecting digital evidence because plastic can produce or convey static electricity and allow humidity and condensation to develop, which may damage or destroy the evidence.
- Ensure that all digital evidence is packaged in a manner that will prevent it from being bent, scratched, or otherwise deformed.
- Label all containers used to package and store digital evidence clearly and properly.
- Leave cellular, mobile, or smart phone(s) in the power state (on or off) in which they were found.
- Package mobile or smart phone(s) in signal-blocking material such as Faraday isolation bags, radio frequency-shielding material, or aluminum foil to prevent data messages from being sent or received by the devices. (First responders should be aware that if inappropriately packaged, or removed from shielded packaging, the device may be able to send and receive data messages if in range of a communication signal.)
- Collect all power supplies and adapters for all electronic devices seized.

Transportation Procedures

When transporting digital evidence, the first responder should:

- Keep digital evidence away from magnetic fields, such as those produced by radio transmitters, speaker magnets, and magnetic mount emergency lights. Other potential hazards that the first responder should be aware of include seats heaters and any device or material that can produce static electricity.
- Avoid keeping digital evidence in a vehicle for prolonged periods of time. Heat, cold, and humidity can damage or destroy digital evidence.

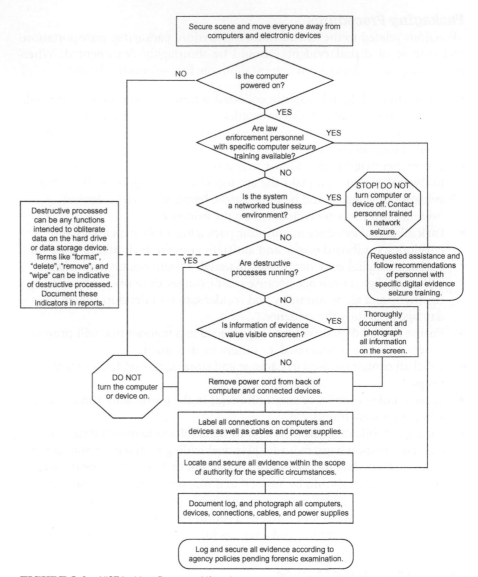

FIGURE 3.1 NIST Incident Response Lifecycle.

- Ensure that computers and electronic devices are packaged and secured during transportation to prevent damage from shock and vibration.
- Document the transportation of the digital evidence and maintain the chain of custody on all evidence transported.

Storage Procedures

When storing digital evidence, the first responder should:

- Ensure that the digital evidence is inventoried in accordance with the agency's policies.
- Ensure that the digital evidence is stored in a secure, climate-controlled environment or a location that is not subject to extreme temperature or humidity.
- Ensure that the digital evidence is not exposed to magnetic fields, moisture, dust, vibration, or any other elements that may damage or destroy it.
- If more than one computer is seized as evidence, all computers, cables, and devices connected to them should be properly labeled to facilitate reassembly if necessary.

It is interesting to see what the Law Enforcement Officer (LEO) community is taught from a management perspective where the focus points are and how the procedures are developed and portrayed to the technicians who are on scene collecting the evidence.

The basic flowchart for evidence collection is found in (Figure 3.1).

The Security Incident Response Team Members

The knowledge and skill of the incident responder is paramount to the successful handling of any incident. The incident responder has to be able to demonstrate impartiality and to know the importance of identification, coupled with collecting and cataloging any evidentiary findings in context with surrounding factors.

- The incident responder needs to be *logical* in their approach to each and every situation. Each event and activity which is to be handled must be approached with an open mind and a sound methodology for investigation and containment.
- The incident responder has to be *thorough* in all actions that they take when responding, analyzing, evaluating and documenting the incident. The full scope of the incident must be accounted for during and after the actual handling activities occur so that nothing is missed and left to continue to create issues in the future.
- The incident responder is required to be as *objective* as possible during and after the response effort to ensure integrity and impartiality of their efforts. The actual data involved in the incident, along with the methods and techniques of exposure need to be identified, cataloged, and traced to ensure the full depth and breathe of the incident is investigated.
- The incident responder must be *observant* of all activities, events, and surrounding environment while responding to gather as much information about the situation as can be gleaned from the incident scene. All sources of data for the investigation must be included in the incident data collection efforts.
- *Resourcefulness* is the hallmark of an incident responder when checking, examining, and reviewing all of the parameters of any type of incident. Utilizing all possible sources of information about surrounding and concerning the hardware and software in relation to the data collected is needed to ensure the full scope of the investigation is covered.
- Above all other criteria, the incident responder must be *accurate* in his findings, results, and reports of the incident, the surroundings, and root cause for the incident. The final and ultimate criteria for the responder

are the need for direct, distinct, and decisive in the examination and development of the results and report of the incident.

An incident responder's responsibilities before, during, and after the incident include the following:

1. Proper information gathering and collection techniques—techniques should be based on the best business practices as well as predefined corporate guidelines.
   The actual performance of data gathering, investigation, analysis, and examination needs to follow proper protocols and documented methods and techniques.
2. Proper documentation—full documentation should be developed as the incident transpires and is contained when possible and also includes the support manuals and vendor documentation. The one basic activity necessary during any event is to document everything that transpires during the event. All actions, activities, evaluations, supporting data collection, and any other relevant act must be fully documented by the responder during the response activity.
3. Proper performance—the obvious key to the whole process in containing and eradicating the incident root cause especially if the incident is caused by external factors. Complete and professional investigative and response performance is paramount for any incident responder.
4. Certification on response tools and techniques—industry certifications in Incident Handling go a long way to ensure the responders have the necessary background to properly respond no matter what the incident may be. Multiple professional certifications in incidence response, malware analysis, reverse engineering of software, penetration testing, and ethical hacking are all available and add to the expertise and standing of the assigned incident responders.
5. Proper methodologies—the proper way to handle an incident always depends on the type and timing of the incident. But, there are documented ways, such as found in Section 3.
6. Detailed, enhanced technical writing capabilities—I often talk about the first job of any security professional is to "secure the data" and the second job is to "report, report, and report." This area is critical to the successful improvement and enhancement of the organizational security posture after the incident is handled as well as the potential further investigative activities in the Forensics arena.

The selection criteria of the Security Incident Response Team (SIRT) members are usually based on two factors: who is available and what skills do they have? Additional factors can include the size and scope of the SIRT itself, what level of executive support is being provided to the SIRT, visibility of the SIRT requirements and needs within the organization, and even possible recent events and incidents. The skills, abilities, and knowledge of the SIRT members are usually in two areas: technical and personal.

TYPES OF TECHNICAL SKILLS NEEDED

These skills, abilities, and knowledge are provided as a guide, not a full set of personnel requirements. Realistically, not many incident handlers will have all of these skills, but they should have a working knowledge of most of them.

- The basic security principles and engineering practices such as found in NIST SP 800-27 are as follows:
    - confidentiality
    - availability
    - authentication
    - integrity
    - access control
    - privacy
    - nonrepudiation.

  The SIRT member needs knowledge about basic security principles in order to understand potential problems that can arise if appropriate security measures have not been implemented correctly, as well as the potential impacts to the customer. SIRT members with this understanding are better prepared to determine their customer needs in securely configuring systems to prevent misuse or compromises and also be better prepared to provide appropriate technical assistance and guidance when breaches do occur.

- Ability to identify risks and threats to data, information, computers, and networks.

  The SIRT member needs to be able to recognize and categorize the most common types of system and network vulnerabilities and associated attacks, such as those that might involve:
    - malicious code (e.g., viruses, worms, Trojan horses),
    - protocol design flaws (e.g., man-in-the-middle attacks, spoofing),
    - implementation flaws (e.g., buffer overflow, timing windows/race conditions),
    - configuration weaknesses or incorrect settings,
    - user errors, omissions, or indifference,
    - physical security issues.

- Understanding the Internet (aspects ranging from architecture and history to future and philosophy)

  Each SIRT member should know about the history, philosophy, and structure of the Internet, and the various infrastructures that support it.

The SIRT member needs to know this information in order to understand why and the way that the various protocols are designed and work across the Internet.

- Detailed knowledge of network protocols (IP, ICMP, TCP, UDP, FTP)
  The SIRT member needs to have a basic understanding of the common network protocols that are used in their operating environment. For each protocol, he/she should have a basic understanding of the protocol, its specification, and how it is used. In addition, the SIRT member should understand the common types of threats or attacks against the protocol, as well as strategies to mitigate or eliminate such attacks.

- In-depth understanding of network infrastructure elements (router, DNS, mail-server)
  The SIRT member needs to have a basic understanding of the concepts of network security and be able to recognize vulnerable points in network configurations. The SIRT member should understand the concepts and basic perimeter security of network firewalls (design, packet filtering, proxy systems, DMZ, bastion hosts, etc.), router security, potential for information disclosure of data traveling across the network (e.g., packet monitoring or "sniffers"), or threats relating to accepting untrustworthy information.

- How network applications, services, and related protocols (SMTP, HTTP, HTTPS, FTP, TELNET, SSH, IMAP, POP3) function and interact with each other.
  The SIRT members need a basic understanding of the common network applications and services that the team and the customer use (DNS, NFS, SSH, HTTP, etc.). For each application or service, the SIRT member should understand the purpose of the application or service, how it works, common usage, secure configurations, and the common types of threats or attacks against the application or service, as well as mitigation strategies.

- Current security vulnerabilities/weaknesses and related attack methodologies (IP spoofing, Internet sniffers, denial of service attacks, and computer viruses)
  The SIRT members need to understand the different types of malicious code attacks (system compromises, denial of service, loss of data integrity, etc.) that occur and how these can affect their customers. Malicious code can have different types of payloads that can cause a denial of service attack or web defacement, or the code can contain more "dynamic" payloads that can be configured to result in multifaceted attack vectors. The SIRT members should understand not only how malicious code is propagated through some of the obvious methods (disks, email, programs, etc.) but also how it can propagate through other means such as website deployments, PostScript, Word macros, MIME, peer-to-peer

file sharing, or boot-sector viruses that affect operating systems running on PC, UNIX, LINUX, or Macintosh platforms. The SIRT members must be aware of how such attacks occur and are propagated; the risks and damage associated with such attacks, prevention and mitigation strategies, detection and removal processes, and recovery techniques.
Team members with special skills in reverse engineering, malicious code review, or detailed code analysis can provide additional support and focused methods for response during incident handling activities.

- Ability to identify host system security issues, from both a user and system administration perspective (backups, patches)
  The SIRT members should have a variety of expertise and exposure to the various types of operating systems (UNIX, Windows, LINUX, MacOS, or any other operating systems used) deployed in their area of responsibility. The members need to have experience in the operating aspects of the operating system, how the operating system is managed, maintained, patched, and how the security parameters of the operating system are installed and monitored.
  Then, for each operating system, the SIRT members need to know how to:
  - configure (harden) the system securely,
  - review configuration files for security weaknesses,
  - manage system privileges,
  - identify common attack methods,
  - determine if a compromise attempt occurred,
  - determine if an attempted system compromise was successful,
  - analyze the results of attacks,
  - review log files for anomalies,
  - recover from a compromise,
  - secure network daemons for non-Windows servers.
- Ability to identify network security issues (firewalls and virtual private networks)
  The SIRT member should have the ability to anticipate, identify, isolate, and describe potential new vulnerabilities that could affect the area of responsibility as a result of changes in network design, hardware, or software. The SIRT member should be able to identify security weaknesses in current network configurations, deployments, and architectures. The SIRT member should be able to identify and develop tools or processes that would mitigate or resolve these potential security weaknesses.
- Which encryption technologies (Triple DES (3DES), AES, IDEA, Blowfish) are in use in the organization
  The SIRT member needs to have awareness and understanding of the basics for use and employment of encryption within the area of responsibility. He/she needs to be aware of both major methods of encryption, symmetric and asymmetric, and how each is used.

The SIRT member must be aware of the core encryption algorithms (AES, 3DES, IDEA, etc.) used in each method and how they function in order to properly identify encryption deficiencies, weaknesses, and attacks. He/she should be familiar with the customer's means of Key Management and Key Distribution in order to understand potential key issues as this is usually the primary area of man-in-the-middle attacks on key systems.

- How digital signatures (RSA, DSA) are used and defined
  The SIRT member should be cognizant of the methods and means used by the customer of Digital Signature activities for verification and validation of message traffic and electronic contract actions. The basic core Digital Signature algorithms (RSA and DSA) and their usage under corporate and federal standards (FIPS-186) are areas of focus for the SIRT member.

- Where cryptographic hash algorithms (MD5, SHA-1) are utilized and under what conditions are they used
  Hashing is often used throughout an organization for multiple requirements, such as password control, digital signatures, software version integrity checking, and file system integrity reviews. The SIRT member should be aware of each version and type of hashing is used, what particular version and algorithm is utilized (MD5, SHA-1, etc.), and how the process is controlled in the particular instance or application where it is employed. The methods for hashing and which algorithm is relevant is often a critical skill and knowledge set for the SIRT member as hashing is used extensively in Incident Response and Forensics for integrity purposes by the investigators and analysts to control evidence and its validity. Therefore, this understanding is vital to the SIRT member and often is a core critical skill necessary for team membership.

- An understanding of public data networks (telephone, ISDN, X.25, PBX, ATM, frame relay)
  The SIRT member should be well versed in the organization's data source provider's services and the telephone service provider's delivery mechanisms. Understanding the delivery and services being provided gives the SIRT member some awareness of the types of security controls inherited by the organization from their service providers and allows the team member to use the "upstream" security to assist in response efforts if the suspicious incident is originating from outside the organization. So the SIRT member needs to know what type of telephone services are provided, what kind of data delivery is provided and through what technologies is the data service delivered to the organization, and what access is provided to the organization from the Internet Service Provider.

- Possibly even domain experts from the fields of:
  - applications,
  - system,

- security,
- network,
- mail,
- database.

TYPES OF PERSONAL SKILLS NEEDED

These skills can become paramount for each team member to have as incidents are investigated, events happen, and breaches are found and disclosed to management, customers, and clients.

- *Common sense* to make efficient and acceptable decisions whenever there is no clear ruling available and under stress or severe time constraints. This one skill can be the most important in a crisis situation—"clear-headed" thinking and even decisive decision-making. The SIRT member who is technically competent and has excellent communication skills can solidify the reputation of the team and strengthen the respect with which a team is held (both by the customer and by others with whom the team interacts). On the other hand, the interactions of a SIRT member who is a technical expert but who possesses poor communication skills or no "common sense" can result in miscommunications and/or actions that can severely damage a team's reputation and standing in the community, especially when those communications are misinterpreted or mishandled.
- Strong, effective oral and written *communication skills* (in native language and English) to interact with clients and other teams. All communications need to be conducted so that there is no misunderstanding or misinterpretation of the needs of the responders. The SIRT member needs to be effective in his/her communications to ensure that they obtain and supply the information necessary to be helpful. They need to be good listeners, understanding what is said (or *not* said) to enable them to gain details about an incident that is being reported. The SIRT member needs to remain in control of these communications to most effectively determine what is happening, what facts are important, and what assistance is necessary.
- *Diplomacy* when dealing with other parties, especially the media, the senior management, and customers. Each response effort will involve the outside response staff personnel and management. Each interchange with these personnel needs to be handled in a proper and secure manner. Diplomacy and tact are essential when dealing with outside parties. The SIRT member needs these skills to be able to anticipate potential points of contention, be able to respond appropriately, maintain good relations, and avoid offending others.

- The dedicated *ability to follow* policies and procedures. Every response team has corporate policies and procedures defined for their efforts, investigations, and reporting mechanisms. Each of these documents needs to be followed during the response effort. To ensure a consistent and reliable incident response service, the SIRT member must be prepared to accept and follow the rules and guidelines, even if these policies, procedures, guidelines, and rules are not fully documented and regardless of whether the team member personally agrees with them. On the other hand, if the SIRT member feels that change is required and if they want to approach management with suggested changes, they should be permitted to propose changes.

- Always willing to *continue education*—learn new ways to handle and contain incidents. One of the hallmarks of a good investigator is the willingness to learn new techniques, tactics, and investigative procedures. The incredible diverse ways of attack available today demand constant learning of response methods and attack mechanisms to stay current.

- Extremely strong *ability to cope with stress* and work under pressure. Any incident response has several focus points which require direct and immediate attention. The identification of the incident, the containment of the harm from the incident, and the quick removal or eradication of the cause of the incident all are "pressure-packed" actions to be accomplished by the response team and its members as expeditiously as possible. The SIRT member, particularly, needs the ability to remain calm in tense situations; ranging from an excessive workload to an aggressive caller to an incident where human life or a critical infrastructure component could be at risk. The SIRT's reputation, and the team member's personal reputation, will be enhanced or will suffer depending on how such situations are handled.

- Must be a *team player*—no "lone wolf" personnel. In a response setting, SIRT members don't usually have the time for individual actions. These efforts are conducted by a team of incident responders which have varying degrees of expertise in different areas, so no one responder needs or should have all of the knowledge needed to completely handle any single incident. The SIRT members need to be aware of their responsibilities, contribute to the goals of the team, and work together to share information, workload, and experiences. Each team member must be flexible and willing to adapt to change as well as having team skills for interacting with other parties, both internal to the team and external to the organization.

- *Integrity and trustworthiness* of the member to keep a team's reputation and standing, especially in the face of possible criticism. Full trust and understanding of the team member's capabilities and expertise must be had by the team leader to ensure the integrity and trust of the team is maintained. Often, in response efforts, data becomes available to the SIRT member which is newsworthy. In this case, the team member must be trustworthy, discrete, and able to handle information in confidence according to the SIRT rules and guidelines, any customer agreements or regulations, and/or any organizational policies and procedures. The SIRT member may find himself in a position where he knows about information and could comment on a topic, but doing so could acknowledge or disclose information that was provided in confidence or that could affect an ongoing investigation or response effort. So the SIRT member must remain aware of his responsibilities and not be caught "off guard" and make unauthorized disclosures of his own.

- A willingness to *admit to one's own mistakes* or knowledge limitations about a topic and then go out and research it. However difficult it may be to admit a limitation, the SIRT member must recognize his or her limitation and actively seek support from their team members, other experts, or SIRT management. Always learning, examining, growing in knowledge and understanding of techniques are areas for each team member to actively pursue and update throughout their career.

- *Problem-solving skills* to address new situations and efficiently handle incidents as they happen. New techniques for attacks, new methods for response, new technologies are always arriving within the organization and need to be added to the repertoire of the team members' skills. SIRT members can become overwhelmed with the volumes of data related to incidents and other tasks that need to be handled if they don't have good problem-solving skills. Problem-solving skills also include an ability for the SIRT members to "think outside the box" or look at issues from multiple perspectives to identify relevant information or data.

- *Time management* skills and abilities, in order to concentrate on priority work. Focusing on the task at hand during the response and subsequent investigation is vitally important to the proper and quick resolution for any incident. Effective time management is important for the SIRT member because they will often be confronted with a multitude of tasks ranging from analyzing, coordinating, and responding to incidents to performing duties such as prioritizing their workload, attending, and/ or preparing for meetings, completing time sheets, collecting statistics, conducting research, giving briefings and presentations, traveling to conferences, and possibly providing onsite technical support.

- Ability to consistently *deliver briefings* and possibly even court testimony. Expert witness testimony is always possible in any incident resolution effort, so each team member must have skills in properly explaining their efforts, and making it straightforward for potential external parties, such as court officers, lawyers, and juries. The SIRT member needs skills to present a technical briefing, management, or sponsor presentations, a panel discussion at a conference or seminar, or some other form of public-speaking engagement as required by the SIRT or management.

The SIRT member presentation skills probably will include providing expert testimony in legal or other proceedings on behalf of the SIRT or a customer.

All of these skills, abilities, and knowledge areas are found best when the team members are blended together to form a cohesive unit for incident response. Not many people are going to have all of these at one time, but the team concept comes into play here with certain skills and expertise on the team, rather than in people. Our response efforts are too varied to try to gather all these skill-sets into one or two individuals.

SP 800-61, the NIST Guide for Incident Response, also provides some guidance on ensuring team members stay active and engaged while participating in team activities and events as follows:

"It is important to counteract staff burnout by providing opportunities for learning and growth. Suggestions for building and maintaining skills are as follows:

- Budget enough funding to maintain, enhance, and expand proficiency in technical areas and security disciplines, as well as less technical topics such as the legal aspects of incident response. Consider sending each full-time team member to at least two technical conferences per year and each part-time team member to at least one.
- Ensure the availability of books, magazines, and other technical references that promote deeper technical knowledge.
- Give team members opportunities to perform other tasks, such as creating educational materials, conducting security awareness workshops, writing software tools to assist system administrators in detecting incidents, and conducting research.
- Consider rotating staff members in and out of the incident response team.
- Maintain sufficient staffing so that team members can have uninterrupted time off work (e.g., vacations).
- Create a mentoring program to enable senior technical staff to help less experienced staff learn incident handling.
- Participate in exchanges in which team members temporarily trade places with others (e.g., network administrators) to gain new technical skills.
- Occasionally bring in outside experts (e.g., contractors) with deep technical knowledge in needed areas, as funding permits.
- Develop incident handling scenarios and have the team members discuss how they would handle them.
- Conduct simulated incident handling exercises for the team. Exercises are particularly important because they not only improve the performance of the incident handlers, but also identify issues with policies and procedures, and with communication."[1]

---

[1] SP 800-61, Guide to Computer Incident Response, 2007.

Incident Evidence

Attacks on information systems and networks have become more numerous, sophisticated, and severe over the past few years. While preventing such attacks would be the ideal course of action for any organization or agency, not all information system security incidents can be prevented. Security incident response team (SIRT) managers are often held responsible for how, when, and where all incident evidence is gathered, collected, analyzed, and evaluated. There are many types of computer- and network-based incidents that produce documentable artifacts, code, and evidence that will be available for investigation. From the latest research data on computer abuse as reported in the media, no one on the Internet is immune. Those affected include banks and financial companies, insurance companies, brokerage houses, consulting organizations, governmental agencies and their contractors, hospitals and medical laboratories, network service providers, utility companies, the textile business, universities, and wholesale and retail corporations.

The consequences of a break-in, an incident cover a broad range of possibilities: a minor loss of time in recovering from the problem, a decrease in productivity, a significant loss of money or staff hours, up to a devastating loss of credibility or market opportunity, a business no longer able to compete, legal liability, and even the loss of life in extreme situations. These incident types include but are not limited to:

1. *Money laundering*
   This is the process of concealing the source of obtained money. This is usually accomplished in three steps: first, cash is introduced into the financial system by some means, the second involves carrying out complex financial transactions in order to camouflage the illegal source, and the final step entails acquiring wealth generated from the transactions of the illicit funds.

2. *Fraud*
   This is an intentional deception made for personal gain or to damage another individual. The international dimensions of the web and ease with which users can hide their location, the difficulty of checking

identity and legitimacy online, and the simplicity with which hackers can divert browsers to dishonest sites and steal credit card details have all contributed to the incredible and very rapid growth of Internet fraud.

3. *Identity theft*
   This is a form of stealing someone's identity in which someone pretends to be someone else by assuming that person's identity, typically in order to access resources or obtain credit and other benefits in that person's name. The victim of identity theft can suffer adverse consequences if they are held accountable for the perpetrator's actions. Identity theft occurs when someone uses your personally identifying information (PII), like your name, Social Security number, or credit card number, without your permission, to commit fraud or other crimes.

4. *Unauthorized computer usage*
   This is where the computer user performs some activity on the computer which has been predefined as being against the corporate policy, acceptable use, or against the law. Often it (the unauthorized use) is found to be in violation of the corporate Acceptable Use Policy as a primary means of intent.

5. *Unauthorized system access*
   This refers to a user gaining access sections or portions of a computing system or network where they do NOT have a legitimate reason or "need-to-know" for use of or access to the data. Users attempting to retrieve or read files they have no right to is often an indication of potentially compromised accounts or an indication of possible insider threat.

6. *Child pornography*
   This refers to images or films (also known as child abuse images) and, in some cases, writings depicting sexually explicit activities involving a child. Abuse of the child occurs during the sexual acts which are recorded in the production of child pornography. Throughout the world, many national and regional governmental bodies have found that child pornography to be one of the most heinous crimes and focus resources on the eradication of this crime and its proponents and users. Often incident responders must, upon discovery of these types of crimes, immediately call law enforcement and remove themselves from any further investigation or actions.

7. *Espionage, both governmental and industrial*
   Espionage or spying involves a government or individual obtaining information that is considered secret or confidential without the permission of the holder of the information. Espionage is inherently clandestine, as it is taken for granted that it is unwelcome and, in many cases illegal and punishable by law. Espionage is often part of an institutional effort by a government or commercial concern; however, the term is generally associated with state spying on potential or actual

enemies primarily for military purposes. Spying involving corporations is known as industrial espionage and is often only a civil offense, not criminally chargeable by the government.

8. *Waste*

   This refers to the intentional and deliberate use of computing equipment or resources with the intent of performing actions which have no legitimate business or service purpose. As an example, developing systems then delivering systems with no business objective can often be considered waste and potentially illegal in some jurisdictions.

9. *Software piracy*

   The copyright infringement of software (often referred to as software piracy) refers to several practices which involve the unauthorized copying of computer software. Copyright infringement of this kind varies globally; most countries have copyright laws which apply to software, but the degree of enforcement varies. Patent and trademark infringement are often areas for incident and forensics involvement when in the corporate arena as these activities often result in civil proceedings and lawsuits, rather than criminal prosecution.

10. *Sexual harassment and abuse*

    Sexual harassment is intimidation, bullying or coercion of a sexual nature, or the unwelcome or inappropriate promise of rewards in exchange for sexual favors. In most modern legal contexts sexual harassment is illegal. Harassment can include "sexual harassment" or unwelcome sexual advances, requests for sexual favors, and other verbal or physical harassment of a sexual nature.

11. *Data breach, leakage, and spillage*

    A data breach is the intentional or unintentional release of secure information to an untrusted environment. Other terms for this activity include unintentional information disclosure, data leakage, and data spillage. In today's Internet-driving world of business and the incredible proliferation of malware, as previously mention, it is no longer if a data breach is going to occur, it is now a matter of when it will occur. Every computing organization, whether it is for-profit or not-for-profit, can and often suffers dramatic losses when subject to a data breach. These can be costly in terms of cleanup efforts, reputational losses, and even company closure for extreme situations. Compliance and governance standard today require companies and organizations to report any breaches almost as soon as they are discovered, even before containment and eradication actions are completed. In the United States, 46 out of 50 states now have data breach laws for reporting and risk management purposes.

A computer system and its components can be valuable evidence in an investigation. The hardware, software, documents, photos, image files, e-mail and attachments, databases, financial information, Internet browsing history, chat logs, buddy lists, event logs, along with data stored on external devices, and identifying information associated with the computer system and components are all potential evidence. One of the main requirements for handling incident evidence is known as the chain of custody. This is the defined process for handling any evidence and how, who, when, and where it is handled by investigators, analysts, examiners, and law enforcement officers (LEOs). There is a detailed explanation of the parts of the Chain of Custody requirements for evidence handling in Section 13, because the investigators are often very familiar with the legal requirements surrounding evidence, but here we will present the preliminary steps for incident responders and handlers. Chain of custody has several requirements:

- First and foremost, all activities performed with the evidence must be logged and documented—as if the evidence is being utilized in a criminal case (because it might happen). The evidence requires an investigation log and tracking methodology to be attached with it. There is an old adage in security where one of the main criteria for any security person is to document, document, document all activities. Within the Incident Response arena, this requirement is especially prevalent and needed. Each and every step performed needs to be recorded by one of the responders during its action. This provides documentation of the steps performed for legal and response purposes and can provide method improvement, technique enhancement, and further analysis for future lessons learned activities. Often, initial responders must perform the following steps upon entering an area of suspect activity:
  - Upon entry to the scene, the response team must first determine the location of all potential digital activity scenes. At this point, the responders touch nothing, being careful to not disturb the evidence in its state and only assessing the evidence and what immediate preservation procedures must be performed.
  - After preserving the evidence as noted in the next step, the responder begins the collection process by documenting the scene using notes, sketches, videos, or pictures, depending on which medium is most appropriate and available. The documentation process should be applied to all potential digital activity scenes. This process might include photographing the screens of running systems and devices.
- Second, the original evidence must *never* be directly investigated, only certified replicas, i.e., hashed copies should be used. There are multiple hashing algorithms, hash tools, and bit-stream imaging tools and devices available to perform this function. There are many methods for capture of both real-time "live" data and the stored data on the many possible storage mediums. These various tools and methods are discussed in other

parts of this book as well as in many other books on the topic of forensics and incident response.

- Third, these replicas must be created *before any* other investigative activity is engaged. All hashed copies are developed at the first possible time after the incident is contained. Completing the data capture during the initial investigative actions is often critical due to time constraints during response efforts as well as ensuring the data captured is the most relevant and current for further review and possible investigation later during the other phases of the response actions.

- Fourth, all evidence and investigative notes must be in a controlled and locked environment when not being examined. There is always a requirement during and after an event response to control the evidence and investigative notes since each case can easily end up supporting court activities and administrative events for the organization. Each item of evidence as well as the notes taken during the investigative activities needs to be identified, controlled through a "Chain of Custody" log, and retained in a secure manner within a secure location with minimal access.

- Fifth, always during the performance of the investigative activity on the evidence, review the entire scope of the available evidence, such as full hard drives including unwritten spaces; all audit logs, network activity records and any other device or network component that may have important evidence recorded. While conducting a response event, always apply full-scope analysis to ensure no potential "back-door" or "out-of-band" activities are overlooked or not considered. There is always the possibility the intrusion could contain additional attack methods and vectors outside the apparent ones when initially reviewing the events and incident particulars.

- Finally, never let the technology used for investigations override the proper techniques for evidence handling in an investigation because the results could and must be able to withstand legal cross-examination in a court of law. Let the evidence lead the analyst to the appropriate conclusions. Follow logical patterns and leads within the technical evidence as captured during the event. Allow the technology to provide the leads but allow the investigator and analyst to evaluate the case parameters directly within the scope of the event or incident.

Evidence handling has four primary areas in any incident response activity. These areas are:

1. *Collection*, which has to do with searching for evidence, recognition and collection of evidence, and documenting the items of evidence. Always ensure the collection includes all of the available data and resources, such as the whole disk drive, not just the used portions. Always document the place, time, and circumstances of each data item collected for evidence.

2. *Hardware evidence examination*, which has to do with origins, significance, and visibility of evidence, often can reveal hidden or obscured information and documentation about the evidence. Dimensions, styles, sizes, and manufacturer of hard drives, other devices, or network items are all important evidence items.

3. *Software and network evidence analysis*, which is where the logs/records/software evidence is actually examined for the incident providing the significance criteria for inclusion and the probative value of the evidence. Always conduct this software and network analysis and interpretation separate from the hardware evidence examination.

4. *Evidence reporting*, it must be written documentation with the processes and procedures outlined and explained in detail in the reports. Pertinent facts and data recovered are the primary keys in the reports. Understand the documentation and reports will always be reviewed, critiqued, and maybe even cross-examined.

One of the critical areas for evidence handling is wherever possible, always keep the evidence safe and secure for further and future review, analysis and evaluation; as it can lead to a better understanding of the attack methods and the techniques to improve the response abilities of the team members. Once the incident is completed and the case is closed, use the parameters of the case to develop training materials for future event awareness and training activities for the incident response and forensics staff members.

The following are examples of electronic devices, components, and peripherals that first responders may need to collect as digital evidence when processing an incident scene:

- Audio recorders
- GPS accessories
- Answering machines
- Computer chips
- Pagers
- Cordless landline telephones
- Copy machines
- Cellular telephones
- Hard drive duplicators
- Facsimile (fax) machines
- Printers
- Multifunction machines (printer, scanner, copier, and fax)
- Wireless access points
- Laptop power supplies and accessories
- Smart cards
- Videocassette recorders (VCRs)

- Scanners
- Telephone caller ID units
- Personal Computer Memory Card International Association (PCMCIA) cards
- PDAs.

All these types of devices can contain digital data, and therefore, can contain evidence of the issue, crime, or problem. These devices are in addition to the standard types of devices at a scene such as computers, laptops, monitors, keyboards, mice, external drives, flash or thumb drives, mass storage devices, network devices with logs on them, and other network components all of which should be examined, data retrieved or stored and then transported to the organization's laboratory for detailed examination and analysis.

Incident Response Tools

There are many different types of tools required for proper incident response. Incident response team members must be trained and tested in these various types of tools. Specific focus on a specific class of tool, by a specific team member, is acceptable and expected. A Windows-server specialist would definitely act different, investigate differently, and have different tools than a UNIX-server specialist or a firewall specialist.

There are many commercial and open source incident response tools available along with or embedded inside full investigative case management systems. All operating systems currently on the market are included in the scope of these available tools.

Types of tools that are available include:

- File system navigation tools
  The standard operating system today comes with an embedded file navigation mechanism.
- Hashing tools
  Each and every time an evidence component is captured, it is to be cryptographically signed to ensure its integrity.
- Binary search tools
  The tools used for binary search have the purpose of examining files to reveal bit patterns within.
- Imaging tools for bit-stream image copies
  One of the basic requirements for any incident response activity is to capture the data in a format that allows for examination of the complete data-set being retrieved.
- Deep retrieval tools
  A forensics-based tool designed to retrieve data that has been deleted or "erased" for long periods of time, as well as the more recent material.
- File Chain & Directory Navigation tools
  A tool designed to trace dependencies and linking of files as they are found in the directories throughout the computer.

- IR Case Management tools
Additional tools for particular Incident Response requirements include tools from Mandiant, Tenable Security, Technology Pathways, and others.

Each of these tool types is explained in detail in Section 14 of this book. I will explain some of the Incident Response specific tools below.

There are many commercial and open source incident response tools available along with or embedded inside full investigative case management systems. All operating systems currently on the market are included in the scope of these available tools. Available resources and tools for investigative activities also include:

1. Resource lists include contact information for all appropriate personnel (e.g., cell phone and pager numbers) and for external sources, such as other department/organization/agency incident response teams and law enforcement.
2. Corporate security activities and procedures, such as those which provide for:
   - All software components are consistently patched for the latest vulnerabilities.
   - All custom coding is through a security review to eliminate any potential buffer overflows and other vulnerabilities.
   - Antivirus software is installed and continually updated on all servers.
   - Backups occur as scheduled, tests backups are performed monthly, and rotation backups are stored offsite.

Investigative tools usage and application require aforementioned corporate security policy and procedures to be in place. These security incident response tools should include:

- evidence gathering tools,
- chain of custody tracking tools and procedures,
- SIRT specialized training and testing,
- corporate media control requirements,
- system and application version control,
- investigation variation procedures.

(NOTE: Most tool data has come from the vendor's websites—please review applicability to your own Incident Response requirements and test tools before deployment.)

Some of the Incident Response tools available today include, but are certainly not limited to, the following packages:

A. First Responder's Evidence Disk (FRED)
The First Responder's Evidence Disk, or FRED, is a script-based incident response tool. It was designed to capture volatile information from a

computer system for later analysis without modifying anything on the victim. It consists of a batch file used to execute a set of known good tools that gather the state of a victim computer system. It was similar to the Incident Response Collection Report (IRCR) program and has been widely imitated by other tools. Many other incident response tools used names similar to FRED. Since 2004, FRED has been maintained by the Air Force Computer Emergency Response Team. The current version of FRED (version 4) has been redesigned as a single executable, with remote collection capabilities, and uses native Application Programming Interface (API) functions. The audit file uses Public Key Infrastructure (PKI) for encryption to protect the contents from tampering and disclosure. The publicly available version has the remote functionality as well as the PKI encryption capabilities turned off.

B. First Response

First Response is an agent-based incident response tool developed by Mandiant and first released in 2006. The current version is 1.1.1. It has since migrated to the Mandiant Platform which connects the dots between network security solutions and endpoints. It equips the handler to hunt for adversaries by identifying evidence of compromise and forensic artifacts on endpoints left behind by attacker activity. The handler can apply Mandiant's intelligence directly and also integrate to Security Information and Event Management (SIEM), log management, and "next generation" network security solutions to automatically identify threats that are present in the network so the handler can stop advanced attacks when they are just beginning to unfold.

C. Helix3 & Helix 3 Pro

Helix3 is a Live CD built on top of Ubuntu as developed by e-fense. It focuses on incident response and computer forensics. Helix focuses on Incident Response and forensics tools. It is meant to be used by individuals who have a sound understanding of Incident Response and forensic techniques. Helix3 Pro is a Live CD built on top of Ubuntu. It focuses on incident response and computer forensics. Live side for Mac OS X, Windows, and Linux. Open source forensic tools included in Helix are:

- dc3dd
- aimage
- The Sleuth Kit (3.0.1, with "light" version of Autopsy, with libewf support)
- foremost
- Volatility
- Several tools for mobile phone forensics

Helix3 Pro can automount some storage devices like firewire devices and Multi-Media Communications (MMC) in read/write mode; Helix3 Pro relies on file system drivers to provide write protection, mounting some file system types (e.g., extension of the Extent File System (XFS)) will result in several data writes to the original media.

D. Incident Response Collection Report

The Incident Response Collection Report is a script-based incident response tool by John McLeod. The latest release was version 2.3 and was intended to work with Helix version 1.8.

E. Knoppix STD

Knoppix STD is a computer forensics/incident response Live CD based on Knoppix. The normal distribution contains the following programs:

- Sleuth Kit 1.66: extensions to The Coroner's Toolkit forensic toolbox.
- Autopsy 1.75: Web front end to Web-based front end to The Coroner's Toolkit (TASK). Evidence Locker defaults to /mnt/evidence
- Biew: binary viewer
- Bsed: binary stream editor
- consh: logged shell (from F.I.R.E.)
- coreography: analyze core files
- dcfldd: US DoD Computer Forensics Lab version of dd
- fenris: code debugging, tracing, decompiling, reverse engineering tool
- fatback: Undelete File Allocation Table (FAT) files
- foremost: recover specific file types from disk images (like all JPG files)
- ftimes: system baseline tool (be proactive)
- galleta: recover Internet Explorer cookies
- hashdig: dig through hash databases
- hdb: java decompiler
- mac-robber: The Coroner's Toolkit's (TCT's) graverobber written in C
- md5deep: run md5 against multiple files/directories
- memfetch: force a memory dump
- pasco: browse IE index.dat
- photorec: grab files from digital cameras
- readdbx: convert Outlook Express .dbx files to mbox format
- readoe: convert entire Outlook Express .directory to mbox format
- rifiuti: browse Windows Recycle Bin INFO2 files
- secure_delete: securely delete files, swap, memory, etc.
- testdisk: test and recover lost partitions
- wipe: wipe a partition securely. Good for prepping a partition for dd

And other typical system tools used for forensics (dd, lsof, strings, grep, etc.). STD is a Linux-based Security Tool. Actually, it is a collection of hundreds if not thousands of open source security tools. It's a Live Linux Distribution, which means it runs from a bootable CD in memory without changing the native operating system of the host computer. Its sole purpose in life is to put as many security tools at your disposal with as slick an interface as it can.

F. Masterkey Linux

Masterkey Linux (or simply Masterkey) is a Live CD based on Slackware developed by Dr. Qin Zhou of Coventry University. It focuses on incident response and computer forensics. While designed for use by students entering the field of Computer Forensics, Masterkey contains a diverse range of free and open source tools that students, computer forensics professionals, and system administrators alike can use.

Masterkey Linux is a new bootable Linux live operating system developed by Qin and focused on incident response and computer forensics. With no installation required, the forensics system is started directly from the CD/DVD-ROM *or* a USB device of a computer and is fully accessible within minutes. Its open source nature and release under the GNU General Public License (GPL) allows university staff, students, and other users to use and redistribute it freely.

Though the Masterkey Linux forensic system was originally developed for educational purpose, it can also be used by computer forensics professionals, system administrators, and incident response individuals for computer-related incident response and investigation.

G. Net/FSE

Net/FSE is a server application for network operations. The system consists of a data capture, indexing, and search services optimized for processing high-volume IP-based network log data. Log data from firewalls, intrusion detection systems, routers, and other network devices is streamed to Net/FSE in near real time, providing network professionals on enterprise networks with fast drill down and analysis of billions of log records.

A web interface built on top of Tomcat and Google Web Toolkit (GWT) is integrated into the codebase. The UI is designed to be an easy to use workflow tool for network operations including security, compliance, troubleshooting, and management. Socket-based APIs and HTTP-based XML APIs make integrating search of network log data fast and easy. The system is also moving towards a plug-in architecture that will allow users to build custom data processing engines to meet individual needs. The core system handles capture and storage, as well as search/query functionality, allowing plug-ins to easily leverage the system's capabilities with minimal coding.

H. ProDiscover IR

ProDiscover®*Incident Response* enables you to quickly and thoroughly examine a live system operating anywhere on your network. When used as part of an incident response procedure or as part of a routine system audit, ProDiscover *Incident Response* enables you to determine if that system has been compromised and allows you to gather the evidence needed to prove it.

ProDiscover *Incident Response* utilizes an agent that runs on the suspect system to read the disk at the bit level. This enables ProDiscover *Incident Response* to work around the suspect system's OS and examine all files, even if they are hidden by Trojans or rootkits. It also prevents any valuable metadata, such as last time accessed, from being altered. ProDiscover *Incident Response* can search the suspect system for over 400 known Trojans or rootkits. And, to insure the integrity of the OS, ProDiscover *Incident Response* can examine all files and compare their hash signature to the signatures of known good files from a user provided baseline or from the National Drug Intelligence Center Hashkeeper database. ProDiscover *Incident Response* allows system administrators to be sure that they uncover any compromised files in the least intrusive manner.

If the system has been compromised, ProDiscover *Incident Response* allows the system administrator to make a bit-stream image of the disk for later analysis and restore the system to proper working order to get it back online quickly. The off-line analysis of the data is easy and allows "evidentiary quality" data to be provided to law enforcement agencies.

I. Regimented Potential Incident Examination Report

The Regimented Potential Incident Examination Report (RPIER or RAPIER) is script-based incident response tool released under the GPL by Intel. It is a modular framework.

RAPIER is a Windows-based information gathering framework. It was designed to streamline the acquisition of information off of systems in a large-scale enterprise network. It was designed with a pretty simple to use GUI so that end-users could be walked through execution of the tool on a system.

RAPIER is a security tool built to facilitate first response procedures for incident handling. It is designed to acquire commonly requested information and samples during an information security event, incident, or investigation. RAPIER automates the entire process of data collection and delivers the results directly to the hands of a skilled security analyst.

J. Windows Forensic Toolchest

The Windows Forensic Toolchest™ (WFT) is designed to provide a structured and repeatable automated Live Forensic Response, Incident Response, or Audit on a Windows system while collecting security-relevant information from the system. WFT is essentially a forensically enhanced batch processing shell capable of running other security tools and producing HTML-based reports in a forensically sound manner.

A knowledgeable security professional can use WFT to help look for signs of an incident, intrusion, or to confirm computer misuse or configuration. WFT produces output that is useful to the admin user, but is also appropriate for use in court proceedings. It provides extensive logging of all its actions along with computing the MD5/SHA1 checksums along the way to ensure that its output is verifiable. The primary benefit of using WFT to perform incident responses or audit is that it provides a simplified way of scripting such activities using a sound methodology for data collection.

From European Network Information Security Agency (ENISA) IR Handbook comes the following list of tool types needed for Incident Response efforts as recommended by the ENISA:

- gathering evidence from the scene of an incident,
- investigating evidence of an incident,
- supportive tools for handling evidence,
- recovering the system after an incident,
- implementing Computer Security Incident Response Team (CSIRT) operational procedures,
- providing secure remote access,
- proactive tools to audit or detect vulnerabilities and prevent incidents.

ENISA has put together a tool for Incident Response Tools and their use called CHIHT, "Clearing House for Incident Handling Tools" (Figure 6.1).

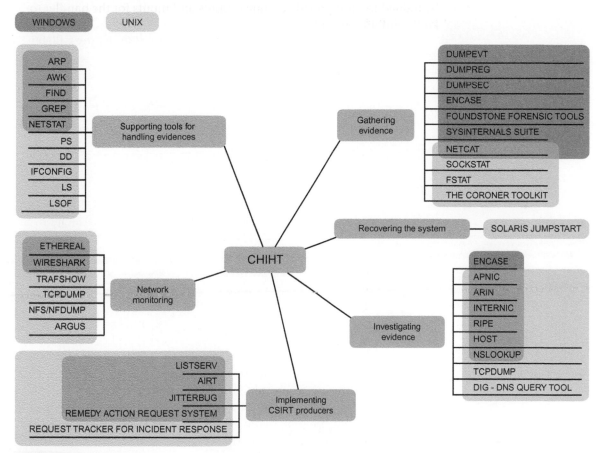

FIGURE 6.1

Clearing for incident handling tools.

Many tools listed in the CHIHT database are simply UNIX or Windows commands; so, if you have a team member with experience in UNIX systems, you do not have to pay special attention to this part of the repository—just remember that system commands (including "programs" such as *awk* or *grep*) can be very helpful tools in incident handling work.

Some final thoughts on tools and management of tool use include the following points:

a. The management of each tool used requires they be tested in the indented environment to make sure the tool will work when needed.

b. The tool under question needs to be officially acquired, approved, and certified by an external organization to allow for potential use in criminal and civil legal cases.

c. Each tool has its own set of particular requirements which will need to be trained for and provide unique outputs and inputs for the handler to know and understand.

Incident Response Policies and Procedures

There are two areas in which the Security Incident Response Team (SIRT) manager has considerable influence within the corporate security environment. These two areas are the policies and strategies for Security Response and Corporate Security activities. Policies describe the "who" and the "what" of an IT or corporate security requirement. Procedures describe the "how" of this same IT or corporate security requirement. These policies and procedures provide a method of risk reduction and liability for the organization and its employees. Policies should be both comprehensive and flexible with respect to what activities are covered, who is covered, when does it apply, and where is the policy in effect.

1. The SIRT should always follow a structured documented process, wherein the content of the items to be investigated need to be preserved, validated, and documented. Any investigation must be understood at the onset as to its dimensions, scope, and investigative methods which are best based upon proven techniques, such as proper and legal collection of evidence and obtaining proper bit-stream "hash encrypted" copies of evidence. The linear nature of investigation always needs documentation and supporting evidence, for technology can give unexpected results. So, always document everything and report everything.

2. Corporate security policies and procedures for computer security, network usage, acceptable use, allowable online activities, etc. are discussed and defined in this section. These procedures are needed and required for any IT support organization. These documents include ones which provide for:
   - All software components are consistently patched for the latest vulnerabilities
   - All custom coding through a security review to eliminate any potential buffer overflows and other vulnerabilities
   - Antivirus software is installed and continually updated on all servers
   - Backups occur as scheduled, tests backups are performed monthly, and rotation backups are stored offsite.

In the corporate security policy framework, these polices have some general structure requirements to ensure user compliance and utilization. These include:

- If too complicated, no one will follow
- If affecting productivity, they will fail and not be followed
- Clear and general as possible, but still cover why they are needed
- Always have consequences of actions
- Keep current with technologies and corporate goals
- Align with regulatory and statutory needs.

SIRT IR POLICIES

Incident Response and evidentiary tools usage and application require aforementioned corporate security policies and procedures to be in place. SIRT policies should allow authorized personnel to monitor systems and networks and perform investigations for legitimate reasons under appropriate circumstances. Legal advisors should carefully review all forensic and incident response policies and high-level procedures. It is always important to include the corporate legal staff in the preparation and review of each policy to ensure compliance and oversight requirements are actually being met by these policies. Each of these policies should mandate what actions are to be executed under what circumstances and they should include:

- Scope, Authority, Role
- Communications
- Chain of Command
- Basic IT Controls
- Guidelines for Recovery
- Training
- Testing
- Reporting Structure
- Jurisdiction
- Data and Media Control
- Privacy—Need to Know
- Audit Trail
- Documentation and Version Control
- Variations to
  - Policy
  - Framework
  - Established Procedures.

These are further defined in the Forensics Chapter on Policies and Procedures.

It is especially important that these security incident response policies include:

- Evidence gathering requirements
- Chain of custody requirements
- SIRT chain of command requirements
- SIRT scope authority
- SIRT roles and responsibility requirements
- SIRT communications training
- SIRT specialized training and testing such as desktop walkthrough simulations
- SIRT jurisdiction and governance
- Corporate media control requirements
- System and application version control
- Investigation variation procedures
- Corporate or organizational privacy requirements.

Several IR focus areas needed within the policy framework include:

Containment: What are the first steps to be taken by the incident responders? When approaching an incident scene—review what is occurring on the computer screen. If data is being deleted, pull the power plug from the wall; otherwise, perform real-time capture of system "volatile" data first. Evaluate what network or systems are being affected.

Chain of Custody: Each examiner and investigator needs to record every single activity with each piece of evidence gathered by the first responders. The process for this effort should be defined in this policy. When the chain of evidence starts, when evidence is handed off to the investigator, when the evidence is transported, where it is stored, etc. should all be recorded and maintained in accordance with this policy.

Business Continuity: In the event that a serious incident should take place, a decision to halt certain information systems may need to be made. For example, during a denial of service attack it may be better to undergo a self-imposed service outage rather than wait for an overwhelming flood of service requests. Who should be responsible for determining when to pull the plug on a service, and under what circumstances is this even an option? The converse is also of importance: who should be allowed to reenable a service, and under what circumstances?

Incident Response Plan

The major portion of the SIRT efforts should be identified and documented in a corporate Incident Response Plan (IRP). This document is the primary business-level documentation which reflects the corporation's due care and due diligence on handling of incidents, methods for response, and business criteria for recovery and restoration of normal business operations after an incident.

Starting out in developing and implementing an IRP, some specific definitions are needed to incorporate into the IRP. They are:

- *Incident* is an adverse event that has caused or has the potential to cause damage to an organization's assets, reputation, or personnel
- *Incident Management* is a process of developing and maintaining the capability to manage incidents within an organization, so that impacts can be continued and recovery is achieved within the specified time objective
- *Incident Response* is the capability to effectively prepare for and respond to unanticipated events to control and limit damage, and maintain or restore normal operations.

It is important to understand, from a business perspective, the managerial requirements for an IRP. Incident Response is the operational part of risk management. It is the activities that take place as a result of unanticipated attacks, losses, theft, accidents, or any other unexpected adverse events that occur as a result of the failure or lack of controls. The business goal of any IRP is to take the action to resolve or mitigate an incident, coordinate and disseminate information, and implement follow-up strategies to prevent recurring incidents.

As with other aspects of risk management, risk and business impact assessments (BIA) form the basis for determining the priority of resource protection and response activities.

Incident response' goal is to detect incidents quickly, manage them properly, contain and minimize damage, and restore affected services. Recent changes in governance regulations, serious breach incidents, and the general advancement of the technologies in use today have led to serious considerations about Incident Response. The following factors have contributed to the criticality of incident management and response:

- The trend of both increased occurrences and escalating losses resulting from security incidents
- The increase in vulnerabilities in software or systems can affect an organizations infrastructure and impact operations
- Failure of technical controls to prevent incidents
- Legal and regulatory requirements
- The growing sophistication and capabilities of profit-oriented attackers.

The IRP focuses on security related breaches that threaten the integrity of systems, networks, applications, and data as well as confidentiality of critical information and nonrepudiability of electronic transactions. Planning considerations must include all business functions that are critical, vital, sensitive as well as nonsensitive and noncritical but necessary support functions. The IRP needs to include the four basic criteria as follows:

- Incident detection capabilities
  This is a function of the type of detective controls the organization has deployed and the type of monitoring capabilities that exist.
- Clearly defined severity criteria
  Determining severity levels is critical to initiating appropriate response efforts.
- Assessment and triage capabilities
  The ability to quickly assess the situation often will be determined by experience and the ability to gather accurate information. The ability to triage effectively will require both good assessment as well as an understanding of where and how to allocate resources and capabilities.
- Declaration criteria
  It is critical that stakeholders and senior management agree about what conditions must exist in order to declare an incident or even worse, a disaster.

The starting point with developing an IRP is to define what the goals are for the IRP capability in the organization. One possible set of goals are:

- Handle incidents when they occur so that the exposure can be contained or eradicated to enable recovery
- Prevent previous incidents from recurring by documenting and learning from past incidents
- Deploy proactive countermeasures to prevent/minimize the probability of incidents from taking place.

Another possible set of goals for an IRP is:

- Containing the effects of the incident
- Notifying the appropriate people for the purpose of recovery or to provide needed information
- Recovering quickly and efficiently from security incidents
- Minimizing the impact of the security incident
- Responding systematically and decreasing the likelihood of recurrence
- Balancing operational and security processes
- Dealing with legal and law enforcement-related issues.

The next step is to define the SIRT team manager's responsibilities. A possible set is like this:

- Developing the information security incident management and response plans
- Handling and coordinating information security incident response activities effectively and efficiently
- Validating, verifying, and reporting of protective or countermeasure solutions, both technical and administrative
- Planning, budgeting, and program development for all matters related to information security incident management and response.

The basic structure to any IRP needs to include the following areas or phases:

A. Preparation
B. Identification
C. Containment
D. Eradication
E. Recovery
F. Lessons learned.

Each of these phases in the IRP is explained below:

A. Preparation is the phase which prepares an organization to develop an IRP prior an incident. Sufficient preparation facilitates smooth execution and includes:
   - Establishing an approach to handle incidents
   - Establishing policy and warning banners in information systems to deter intruder and allows information collection
   - Establishing communication plan to stakeholders
   - Developing criteria on when to report incident to authorities
   - Developing a process to activate incident management team
   - Establishing a secure location to execute IRP
   - Ensuring equipment needed are available.
B. Identification is the phase which aims to verify if an incident has happened and find out more details about the incident. Reports on possible incidents may come from information systems, end users or other organizations. Not all reports are valid incidents, as they may be false alarms or may not qualify as an incident. This phase includes:
   - Assigning ownership of an incident or potential incident to an incident handler
   - Verifying that reports or events qualify as an incident
   - Establishing chain of custody during identification when handling potential evidence
   - Determining the severity of an incident and escalating it as necessary.

C. Containment is the phase that provides the limitation of exposure. After an incident has been identified and confirmed, the SIRT is activated and information from the incident handler is shared. The team will conduct a detailed assessment and contact the system owner, business manager of the affected information systems/assets to coordinate further action. The action taken in this phase is to limit the exposure and includes:

- Activating incident management/response team to contain the incident
- Notifying appropriate stakeholders affected from the incidents
- Obtaining agreement on actions taken that may affect availability of a service or risks of the containment process
- Getting IT representative and relevant virtual team members involved to implement containment procedures
- Obtaining and preserving evidence
- Documenting and taking backups of actions taken from this phase onward
- Controlling and managing communication to public by public relations team.

D. Eradication is the phase when containment measures have been deployed and it is time to determine the root cause of the incident and eradicate it. Eradication can be done in a number of ways: restoring from backups to achieve a clean state of system, removing the root cause, improving defenses and performing vulnerability analysis to find further potential damages from the same root cause. This phase includes:

- Determining the signs and cause of incidents
- Locating the most recent version of backups or alternative solutions
- Removing the root cause—in the event of worm or virus infection, it can be removed by deploying appropriate patches and updated antivirus software
- Improving defenses by implementing protection techniques
- Performing vulnerability analysis to find new vulnerabilities introduced by the root cause.

E. Recovery phase ensures that affected systems or services are restored to a condition specified in the Recovery Point Objective (RPO) from the Business Impact Analysis for the affected line of business. The time constraint up to this phase is documented in the Recovery Time Objective (RTO) from the same BIA document. The primary steps to this phase are:

- Restoring operations to normal
- Validating that actions taken on restored systems were successful
- Getting involvement of system owners to test the system
- Facilitating system owners to declare normal operation.

F. The final part is the lessons learned process, occurring at the end of the incident response activity, providing a report which should always be developed to share what has happened, what measures were taken and the results after the plan was executed. Part of the report should contain lessons learned that provide Information Management Team (IMT) and other stakeholders valuable learning points of what could have been done better. These lessons should be developed into a plan to enhance the incident management capability and the documentation of the IRP. The steps are:

- Writing incident report
- Analyzing issues encountered during incident response efforts
- Proposing improvement based on issues encountered
- Presenting report to relevant stakeholders.

The basic full structure of the IRP is:

1. Overview
2. Roles and Responsibilities
3. Incidents Requiring Action
4. Current Network Infrastructure
5. Existing Security Safeguards
6. Response Steps
   a. Preparation
   b. Identification
   c. Containment
   d. Eradication
   e. Recovery
   f. Lessons learned.
7. Call List
8. Training and Awareness
9. Testing
10. Revisions.

Several example IRP plans are located at the associated site with this book and one example plan is included in Appendix C. Included in the appendix is an IT System-Specific IRP template for actual response requirements for any IT system.

CORPORATE IR STRATEGY AND GENERAL USE SECURITY POLICIES

The Corporate Security strategy starts off with what policies are needed for all users and the organization. The SIRT manager can influence and possibly even help draft some of these critical documents for the corporation. Always remember as the SIRT manager, it is your responsibility to ensure all corporate policies allow for secure, effective and efficient operations. In other words, within the policy framework of your organization, keep the focus on the objectives, secure the corporate data and keep all active threats outside the corporation. It is especially important that these corporate security policies include the following areas:

- Definition of Information Security
- Management Intent for Information Security in the Corporation
- Compliance requirements
- Security Awareness Training requirements for all employees
- Acceptable Use of corporate equipment
- Business Continuity management
- Reporting of Incidents
- Data Classification requirements
- Access Control requirements
- System and application version control
- Corporate or organizational privacy requirements.

The top six corporate security policies necessary to help prepare for an incident response effort are:

1. *AUP*: The corporate Acceptable Use Policy defines the actions allowed by the computer user on the machine or network. IR personnel need to know this policy so they can determine what activities are normal and what activities are not acceptable on the computer or the network.
2. *Privacy*: What is the expectation of privacy for each computer user when performing the various activities on the system? Each user will perform actions during the normal course of events which can impact privacy. The overarching privacy policy can provide guidance to the user when performing typical activities such as searching websites, "online" banking, social networking, etc. All of these can have major impacts on IR events or incidents.
3. *Version Control*: What is the corporate patch management policy? Who and when are patches tested, loaded, and evaluated? Who controls the configurations of the servers and network devices? All these questions are answered in the version control policy which gives the incident responder the baseline to work from when investigating and incident.
4. *Communications*: This policy covers who communicates to the corporate staff, the users, the workers, and the customers and clients of your organization when something happens. Who and how the issue is communicated to the shareholders, the public, the media and even the local emergency and law enforcement officials is also included in this policy.
5. *Reporting*: When the incident is responded to, whom and when the various activities are reported about needs clear definition in this policy. Just as important is who is NOT reported to as who is reported to since the incident can always have some "insider" component to it.

6. *Backup*: This policy sets the boundaries for recovery from the incident. How far back in time is the data retained, where is it, what are the procedures for the daily, weekly, and monthly backups of the server or network data? These questions are answered in this backup policy which the incident responders need to properly return the system or network to normal business operations.

Legal Requirements and Considerations

Legal disclaimer: This section's information is merely to explain the process and foundation for the incident response activities. It is not meant to be a legal opinion, please consult your corporate legal counsel for full legal opinion and advise.

There are three main areas within the legal scope of incident response to be considered.

1. First—privacy
2. Second—ethics
3. Third—investigations themselves.

Then several legal areas of focus on Incident Response and evidence gathered during incident handling activities are covered.

PRIVACY

National and international privacy laws and regulations require that all incident response activities be conducted as privately as possible. There could be liability of some sort on the part of the corporation or organization if the incident response results are given to the wrong party or publicly released. Additionally, there could be severe financial repercussions for the corporation, the organization, and/or the individuals involved if the privacy requirements are not maintained. Additional reviews of the actual national and international privacy requirements are found in Section 9 on the governmental statutory and regulatory requirements for incident response.

The SIRT leader always needs to keep in his/her mind who can receive the information, who can receive the evidence and who has the authority to give instructions and make decisions about the incident. Security incidents often end up in courts of law—criminal or civil or administrative proceedings;

therefore, privacy must be of the utmost importance during the investigation. The privacy areas for consideration by the SIRT manager include:

- Importance of privacy for actual investigations
  The actual IR response will require the data involved be protected under the normal statutory and regulatory requirements for the location of the investigation of the incident. Are there any external Privacy regulations or legal requirements? If so, how do they apply to this SIRT response effort? These are questions the SIRT Manager needs to have answered as the response progresses. Each location and jurisdiction has its own privacy requirements for the protection of data and its use throughout the organization. Additional requirements may be placed on the data as it is used by associated third-party organizations of the retaining organization. So, always research and be aware of the privacy laws and regulations surrounding the retention and use of data, whether it is customer data, client corporate data, or general consumer data.
- Liability if data is given to wrong party
  When the data involved in the investigation is determined, the actual legal needs for protection of the data will need to be reviewed and determined. What are the parameters for privacy surrounding the data? Who is allowed to know what data is involved? What are the data disclosure regulations which govern this event or incident? What are the internal human relations issues relating to payroll and employee privacy that are to be covered? These are just a few questions which need answers concerning the data.

Also, keep in mind not to allow the SIRT Members to discuss the cases with unknown or not authorized personnel so as to prevent a data breach directly from the Team. Only allow the media relations staff to discuss any current investigation or response effort with outside of the team personnel not in the reporting chain.

- Know who can receive information from the investigation.
  Based upon the data found to be under investigation, the reporting requirements are vital on who can receive the IR reports and at what point during the investigation can they receive these reports. Certain types of data (Personal identity, Health-related, etc.) must be reported under investigation as soon as possible when providing Incident Response services for various types of organizations (federal, financial, etc.) due to statutory or regulatory reporting requirements.
  As an example, in the US federal and health-care-related fields, Personally Identifiable Information (PII) data breaches must be reported to federal authorities within 1 h of the discovery of a POTENTIAL breach. This requirement is in the statutes and regulations for both industries and concerns even potential data breaches, not just confirmed ones.

- Know who has the authority to give instructions and make decisions related to the incident.
  Within the framework of the SIRT operating instructions and policies, there should be the reporting and decision mechanisms for the type of incident under investigation. Given there are seven basic types of investigations (see Section 3) which the SIRT will provide services for, each type needs to have identified who is the Senior Executive which will oversee the effort, and under what circumstances can they make investigative decisions concerning the SIRT response to the incident.

ETHICS

Ethics are usually the corporate rules of conduct, rules of behavior, moral codes, and acceptable use activities for users, supervisors, managers, executives, and any third party outside entity to follow when conducting investigations. Ethics are usually judged by the society's acceptable practices which can include corporate accounting practices, public information dissemination requirements, and legal statutory or regulatory demands. Ethics often refers to well-founded standards of right and wrong that prescribe what humans ought to do, usually in terms of rights, fairness, obligations, benefits to society, and specific virtues. These ethical needs include various standards relating to rights, such as the right to life, the right to freedom from injury, the right to choose, the right to privacy, and right to freedom of speech and expression. Such standards are often found to be adequate measures of ethics because they are supported by consistent and well-developed reasons.

Ethics also refers to the study and development of personal ethical standards, as well as community and corporate ethics, in terms of behavior, feelings, laws, and social habits and norms which can deviate from more universal ethical standards. Ethics are based in the notion of responsibility (as free moral agents, individuals, organizations, and societies are responsible for the actions that they take) and accountability (individuals, organizations, and society should be held accountable to others for the consequences of their actions). So there are two areas that the organization needs to have ethics addressed in its corporate documentation:

- Corporate Policy in place defining ethics—Focus on Responsibility
  The corporate policy for ethical behavior should reflect the senior executive and board of directors' stance on the expected employee and corporate behaviors at all times, especially when representing the company. The Internet Use Policy, the Data Handling Policy, and the Corporate Compliance Policy are all examples of this type of Policy.

- Rules of Conduct—Focus on Accountability
  Employee rules of conduct will reflect the expected day-to-day behaviors during the normal conduct of work-related efforts. The Acceptable Use Policy and the Password Policy are examples of this type of policy.

There are many ethics guides and policy templates available on the Internet and through the various professional security organizations such as International Information Systems Security Certification Consortium (ISC2) and Information Systems Audit and Control Association (ISACA). Each of these organizations requires their certificate holders to adhere to a professional code of ethics and publishes these documents publicly for all to see and read.

Another source for personal ethical behavior is the Brookings Institute Computer Ethics Institute 10 Commandments of Computer Ethics[1]:

1. Thou shalt not use a computer to harm other people
2. Thou shalt not interfere with other people's computer work
3. Thou shalt not snoop around in other people's files
4. Thou shalt not use a computer to steal
5. Thou shalt not use a computer to bear false witness
6. Thou shalt not copy or use proprietary software for which you have not paid
7. Thou shalt not use other people's computer resources without authorization or proper compensation
8. Thou shalt not appropriate other people's intellectual output
9. Thou shalt think about the social consequences of the program you write or the system you design
10. Thou shalt use a computer in ways that show consideration and respect for your fellow humans.

INVESTIGATION GUIDELINES

All responders and senior executives that oversee incident response activities must be familiar with the current local, regional, national and international law rules, guidelines and current litigations surrounding the incident response efforts and evidence. There are differences within governmental and corporate jurisdictions with respect to evidence, search and seizure, self-incrimination, and privacy.

- Familiar with Laws
  There is an old law enforcement saying the "ignorance of the law is no excuse for violating the law." Each responder and executive must ensure

---

[1] 10 Commandments of Computer Ethics, The Computer Ethics Institute, http://computerethicsinstitute.org/; 2003.

they are aware of any statutory or regulatory requirement during the performance of their duties and activities.

- Violation of laws

Each responder must know what the repercussions are for violating the standard laws of the local area as well as the regional, national, and potentially even international laws when investigation an incident.

- Successful Litigation

The responder takes the first critical steps during the investigation which provide the successful framework for future litigation involving the potential crime, event, or administrative action. These steps include following the appropriate chain of custody actions, full and complete analysis and other actions explained in previous sections.

- Familiar with Rules

Familiarity with the rules of evidence, chain of evidence, meaningful use, eDiscovery rules, and many other standards for investigation and analysis are all important for the SIRT manager to provide guidance and direction on to the team members.

- Familiar with Guidelines

SIRT members will require the Team Manager to provide them the necessary corporate guidance, the response guidelines for the actual situation being investigated, the forensics/evidentiary guidance for the hardware, network and software involved, as well as the direct on-site guidance for handling of the people, situation, and environment during the incident response.

- Differences with governmental jurisdictions

Order of precedence for legal jurisdiction is always needed and should be reviewed by the SIRT Manager when getting ready to respond to an incident. This order is dependent upon your local, regional, and national legal structure and should be identified and defined by your corporate legal counsel during the team set-up process.

Now a couple of focus areas for consideration by the SIRT Manager are needed at this point during the review of what are the legal and ethical standings for the SIRT actions and activities. There are two primary US-based areas to always keep in mind when overseeing and managing SIRT actions.

US Federal Rules of Evidence

The Federal Rules of Evidence (FRE) are the guides for investigators and responders in the actual collection and use of evidence in court cases. The FRE is the code of evidence law governing the admission of facts by which parties in the US federal court system may prove their cases, both civil and criminal. The FRE were the product of protracted academic, legislative, and judicial examination before being finally approved in 1975. US states are free to adopt or maintain evidence rules different from the Federal Rules, but a significant majority (47 out of 50) has adopted codes in whole or part based on the FRE.

The FRE primarily serve to govern federal trial courts rather than appellate courts, because they (FRE) govern the initial presentation of evidence in a trial; especially since appellate courts, due to their function and scope address very few questions touching upon the facts of a case. Primarily the purpose of these FRE is to regulate the evidence that the US Federal Court judge and/or jury may use to reach a verdict. The FRE strive to eliminate the historical distrust of jurors, and encourage admitting evidence in close cases. The many types of information presented to a judge or jury are designed to convince them of the truth or falsity of key facts. Strict rules limit what can be properly admitted as evidence, but dozens of exceptions to these rules often mean that lawyers find a way to introduce such testimony or other items into evidence.

At the same time, the FRE centers on a few basic ideas—relevance, efficiency, reliability of evidence, unfair surprise, and overall fairness of the adversary (prosecution/defense) process. The FRE grant trial judges broad discretion to admit evidence in the face of competing arguments from the parties. This ensures that the jury has a broad spectrum of evidence before it, but not so much evidence that is repetitive, inflammatory, or unnecessarily confusing. The FRE define relevance broadly and relax the common-law prohibitions on witnesses' competence to testify. Hearsay standards are similarly relaxed, as are the standards for authenticating written documents. At the same time, the judge retains power to exclude evidence that has too great a danger for unfair prejudice to a party due to its inflammatory, repetitive, or confusing nature or its propensity to waste the court's time.

There are 67 individually numbered rules, divided among 11 articles within the FRE:

1. General Provisions
2. Judicial Notice
3. Presumptions in Civil Actions and Proceedings
4. Relevancy and Its Limits
5. Privileges
6. Witnesses
7. Opinions and Expert Testimony
8. Hearsay
9. Authentication and Identification
10. Contents of Writings, Recordings, and Photographs
11. Miscellaneous Rules.

The FRE embody some very common concepts, and attorneys frequently refer to those concepts by the rule number. The most important concept—the balancing of relevance against other competing interests—is embodied in Rule 403.

> Although relevant, evidence may be excluded if its probative value is substantially outweighed by the danger of unfair prejudice, confusion of the issues, or misleading the jury, or by considerations of undue delay, waste of time, or needless presentation of cumulative evidence.

US Federal Rules for Civil Procedures

The Federal Rules for Civil Procedures (FRCP) govern the procedure in all civil actions and proceedings in the US district courts, except as stated in Rule 81. They should be construed and administered to secure the just, speedy, and inexpensive determination of every action and proceeding. The FRCP was adopted and went into effect on December 1, 2010.

Specifically relevant to SIRT activities is the Rule 34 related to producing documents, electronically stored information (ESI) and tangible things, or entering onto land for inspection and other purposes.

Rule 34 states that any party may serve onto the other party in a litigation action, a request to produce and permit the requesting party or its representative to inspect, copy, test, or sample the following items in the responding party's possession, custody, or control:

A. any designated documents or electronically stored information— including writings, drawings, graphs, charts, photographs, sound recordings, images, and other data or data compilations—stored in any medium from which information can be obtained either directly or, if necessary, after translation by the responding party into a reasonably usable form; or
B. any designated tangible things; or
C. to permit entry onto designated land or other property possessed or controlled by the responding party, so that the requesting party may inspect, measure, survey, photograph, test, or sample the property or any designated object or operation on it.

This requires each party within a legal case to produce the ESI related to the case which can include e-mails, documents on a server, and any other related electronic information. *This has resulted in the entirely new field with SIRT and Forensics known as "eDiscovery" and created a new arena for SIRT managers to monitor and oversee during incident response and investigations.*

See Section 13 for a further explanation and detailed examination of the eDiscovery field and the forensics involved in eDiscovery.

Governmental Laws, Policies, and Procedures

Over the past 50 years, various governments around the world have developed and passed laws within their country to govern and oversee Incident Response, Computer Security, and Forensics activities. This section is designed to provide the reader with a "snapshot" of these laws in some of the larger countries.

US GOVERNMENT

The US government has documented many incident response policies and procedures over the past 40 years, starting with US Privacy Act of 1974. The Federal Information Security Management Act (FISMA), passed into public law as part of the E-Government Act in 2002, documented the requirements for computer security for all US government information systems and designated the National Institute of Standards and Technology (NIST) as the single US governmental agency responsible for security procedures and standards development. NIST provides multiple computer security guidelines known as special publications (SP) for various computer security related requirements. As an example, the NIST SP 800-61 REV.1, entitled "Computer Security Incident Handling Guide," dated March 2008, is a very well developed and extremely well thought out document to start with for your incident response program development. This document covers developing an incident response capability handling an incident, team management, and development of check lists and recommendations for various incident response requirements. This document is great for use by private organizations and corporations to adapt and utilize in their own environment. Always review local, national, and international organizational and governmental requirements for security policies, procedures, and guideline.

Explanations and resources for local, national, and international organizational and governmental requirements for security policies, procedures, and guidelines are provided.

Privacy Act

Passed in 1974 as a result of the Watergate episode, the US Privacy Act places personal citizen data in a protected mode for all governmental agencies that retain citizen data.

The Privacy Act establishes a Code of Fair Information Practice that governs the collection, maintenance, use, and dissemination of personally identifiable information about individuals that is maintained in systems of records by federal agencies. A system of records is a group of records under the control of an agency from which information is retrieved by the name of the individual or by some identifier assigned to the individual. The Privacy Act requires that agencies give the public notice of their systems of records by publication in the Federal Register. The Privacy Act prohibits the disclosure of information from a system of records absent the written consent of the subject individual, unless the disclosure is pursuant to 1 of 12 statutory exceptions. The Act also provides individuals with a means by which to seek access to and amendment of their records, and sets forth various agency record-keeping requirements.

The Privacy Act states in part:

> No agency shall disclose any record which is contained in a system of records by any means of communication to any person, or to another agency, except pursuant to a written request by, or with the prior written consent of, the individual to whom the record pertains....

There are specific exceptions for the record allowing the use of personal records:

- For statistical purposes by the Census Bureau and the Bureau of Labor Statistics
- For routine uses within a US government agency
- For archival purposes "as a record which has sufficient historical or other value to warrant its continued preservation by the United States Government"
- For law enforcement purposes
- For congressional investigations
- Other administrative purposes.

The Privacy Act mandates that each United States Government agency has in place an administrative and physical security system to prevent the unauthorized release of personal records.

To protect the privacy and liberty rights of individuals, federal agencies must state "the authority (whether granted by statute, or by Executive order of the President) which authorizes the solicitation of the information and whether disclosure of such information is mandatory or voluntary" when requesting information. This notice is common on almost all federal government forms which seek to gather information from individuals, many of which seek personal and confidential details.

Computer Security Act

Passed in 1987, it is designed to improve the security and privacy of sensitive information in Federal computer systems and to establish a minimum acceptable security practices for such systems. It requires the creation of computer security plans and the appropriate training of system users or owners where the systems house sensitive information.

- Improve security/privacy of sensitive information in federal systems.
- Federal agencies to establish standards and guidelines under NIST direction and guidance.
- Requires that any federal computer system that processes sensitive information have a customized security plan (System Security Authorization Agreement (SSAA)).
- Requires that users of those systems undergo security training.

NIST responsible, National Security Agency (NSA) to advise:

- assessing the vulnerability of federal computer systems,
- developing standards,
- providing technical assistance with NSA support,
- developing training guidelines for federal personnel.

Clinger–Cohen Act

Passed in 1996 as the *Information Technology Management Reform Act of 1996*, this law is designed to improve the way the federal government acquires, uses, and disposes of information technology (IT).

The Clinger–Cohen Act supplements the information resources management policies by establishing a comprehensive approach for executive agencies to improve the acquisition and management of their information resources, by:

1. focusing information resource planning to support the agency's strategic missions;
2. implementing a capital planning and investment control process that links to budget formulation and execution;
3. rethinking and restructuring the way the agency does their work before investing in IT systems.

The Clinger–Cohen Act directed the development and maintenance of Information Technology Architectures (ITA) by federal agencies to maximize the benefits of information technology (IT) within the US Government. In subsequent guidance on implementing the Act, the Office of Management and Budget (OMB) stipulated that agency IT Architecture's "… should be consistent with Federal, agency, and bureau information architectures." In keeping with this mandate, in 1999, the US Federal CIO Council initiated the Federal Enterprise Architecture, essentially a federal-wide ITA that would "… develop, maintain, and facilitate the implementation of the top-level enterprise architecture for the Federal Enterprise."

Computer Fraud & Abuse Act

Passed in 1986, the Computer Fraud and Abuse Act (CFAA) is designed to reduce cracking and hacking of computer systems and to address federal computer-related offenses. The CFAA governs cases with a compelling federal interest, where computers of the federal government or certain financial institutions are involved, where the crime itself is interstate in nature, or where computers are used in interstate and foreign commerce. The CFAA essentially states that, whoever intentionally accesses a computer without authorization or exceeds authorized access, and thereby obtains information from any protected computer if the conduct involved an interstate or foreign communication shall be punished under the Act. In 1996 the CFAA was, again, broadened by an amendment that replaced the term "federal interest computer" with the term "protected computer." While the CFAA is primarily a criminal law intended to reduce the instances of malicious interferences with computer systems and to address federal computer offenses, an amendment in 1994 allows civil actions to be brought under the statute, as well.

There are seven types of criminal activity enumerated in the CFAA:

1. obtaining national security information,
2. compromising confidentiality,
3. trespassing in a government computer,
4. accessing to defraud and obtain value,
5. damaging a computer or information,
6. trafficking in passwords,
7. threatening to damage a computer.

A violation of the CFAA can be committed in two ways:

1. either by an outsider who trespasses into a computer or
2. by an intruder who goes beyond the scope of his given authorization.

COPPA

Passed in 1998, the Children's Online Privacy Protection Act of 1998 (COPPA), effective April 21, 2000, applies to the online collection of personal information by persons or entities under US jurisdiction from children under 13 years of age. It details what a web site operator must include in a privacy policy, when and how to seek verifiable consent from a parent or guardian, and what responsibilities an operator has to protect children's privacy and safety online including restrictions on the marketing to those under 13. While children under 13 can legally give out personal information with their parents' permission, many web sites altogether disallow underage children from using their services due to the amount of paperwork involved.

This is an American law, however, the Federal Trade Commission has made it clear that the requirements of COPPA will apply to foreign-operated web sites if such sites "are directed to children in the US or knowingly collect information from children in the US."

Electronic Communications Privacy Act of 1986 (ECPA)

- Extend government restrictions on wire taps from telephone calls to include transmissions of electronic data by computer.
  Title I of the ECPA protects wire, oral, and electronic communications while in transit. It sets down requirements for search warrants that are more stringent than in other settings.
- Added new provisions prohibiting access to stored electronic communications.
  Title II of the ECPA, the Stored Communications Act, protects communications held in electronic storage, most notably messages stored on computers. Its protections are weaker than those of Title I, however, and do not impose heightened standards for warrants.
- Added so-called pen/trap provisions that permit the tracing of telephone communications.
  Title III prohibits the use of pen register and/or traps and trace devices to record dialing, routing, addressing, and signaling information used in the process of transmitting wire or electronic communications without a court order.

FISMA

Passed in 2002, FISMA requires all US governmental agencies to protect their sensitive data as part of its annual security requirement, because information security is important to both the economics and security of the United States. FISMA requires each federal agency to develop, document, and implement an agency-wide program to provide information security for the information and information systems that support the operations and assets of the agency, including those provided or managed by another agency, contractor, or other outside source. FISMA has brought attention within the federal government to cybersecurity and explicitly emphasized a "risk-based policy for cost-effective security."

OMB has oversight over E-Government

- Federal Government (Organizations and IGs) must report IA status to OMB annually and quarterly.
- OMB provides reports to Congress annually.
- Congressional Cybersecurity Grade.

NIST publishes Standards and Guidelines and NSA serves as Technical Advisor.

- All Federal Government must follow NIST C&A processes, with the exception of Defense and Intelligence organizations.

USA Patriot Act

Uniting and Strengthening America by Providing Appropriate Tools Required to Intercept and Obstruct Terrorism Act was originally passed in 2001, subsequent to the 9/11 terrorist attacks, and has been renewed by the US Congress several times since then. It includes the following areas for focus for SIRT and Forensics areas:

a. Amended the definition of "electronic surveillance" to exclude the interception of communications done through or from a protected computer where the owner allows the interception, or is lawfully involved in an investigation.

b. Secret Service jurisdiction was extended to investigate computer fraud, access device frauds, false identification documents or devices, or any fraudulent activities against US financial institutions.

c. Specified the development and support of cybersecurity forensic capabilities.

   i. Directs the Attorney General to establish regional computer forensic laboratories that have the capability of performing forensic examinations of intercepted computer evidence relating to criminal activity and cyberterrorism, and that have the capability of training and educating Federal, State, and local law enforcement personnel and prosecutors in computer crime, and to facilitate and promote the sharing of Federal law enforcement expertise and information.

CANADIAN GOVERNMENT

This data is from the Operational Security Standard: Management of Information Technology Security (MITS) of the Canadian Government found at http://www.tbs-sct.gc.ca/pol/doc-eng.aspx?id=12328

Section 18. Response and Recovery

18.1 Incident Response Coordination

Section 10.12.3 of the *Government Security Policy* requires departments to establish mechanisms to respond effectively to IT incidents and exchange incident-related information with designated lead departments in a timely fashion. To do so, departments must appoint an individual or establish a centre to coordinate incident response and act as a point of contact for communication with respect to government-wide incident response. Departments that do not have an Information Protection Centre should assign this function to the IT Security Coordinator.

The Government of Canada systems and networks should be viewed as a single interconnected entity that requires a coordinated incident response. PSEPC is responsible for coordinating incident response across the federal government and, with other lead agencies, providing technical assistance, advice and information on the handling of IT security incidents.

Incident handling generally follows five stages:

- Identification—determine the type, severity and cause of the incident(s) (e.g. virus, worm, denial-of-service-attack),
- Response—determine the best approach and take action to contain the damage (e.g. disconnect, disable, block, or update computer or network configurations),
- Reporting—communicate the incident specifics, including the impact and the response, to PSEPC and departmental management,
- Recovery—identify an approach to restore and recover systems and implement approved changes to security devices (e.g. firewall and incident detection rules), and
- Post-Analysis—assess the incident and recommend changes in processes and procedures, if required.

18.2 Incident Identification and Prioritization

If monitoring reveals an anomaly, departments must determine whether the cause is a security incident, a hardware or software problem, or an increase in client demand. An IT security incident refers to an adverse event in an information system or network or the threat of the occurrence of such an event. Incidents can include but are not limited to:

- Denial of Service (DoS)—an attack that could prevent the usage of networks, systems, or applications,
- Malicious Code—a virus, worm, Trojan horse, or other code-based malicious entity that infects a host,

- Unauthorized Access—a user who gains access without permission to a network, system, applications, data, or other resource, and
- Multiple Impacts—a combination of a number of computer events occurring at the same time or a computer event in coordination with other malicious or accident incidents.

To analyze IT security incidents effectively, departments must understand the types of IT security incidents that can occur, their potential impact, the technical and operational environment, and service delivery priorities.

Typically this analysis involves the following steps:

- Determine if an incident has occurred
- Perform an assessment of the severity of impact or potential impact
- Identify the type, cause, and source
- Log the event

If more than one incident occurs at the same time or is too complex, departments should prioritize and focus on the most significant incident event first. Factors to consider include risks related to:

- Human life and safety,
- Valuable, sensitive and critical information and assets,
- Disruption to operations or services, and
- Public confidence

18.3 Incident Response

Departments must develop incident response procedures to follow in order to mitigate damage, contain the cause of the incidents and restore services.

Given the interconnectivity of the Government of Canada, departments must always, when responding to an IT security incident, consider the impact of their actions or inaction on other federal organizations.

Departments must maintain operational records that show how incidents were handled, documenting the chain of events during the incident, noting the time when the incident was detected; the actions taken; the rationale for decisions; details of communications; management approvals or direction; and external and internal reports.

EU

Within the European Union, privacy and data protection are considered as two separate fundamental rights.

Protection of personal data is a right which is separate, but closely linked to the right to privacy:

a. Respect for private life was established in 1950 with the adoption of the European Convention of Human Rights—in the framework of the Council of Europe. Put in short terms, the right to privacy may be described as a right which prevents public authorities from measures which are privacy invasive, unless certain conditions have been met.

b. The right to data protection was introduced in the 1980s as a consequence of technical developments. Put in short terms, data protection principles aim to establish conditions under which it is legitimate and lawful to process personal data. Data protection legislation obliges those responsible to respect a set of rules and empowers the people concerned by granting them rights. Finally, it provides for supervision by independent authorities.

EU Security Requirements for Incidence Response:

Article 13a of the Framework directive: *"Security and Integrity"*

The Telecoms reform, passed into law in 2009, adds Article 13a to the Framework directive, regarding security and integrity of public electronic communication networks and services. Article 13a states:

- Providers of public communication networks and services should take measures to guarantee security and integrity (i.e. availability) of their networks.
- Providers must report to competent national authorities about significant security breaches.
- National authorities should inform ENISA and authorities abroad when necessary, for example in case of incidents with impact across borders.
- National authorities should report to ENISA and the EC about the incident reports annually.

Article 13a also says that the EC may issue more detailed implementation requirements if needed, taking into account ENISA's opinion.

The EC, ENISA, and the national regulators have been collaborating for the past 2 years to implement Article 13a and to agree on a single set of security measures for the European electronic communications sector and a modality for reporting about security breaches in the electronic communications sector to authorities abroad, to ENISA, and the EC.

In May 2012, ENISA received the first set of annual reports from Member States, concerning incident that occurred in 2011. ENISA received 51 incident reports about large incidents, which exceeded an agreed impact threshold.

The reports describe services affected, number of users affected, duration, root causes, actions taken, and lessons learnt. While nationally incident reporting is implemented differently, with different procedures, thresholds, etc., nearly all national regulators use a common procedure, a common template and common thresholds for reporting to the EC and ENISA.

2.2 Article 4 of the e-Privacy directive: *"Security of processing"*

The Telecoms reform also changed the e-Privacy Directive, which addresses data protection and privacy related to the provision of public electronic communication networks or services. Article 4 of the e-Privacy directive requires providers to notify personal data breaches to the competent authority and subscribers concerned, without undue delay. The obligations for providers are:

- To take appropriate technical and organizational measures to ensure security of services,
- To notify personal data breaches to the competent national authority,
- To notify data breaches to the subscribers or individuals concerned, when the personal data breach is likely to adversely affect their privacy, and
- To keep an inventory of personal data breaches, including the facts surrounding the breaches, the impact and the remedial actions taken.

Article 4 also says that the EC may issue technical implementing measures regarding the notification formats and procedures, in consultation with the Article 29 Working Party, the European Data Protection Supervisor (EDPS), and ENISA.

2.3 Articles 30, 31 and 32 of the Data Protection regulation

The EC has proposed to reform the current European data protection framework (Directive 95/46/EC), and has proposed an EU regulation on data protection. The regulation regards organizations that are processing personal data, regardless of the business sector the organization is in. Security measures and personal data breach notifications are addressed in Articles 30, 31, and 32:

- Organizations processing personal data must take appropriate technical and organizational security measures to ensure security appropriate to the risks presented by the processing.
- For all business sectors the obligation to notify personal data breaches becomes mandatory.
- Personal data breaches must be notified to a competent national authority without undue delay and, where feasible, within 24 hours, or else a justification should be provided.
- Personal data breaches must be notified to individuals if it is likely there will be an impact on their privacy. If the breached data was unintelligible, notification is not required.

2.4 Article 15 of the e-Sig and e-ID regulation: *"Security requirements"*

The EC recently released a proposal for a regulation on electronic identification and trust services for electronic transactions in the internal market. Article 15 in this proposal introduces obligations concerning security measures and incident reporting:

- Trust service providers must implement appropriate technical and organizational measures for the security of their activities.
- Trust service providers must notify competent supervisory bodies and other relevant authorities of any security breaches and where appropriate, national supervisory bodies must inform supervisory bodies in other EU countries and ENISA about security breaches.
- The supervisory body may, directly or via the service provider concerned, inform the public.
- The supervisory body sends a summary of breaches to ENISA and the EC.

There are other countries with Incident Response directives, legislation, and regulation. It is always paramount when managing an SIRT, the manager knows the statutory and regulatory requirements for Incident Response reporting and coordination with the national and international IR organizations.

PART

2

Forensics Team

This part will present the concepts and principles security professionals and managers need to know to conduct or oversee a forensics investigation team. It will discuss how managers are responsible for establishing and following policies and procedures, as well as certifying personnel and their levels of expertise. The sections will explore forensics team management, critical chains of evidence collection and custody, and the laws, ethics, regulations, and boundaries for investigations, and the investigators. This part also will present the relationships the forensics manager should develop including technical, management, law enforcement, and civil relationships with professionals and organizations.

The First Digital Forensics Research Workshop defined Digital Forensic Science as:

"The use of scientifically derived and proven methods toward the preservation, collection, validation, identification, analysis, interpretation, documentation and presentation of digital evidence derived from digital sources for the purpose of facilitating or furthering the reconstruction of events found to be criminal, or helping to anticipate unauthorized actions shown to be disruptive to planned operations."[1]

This definition covers the broad aspects of digital forensics from data acquisition to legal actions. This is the base requirement for any forensics investigation and examination that will be conducted by the Forensics team.

As with any investigation, to find the truth one must identify data that:

- verifies existing data and theories (Inculpatory Evidence),
- contradicts existing data and theories (Exculpatory Evidence).

"To find both evidence types, all acquired data must be analyzed and identified. Analyzing every bit of data is a daunting task when confronted with the increasing size of storage systems. Furthermore, the acquired data is typically only a series of byte values from the hard disk or network wire. Raw data like this are typically difficult to understand. In cases of multi-disk systems, such as RAID and Volume Management, acquired data from a single disk cannot be analyzed unless they are merged with the data from other disks using complex algorithms."[2]

It is often very important for an Incident Responder to conduct Forensics-based investigations just to identify the source of the incident and any attendant artifacts or malware. The NIST Special Publication SP 800-61, revision 1 has many key points for developing and working with the combination of Incident Handling and Forensics. I have included one key section on Forensics in Incident Response cases from pages 3 to 20 as an example of what to look for when reviewing this document.

"Before copying the files from the affected host, it is often desirable to capture volatile information that may not be recorded in a file system or image backup, such as current network connections, processes, login sessions, open files, network interface configurations, and the contents of memory. This data may hold clues as to the attacker's identity or the attack methods that were used. It is also valuable to document how far the local clock deviates from the actual time. However, risks are associated with acquiring information from the live system. Any action performed on the host itself will alter the state of the machine to some extent. Also, the attacker may currently be on the system and notice the handler's activity, which could have disastrous consequences.

A well-trained and careful incident handler should be able to issue only the minimum commands needed for acquiring the dynamic evidence without

---

[1] Palmer G. A road map for digital forensic research. Technical Report DTR-T0010-01, DFRWS, November 2001. Report from the First Digital Forensic Research Workshop (DFRWS).
[2] Defining digital forensic examination and analysis tools using abstraction layers. Brian Carrier Int J Digit Evidence Winter 2003;1(4).

inadvertently altering other evidence. A single poorly chosen command can irrevocably destroy evidence; for example, simply displaying the directory contents can alter the last access time on each listed file. Furthermore, running commands from the affected host is dangerous because they may have been altered or replaced (e.g., Trojan horses, rootkits) to conceal information or cause additional damage. Incident handlers should use write-protected removable media that contains trusted commands and all dependent files so that all necessary commands can be run without using the affected host's commands. Incident handlers can also use *write blocker* programs that prevent the host from writing to its hard drives.

After acquiring volatile data, an incident handler with computer forensics training should immediately make a full disk image to sanitized write-protectable or write-once media. A disk image preserves all data on the disk, including deleted files and file fragments. If it is possible that evidence may be needed for prosecution or internal disciplinary actions, the handlers should make at least two full images, label them properly, and securely store one of the images to be used strictly as evidence. (All evidence, not just disk images, should be tagged and stored in a secure location.) Occasionally, handlers may acquire and secure the original disk as evidence; the second image can then be restored to another disk as part of system recovery.

Obtaining a disk image is superior to a standard file system backup for computer forensic purposes because it records more data. Imaging is also preferable because it is much safer to analyze an image than it is to perform analysis on the original resource—the analysis may inadvertently alter or damage the original. If the business impact of taking down the system outweighs the risk of keeping the system operational, disk imaging may not be possible. A standard file system backup can capture information on existing files, which may be sufficient for handling many incidents, particularly those that are not expected to lead to prosecution. Both disk imaging and file system backups are valuable regardless of whether the attacker will be prosecuted because they permit the target to be restored while the investigation continues using the image or backup."

This section will cover the critical parts of a Forensics Team structure, team membership, training, activities, and general management of the actions within the corporate governance and security infrastructure. Techniques for managing forensics investigations, tools for forensics use, a forensics examination process definition, and the overarching corporate security policies and compliance requirements are all discussed in this section.

Forensics Process

Digital Forensics is the *process for any forensics scene activity or investigation involving computer-based or network-based digital data in a system and/or network.*

NIST developed and produced a Special Publication for Forensics as applied in Incident Response known as SP 800-86. In this document, the term data refers to distinct pieces of digital information that have been formatted in a specific way. This document continues: "The expansion of computers for professional and personal use and the pervasiveness of networking have fueled the need for tools that can record and analyze an ever-increasing amount of data from many sources. For example, data can be stored or transferred by standard computer systems (e.g., desktops, laptops, servers), networking equipment (e.g., firewalls, routers), computing peripherals (i.e., printers), personal digital assistants (PDA), CDs, DVDs, removable hard drives, backup tapes, flash memory, thumb drives, and jump drives. Many consumer electronic devices (e.g., cell phones, video game consoles, digital audio players, and digital video recorders) can also be used to store data. This increasing variety of data sources has helped spur the development and refinement of forensics tools and techniques. This has also been caused by the realization that such tools and techniques can be used for many purposes, such as investigating crimes, reconstructing computer security incidents, troubleshooting operational problems, and recovering from accidental system damage."

This activity is usually in response to some incident, event, or activity that resulted in an Incident Response action. Forensics is the detailed process invoked during Incident Response when the event is found to have some legal, criminal, or civil component or potential result for the organization.

Always keep in mind as the forensics process is conducted, the four main sources of data within any network or computer:

A. files,
B. operating systems,
C. network traffic,
D. applications.

We will discuss these areas and will detail their criticality and sensitively in Section 14 when looking at forensics tools and techniques for investigation.

There are many methods and techniques which define the steps to a forensics investigation; however, it has been my experience in performing investigations and teaching higher level forensics courses, the following methodology seems to work the best. So the basic steps to a forensics investigation are as follows:

1. *Prepare*—Specific forensics training, overarching corporate policies and procedures, as well as practice investigations and examinations will prepare you for an "event." Specialized forensics or incident handling certifications are considered of great value for forensics investigators.
2. *Identify*—When approaching an incident scene—review what is occurring on the computer screen. If data is being deleted, pull the power plug from the wall; otherwise perform real-time capture of system "volatile" data first.
3. *Preserve*—Once the system-specific "volatile" data is retrieved, then turn off machine, remove it from scene, and power it up in an isolated environment. Perform a full system bit-stream image capture of the data on the machine, remembering to "hash" the image with the original data for verification purposes.
4. *Select* —Once you have a verified copy of the available data, start investigation of data by selecting potential evidence files, datasets, and locations data could be stored. Isolate event-specific data from normal system data for further examination.
5. *Examine*—Look for potential hidden storage locations of data such as slack space, unallocated space, and in front of File Allocation Table (FAT) space on hard drives. Remember to look in registry entries or root directories for additional potential indicators of data storage activity.
6. *Classify*—Evaluate data in potential locations for relevance to current investigation. Is the data directly related to case, or does it support events of the case, or is it unrelated to the case?
7. *Analyze*—Review data from relevant locations. Ensure data is readable, legible, and relevant to investigation. Evaluate it for type of evidence: Is it direct evidence of alleged issue or is it related to issue?
8. *Present*—Correlate all data reviewed to investigation papers (warrants, corporate documents, etc.). Prepare data report for presentation—either in a court of law or to corporate officers.

These eight steps are further discussed on the following pages.

PREPARE

What policies and procedures are in place at the corporate level for any forensics endeavor? These policies should cover evidence collection, retention, chain of custody requirements, chain of reporting for the investigation, as well as use and employment of the forensics reports and evidence itself. Managers must mast sure the corporate level approvals and policies are in place, approved by the corporate counsel, and in accordance with the statutory and regulatory guidance and compliance for their organization. The best practices for the industry they are operating in must also be adhered to within these policies and procedures. A lot of these policies were discussed in Section 7, but there are some specific forensics-based policies and procedures which the manager needs to develop and produce for the organization. "Handover" policy of evidence to law enforcement, corporate reporting and governance policy for data breaches, and "chain of custody" policy for evidence control are just some of these specific policies and procedures which are discussed in Section 12.

Specific forensics training of the investigators, analysts, examiners, and data handlers is all needed to ensure proper legal and regulatory compliance for the actual forensics activity along with specialized forensics or evidence handling certifications for the forensics team. Each SIRT member needs to be well versed in evidence gathering and collection, evidence handling, investigative techniques and procedures, and the proper corporate method for reporting the results of any forensics activity. The manager is responsible for the training and detailed forensics instruction that the team receives, reviews, and is exposed to during the course of their tenure on the forensics team.

One method for the manager to gain the trust and confidence in the team member is to require professional certification of the skills and abilities of the team member. There are numerous certifications available in the industry for forensics, data handling, data capture, incident handling, and other related technical fields. These various types of certifications include Windows-based forensics, Unix-based forensics, cell phone forensics in today's modern "always-connected" corporate environment, Internet-based forensics, and volatile memory data collection. Other areas also include image and data evidence gathering techniques, "eDiscovery" data gathering techniques, Web Browser data gathering techniques, malware analysis tools and techniques, and others.

Another activity under prepare for the forensics team is to practice evidence gathering techniques and procedures during training sessions and exercises. The more the team has exposure to various different types of attacks and potential evidence, the better their ability to respond during an actual forensics activity. So, in order for the manager to conduct these types of event, the organization will need to have an independent laboratory equipped with the full scope of corporate machines, operating systems, and applications that are deployed throughout the corporation. This allows the manager to properly prepare the team for potential types of forensics events before the "real" event occurs. So, preparation covers many areas that the team manager must account for before the forensics team performs their first data collection and analysis activity.

IDENTIFY

At the start of any investigation, several questions must be answered by the responders and the manager right away. When entering the scene, does the machine under scrutiny reflect any current activity? If so, are there activity file deletions? And if that is occurring, the responder must cease the activity immediately by usually pulling the power cable out of the wall. This will freeze the machine and allow the responder to obtain the potential evidence before it is actually removed from the machine.

Otherwise, the responder can begin "real-time" capture of the volatile data on the machine. This would include the system registers, RAM data loaded in memory, system processes currently active on the machine, cache memory, currently open ports running on the machine, and system temporary and swap space files and data. All of this data is lost and removed once the machine is turned off and needs to be retained before removing power from the machine. There are critical data components within these areas that can aid in the investigation later during the analysis process. Because volatile data has a propensity to change over time, the order and timeliness with which volatile data is collected is important. In most cases, analysts should first collect information on network connections and login sessions, because network connections may time out or be disconnected and the list of users connected to a system at any single time may vary. Volatile data that is less likely to change, such as network configuration information, should be collected later. The recommended order, in which volatile data generally should be collected, from first to last, is as follows:

1. RAM contents
2. Login sessions
3. Contents of memory: registers and cache
4. Running processes
5. Open files
6. Network connections
7. Network configuration: routing tables and config. files
8. Operating system time.

The forensics team manager must make the initial decision when performing the initial response or must be sure the responder has the ability to make the initial decision if the manager is not present. This process can become important during the further events to follow the first steps.

PRESERVE

The next step in the standard forensics response process is to perform a "bit-stream" image copy of the hard drive and other data storage devices at the scene of the response. The manager must ensure the responders have the appropriate tools, training, and procedures to perform this capture activity successfully and completely. Forensic analysts take precautions to be sure that the information saved on data storage media designated for examination will be protected from alteration during the examination. This process is where the original media (hard drive, removable drive, smartphone, SSD Memory, etc.) is copied, physically inspected, and stored without alteration to the data. The forensic examiner will then examine the copy, not the original media. In forensic terminology, the copy is called an "image." This image capture should be performed as soon as possible once the scene is controlled to restrict potential outside influences on the data or the machine.

This image capture can be performed at the scene or immediately upon return to the forensics laboratory with the machine. The manager will provide the procedures and the oversight to make sure the process is controlled, performed correctly, and all "chain of custody" actions are recorded with respect to the machine and data storage devices now in the control of the forensics personnel.

During the image capture, the recording of the types and kinds of devices is vital to the success of the investigation, along with the encrypting of the data image, known as "hashing." This step is performed by the collection person to ensure the "bit-stream" image copy is an exact match for the actual data device for integrity purposes of the investigation and analysis which will follow.

Another area for management oversight during this capture process is to verify the capture technician is utilizing "write-blocker" hardware or software during the imaging process to ensure no data is being written back to the capture device. This provides additional "chain of evidence" proof of noncorruption of evidence that can be used in litigation efforts or criminal cases.

SELECT

When performing an initial evaluation of data within an investigation, selection of area for examination based upon the particulars of the case is the usual starting point. Each investigator would select the area individually which the manager would expect from his team. The manager's oversight in this area would be to guide the examination into areas possibly not considered or reviewed by the initial investigation.

Various techniques and types of data searches are performed by the investigator or examiner during this initial process including string searches, data carving, registry examinations, history files review, and log file reviews. The object here is to get the data which can be vital to the case out and available for further analysis and evaluation. The forensics team manager in this arena provides potential areas for data retrieval and consideration, such as external smartphone connections, USB device controllers, and modem connection and drivers. The examiner needs to isolate event-specific data from normal system data for further examination during this process. Always keep in mind that text-based searches have some limitations based upon any technique that would alter the ASCII-based data to another format including:

A. Bit shifting
B. Encryption
C. Compression
D. Bit-mapping.

Another area to focus on in this selection phase is the string search and data search arena. Utilizing a standard string search mechanism, such as found in the standard forensics toolkits starts off this process, but should not be the only means of searching and selecting files for further review. String searching is an efficient technique for finding any type of text string, including names, number sequences, and words. This type of search—a search across the media for the particular name, number sequence, phrase, or word—will often produce suspect files and data elements which warrant further examination and evaluation. Utilizing an independent search tool for data elements, such as the SiTe tool, found at Cylab.com can develop and product additional data components worth additional review.

Mechanisms for data carving, the process of retrieving the data from hidden or deleted files, is also important in this phase. Data carving is defined as a data recovery search technique. It allows for users to recover data with no file system allocation information to be extracted by identifying clusters and sectors belonging to the file. Data carving searches through the raw sectors looking for specific desired file signatures, but by having no allocation information means that the investigator must specify a block size of data to carve out when a matching file signature is located. Given this, the beginning of the file is still present and there is a risk of numerous false hits. Data carving also requires that the files recovered be located in sequential sectors as there is no allocation information to point to fragmented file portions. This method can be time and resource intensive.

Also, most data files have a file extension. A file extension is typically a two or three character alphanumeric code grouped with a file name. Operating systems use the file extension to identify the proper application to open and use the file. Simply renaming the file extension to something innocuous disguises the true content of the file to the examiner looking only at the file extension.

EXAMINE

The forensics team manager guides the examiner here to look for potential hidden storage locations of data such as slack space, unallocated space, and in front of FAT space on hard drives. The current technology available allows for multiple areas for storage of data commonly unavailable to normal processing software such as word processors and spreadsheet programs. Data can be stored anywhere there is a storage activity with memory, real or virtual, so the manager must guide the examiner to proper storage areas and mechanisms for retrieval of this type of data.

There are many simple techniques that are employed to disguise or hide files. Files can be password protected, saved in places on data storage media that typically only contain innocuous system files, encrypted, or compressed. Files or data may be saved with innocuous sounding file names by the user in an attempt to avoid detection. Remember to look in registry entries or root directories for additional potential indicators of data storage activity. USB devices, external storage devices, smartphone devices all contain memory and indicate their use and data file transfers in the typical registry entry activity.

E-mail systems, Internet browser systems, and other Internet-based programs all retain some or all of the data related to file transfers, exchanges of data, and location and time of data actions, so these are all areas for further consideration during this phase of the forensics investigation. History files, "cookies" in the browser, link files are all potential indicators of data which can be used for evidence.

Many different forensics tools which are used to perform the activities in this phase are found in Section 14. Each type of examination tool has its advantages and its limitations so each examiner may actually have his own forensics toolkit, so as the team manager, ensure the tools used are approved and certified by an outside agency and the user is appropriately trained on the use of the tools.

CLASSIFY

Each dataset retrieved by the examiner must be evaluated for its relevance to the current case or effort. Several questions must be answered about the data: Is the data directly related to case, or does it support events of the case, or is it unrelated to the case? How is the data related and what additional examinations does it indicate are needed?

Data found in unallocated space can be overwritten with files or by automated processes. In many situations, unallocated space contains vast quantities of data, including deleted files. Forensic examiners must identify and extract data and files from unallocated space, and review it to determine if it is of evidentiary significance.

Each piece of significant evidence is documented at to its location, time of creation, access and modification, if any, and the relevance to the case. Primary areas to consider in the analysis include relationship to the warrant or other official documentation used to retrieve the data, relationship to the person or organization under investigation, actual data facts about the evidence (what is it? what does it show?), and the relationship of this specific piece of evidence to the overall "picture" of all evidence in the case. The manager will review this analysis to ensure the logic and construct of the evidence actually follows the evidence and substantiates the case.

Remember the disclosure requirements for exculpatory and inculpatory evidence while performing the research and evaluation under this classify phase. Exculpatory evidence is the evidence favorable to the defendant in a criminal trial, which clears or tends to clear the defendant of guilt. It is the opposite of inculpatory evidence, which tends to prove guilt. Each side of the case has the right to the original evidence so as to perform its own review and evaluation.

ANALYZE

The final analysis reviews the data from relevant location to ensure data is readable, legible, and relevant to investigation. The manager evaluates it for type of evidence: Is it direct evidence of alleged issue or is it related to issue? Typically, the manager knows there are two major types of evidence that guide arguments in court and legal cases:

A. Circumstantial evidence requires inference to reach a desired conclusion. If the person on trial went out and bought a gun and bullets the day before the victim was shot, the prosecution will want the judge or jury to infer that the accused bought the gun to shoot the victim. Enough telling circumstantial evidence can convince people to believe that someone is innocent or guilty, but by itself cannot prove that an event took place.

B. True direct evidence, in contrast, leaves little or no possibility of a different conclusion. In American courts, juries and judges must believe that the accused person committed the crime beyond a reasonable doubt. Direct evidence, such as a video showing a crime, can help remove any lingering doubts about what actually happened. Although there is no legal distinction between circumstantial and direct evidence, the latter is often seen as more objective.

Additionally there is consideration for other types of evidence to be included in the forensics investigation. Documentation evidence is any evidence introduced at a trial in the form of documents. Although this term is most widely understood to mean writings on paper (such as an invoice, a contract, or a will), the term actually include any media by which information can be preserved. Photographs, tape recordings, films, and printed e-mails are all forms of documentation evidence.

The investigation can include many forms of documentation evidence, business standards employed by the firm, and standard business practices for the employees of the firm under review. Each of these documents can be considered as part of the case package for the legal and/or administrative review of the evidence of the case.

See the references cited in Section 8 for further consideration.

PRESENT

During the course of a forensics activity, the investigators and examiners are required to document every event as they perform it. This process is often extremely critical to the outcome of the investigation and potential litigation of the case. Here are some steps for the manager to use and advise the investigators to properly document and report these events and actions:

1. Ensure the documentation and reports reflect the objective of the investigation, the time frame and outside parameters for the investigation, and the results. Always making sure the parameters of the investigation are important to the analysis and results, as well as the interpretation of the evidence in the report and documentation. Correlate all data reviewed to investigation papers (search warrants, corporate documents, etc.).

2. The investigators and analysts have to define and document the technical and operational procedures used during the investigation. This is required to show repeatability, objectivity, and the validity of the investigative process.

3. The process of investigating and documenting the contents of the evidence for the case can take a significant amount of time. When providing the results reporting actions, make sure the amount of time documented is reasonable and actual.

4. Once items are assigned to the case, make sure they are documented as to their significance to the case and they are analyzed for value and inclusion. Keep all evidence documents together for full analysis of all relevant items.

5. During the review of these documents and reports, check for completeness of the process and evidence review—outline the examination process and the procedures used; watching out for evidence that is not reviewed and reported on.

6. Always include the facts of the case within the report and documentation. When conducting the investigative actions, leave the interpretation of the facts to the legal profession and just provide the facts as discovered.

7. The investigator is preparing a data report for presentation—either in a court of law or to corporate officials, so pertinent facts and data recovered are the primary keys to be defined and explained in the reports. The team manager must ensure the investigators understand the documentation and reports will always be reviewed, critiqued, and maybe even cross-examined in a court of law, so they must be precise, exact, truthful, and above all accurate.

Forensics Team Requirements Members

Team membership requires logical, thorough, objective, observant, resourceful, and accurate investigator characteristics. These basic criteria for team membership are explained in Section 4. The specific needs for forensics team members are explained below.

MEMBER CRITERIA

The criteria for the forensics team members are identified below. Each team member is identified, trained, and certified in their areas of expertise and experience. The manager needs to review these team member's criteria and determine the needs of his own forensics team and provide requirements, skills, and expertise needs to his HR department for the proper person or people to be retained and hired for his team. The forensics team manager needs to ensure each team member has the basic forensics expertise to perform the analyst activities under multiple circumstances and under any condition. Once that basic requirement is found to be functional, then each analyst, investigator, and examiner gets their special forensics domain approved and listed as part of the basic qualifications for the overall team. As an example, the forensics investigator that is also certified with an MSCE or an MCITP then gets listed as the forensics point person for Windows responses and investigations. The same goes for the UNIX, Linux, and the Macintosh focused personnel.

Forensics Analyst or Specialist

The forensic specialist has to be able to demonstrate impartiality and know the importance of data identification during the image capture and initial data gathering activities. The forensics specialist is the primary initial forensics person involved with the gathering of the evidence at the scene during the data capture actions conducted at the beginning of the forensics process.

The forensics specialist applies the basic techniques for bit-stream image capture actions since he is responsible for gathering evidence and collecting the data from the storage devices identified during the initial data identification activities when the forensics team is first deployed to the scene of the forensics event. This process is core to the proper chain of custody for the forensics evidence, hence the forensics specialist can easily "make or break" the actual outcome of any forensics case by their action during this initial phase of data gathering.

The forensics specialist needs to be extremely well versed in the processes of image capture from any type of data storage device, including cell and mobile phones, external hard drives, smartphones, personal data devices, SIM cards, cloud storage locations, SAN and network storage devices, network application appliances, logging servers, file servers, standard workstation and server machines, network devices with storage attached to them, and the other varied locations which retain data on the network. Every place data can be stored is a "potential" location the forensics specialist needs to be able to access and capture data for further investigation and evaluation by the forensics team members. The basic steps for the forensics specialist include the following, but are not necessarily limited to:

a. For target drives, use only recently wiped media that have been reformatted and inspected for computer viruses.
b. Inventory the hardware on the suspect computer/device and note the condition of the computer when seized
c. Remove the original drive from the computer and then check the date and time values in the system's CMOS.
d. Perform the bit-stream image capture of the entire dataset identified.
e. Conduct a cryptological "hash" of the dataset.
f. Notate the "hash" of the captured dataset for reference.

Forensics Investigator

The forensics investigator is the person initially responsible for examining the "captured" evidence from the scene of the incident or event. The investigator documents the various types of data captured, provides the research in the parameters and technical specifications of the data storage devices, and details the types and locations of the various data components of the evidence as it is presented to him by the data capture specialist identified above. The forensics investigator needs to have "expert-level" skills and technical knowledge for:

1. The operating system under review
2. The application and its data structures under review
3. The hardware and machines under review
4. Any databases being reviewed for data
5. The network appliances and devices and their data.

The basic steps for the forensics investigator process include:

a. Record how the data was acquired from the suspect drive or dataset.

b. Process the data methodically and logically.

c. List all folders and files on the image or drive.

d. If possible, examine the contents of all data files in all folders, starting at the root directory of the volume partition.

e. For all password-protected files that might be related to the investigation, make a best effort to recover file contents.

f. Identify the function of every executable (binary or .exe) file that doesn't match known hash values.

g. Maintain control of all evidence and findings, and document everything as the examination is conducted.

h. Document every step as the reason for each step of the examination.

Forensics Examiner

The forensics examiner is responsible for independently analyzing evidence as it is presented to him by the forensics investigator. His job is to provide logical conclusions of the dataset and what it reveals as to the nature and purpose of the evidence. The forensics examiner is the person who examines the data and develops "expert" evaluation and opinions about the data and its use. They then document this evaluation into the forensics report provided to the manager, who then reviews it and passes it along to the client, the attorneys, and/or the law enforcement officers involved in the case.

The forensics examiner is usually the most senior person on the forensics staff and is certified in forensics or extremely knowledgeable in computer forensics. This person needs to be technically proficient with the "court accepted" forensic tools for the location they are working in, such as in the United States, United Kingdom, or European Union. Additionally, by being certified with these tools, it enhances their credibility as a "potential" expert witness and lends weight to their conclusions and opinions of the use and value of the evidence. The forensics examiner is usually considered the subject matter expert in the areas of their expertise, such as cell phone forensics, Internet forensics, network forensics, or server forensics.

The forensics examiner provides the detailed string of cause and effect for the history, data components, and artifacts found during the examination. They "tie" together the various components into an observation of the activities and artifacts that show what has transpired, where it took place, and timing and location of each part. By doing this process, they end up with an "expert" conclusion of what has happened, when it happened, where did it take place, and who conducted these actions. They often become "expert witnesses" within the court system based on their expertise, conclusions, and background. As an expert witness, the forensics examiner testifies in a court of law on their evaluations, observations, and "accepted" opinions. In order for this to occur, the court procedures will typically include the presentation of the examiner as a competent expert in the field of forensics, the court will then review the examiner's credentials and history and accept the examiner as an expert with the ability to allow "opinion" testimony, which normally is not allowed in court. Once that process is concluded, the examiner testifies on the evidence, examination, and conclusions. The opposing attorney will often cross-examine the examiner and the evidence in an attempt to discredit either the process or the results. This process has been known to be contentious at times since often the defendant is on trial for an offense which can result in long jail time, can be criminal, or can result in large fines.

The forensic examiner should know that he will need to be able to explain the forensic report in court in such a way that the average person (member of jury) can understand the evidence that has been discovered. Knowing where the data came from, how it was acquired, verifying the authenticity of the data, and being able to answer questions about the devices examined, and the forensic process followed all the way to the report which was produced, will ensure the Forensic examiner is a reliable experienced professional in which the end result can produce a complete result of the evidence so an informed decision can be made in the case.

MEMBER EXPERTISE

Forensics Expertise Areas

Team membership should include personnel who can examine any storage or computing device wherein the data relevant to the case is found during the initial data capture events. Areas of consideration include:

1. Windows-based machines
2. Unix-based machines
3. Apple-based machines
4. Linux-based machines
5. Network appliances
6. Storage area network (SAN) devices
7. "Smartphone" devices
8. Cell phone devices
9. Internet-based storage mechanisms
10. Specific applications used in client environment
11. Specific database management systems used in client environment
12. Various hard drive equipment
13. Various network connection hardware components
14. External hard drive equipment and components

15. Various USB-based storage devices
16. Cloud storage mechanisms in place, if any
17. External third-party interconnections
18. Mainframe computing hardware, if needed
19. Mid-range computing hardware, if needed
20. Supercomputing hardware, if needed.

Developing and Refining the Investigation Plan

1. The forensics team member is expected to be able to develop an investigation plan for the case when initiating the process for investigation. Some of the considerations to include in an investigation plan:
   a. Determine the scope of the investigation
   b. Estimate number of hours to complete the case
   c. Decide what information to collect
   d. Whether all information available should be collected
   e. What happens if the investigation leads into areas not included in the original set of requirements (dealing with scope creep)
2. The team member must understand that the key is to start with a plan but remain flexible in the face of new evidence. This is where the team manager provides guidance and advise based upon client relations, legal and operational considerations, regulatory or statutory guidance, and operational logistics of the investigation itself.

MEMBER CERTIFICATION

Forensics certifications of the forensics team members are one area of focus for the team manager to oversee and provide guidance and direction to the team members. There are many professional certifications available today within the forensics community which provide training and verification of the expertise and validate the skills and abilities of the forensics practitioner. Most of the information listed by certification is from the organization responsible for the certification. These certifications include the following two categories, vendor neutral and vendor specific.

Vendor Neutral Certifications
Certified Computer Examiner
This is a certification offered industry-wide through the International Society of Forensic Computer Examiners (ISFCE) to qualified applicants who complete an examination process. The purpose of the Certified Computer Examiner (CCE) certification is to

- professionalize and further the field and science of computer forensics;
- provide a fair, vendor neutral, uncompromised process for certifying the competency of forensic computer examiners;

- certify computer forensic examiners solely based on their knowledge and practical examination skills and abilities as they relate to the practice of digital forensics;
- set high forensic and ethical standards for forensic computer examiners;
- provide a universally recognized, unblemished certification that is available to all who can qualify, for a reasonable cost.

To learn more about the CCE and the ISFCE, visit their web site at www.isfce.com.

Certified Forensic Computer Examiner

This is a certification offered only to those meeting membership criteria through the International Association of Computer Investigative Specialists (IACIS). The Certified Forensic Computer Examiner (CFCE) program is a two-part process, consisting of a "Peer Review" phase and a "Certification" phase. The CFCE Peer Review Subcommittee is responsible for the administration of the Peer Review phase of the CFCE program. Upon entry, each candidate is assigned a "coach" who mentors the candidate through a series of practical exercises (also known as problems) which are based on the CFCE core competencies. Candidates are required to successfully complete the entire peer review phase in order to qualify for the CFCE Certification phase. Candidates who fail the peer review process, or otherwise fail to meet deadlines and other requirements, will not qualify for entry into the CFCE Certification phase. To learn more about the CFCE and the IACIS, including their membership criteria, visit their web site at www.cops.org.

CyberSecurity Forensic Analyst

This is a certification offered industry-wide through the CyberSecurity Institute to those who complete the certification process. Possessing the CyberSecurity Forensic Analyst (CSFA) certification is proof that the analyst can conduct a thorough and sound forensic examination of a computer system and other digital/electronic devices, properly interpret the evidence, and communicate the examination results effectively and understandably. The CSFA designation is held exclusively by the most qualified digital forensic professionals and is a testament that the holder has the skills necessary to perform a comprehensive analysis within a limited time frame. Testing scenarios are based on actual cases and are constantly being reviewed and updated by a team of professionals representing both law enforcement and the corporate sector. To learn more about the CSFA and the CyberSecurity Institute, visit their web site at www.cybersecurityforensicanalyst.com.

Certified Hacking Forensics Investigator

Computer hacking forensic investigation is the process of detecting hacking attacks and properly extracting evidence to report the crime and conduct audits to prevent future attacks. Computer crime in today's cyber world is on the rise. Computer investigation techniques are being used by police, government, and corporate entities globally, and many of them turn to EC-Council for the Computer Hacking Forensic Investigator CHFI Certification Program. Computer security and computer investigations are changing terms. More tools are invented every day for conducting computer investigations, be it computer crime, digital forensics, computer investigations, or even standard computer data recovery. The tools and techniques covered in EC-Council's CHFI program will prepare the student to conduct computer investigations using groundbreaking digital forensics technologies.

Computer forensics is simply the application of computer investigation and analysis techniques in the interests of determining potential legal evidence. Evidence might be sought in a wide range of computer crime or misuse, including but not limited to theft of trade secrets, theft of or destruction of intellectual property, and fraud. CHFI investigators can draw on an array of methods for discovering data that resides in a computer system, or recovering deleted, encrypted, or damaged file information known as computer data recovery. To learn more about the CHFI and the EC-Council, visit their web site at www.ec-council.org.

Certified Information Forensics Investigator

The *Certified Information Forensics Investigator (CIFI) Certification* is a designation earned exclusively by the most qualified information forensic professionals in the field. Along with adherence to the highest standards of ethical conduct, the CIFI epitomizes the highest standards in knowledge requirements and expertise. The CIFI encompasses multiple domains of knowledge, practical experience, and a demonstration of expertise and understanding accomplished through a rigorous exam proctored under the most controlled of environments. Unlike many vendor certifications, the CIFI maintains vendor neutrality and is independent of dependency requirements such as sponsored training, purchasing of product, or requirements other than ability. In fact, candidates may choose to sit for the exam without any restrictions other than adherence to the IISFA code of ethics and the exam fee. The CIFI is recognized as the only certification that truly represents the abilities of field information forensics investigators and is the benchmark by which they are measured. Earning the CIFI designation is a significant accomplishment and identifies the best in the profession of information forensics investigator.

Certified Computer Forensics Examiner

The Certified Computer Forensics Examiner (CCFE) tests a candidate's fundamental knowledge of the computer forensics evidence recovery and analysis process. Candidates are evaluated on their relevant knowledge of both hard and soft skills. Candidates will be tested on soft skills; they must prove that they have the requisite background knowledge of the complex legal issues that relate to the computer forensics field. Candidates' hard skills are vetted via a comprehensive practical examination that is given to candidates that pass the online multiple choice exam. Only candidates that complete both the online multiple choice exam and the practical exam are granted active CCFE certification status. To learn more about the CCFE and the IACRB, visit their web site at http://www.iacertification.org

SANS Forensics
Global Information Assurance Certification Forensic Analyst (GCFA)

The Global Information Assurance Certification Forensic Analyst (GCFA) certifies that the individual has the knowledge, skills, and abilities to utilize state-of-the-art forensic analysis techniques to solve complicated Windows- and Linux-based investigations. GCFA experts can articulate complex forensic concepts such as the file system structures, enterprise acquisition, complex media analysis, and memory analysis.

GCFAs are front line investigators during computer intrusion breaches across the enterprise. They can help identify and secure compromised systems even if the adversary uses anti-forensic techniques. Using advanced techniques such as file system timeline analysis, registry analysis, and memory inspection, GCFAs are adept at finding unknown malware, rootkits, and data that the intruders thought had eliminated from the system.

This certification will ensure you have a firm understanding of advanced incident response and computer forensics tools and techniques to investigate data breach intrusions, tech-savvy rogue employees, advanced persistent threats, and complex digital forensic cases.

GCFA certification tests knowledge that is not geared for only law enforcement personnel, but for corporate and organizational incident response and investigation teams that have different legal or statutory requirements compared to a standard law enforcement forensic investigation.

To learn more about the GCFA and the SANS Institute, visit their website at http://computer-forensics.sans.org/certification/gcfa.

Global Information Assurance Certification Forensic Examiner

When a person obtains the Global Information Assurance Certification Forensic Examiner (GCFE) ensure that all candidates who successfully pass the exam have the knowledge, skills, and abilities required to acquire and examine evidence from digital systems to find and recover known essential artifacts to prove or disprove a fact in order to produce a formal report or presentation that could be used internally or in civil/criminal litigation.

The GCFE certification is for professionals working or interested in the information security, legal and law enforcement industries with a need to understand computer forensic analysis. The certification focuses on core skills required to collect and analyze data from Windows computer systems.

The GCFE certifies that candidates have the knowledge, skills, and ability to conduct typical incident investigations including eDiscovery, forensic analysis and reporting, evidence acquisition, browser forensics, and tracing user and application activities on Windows systems.

Certified Skills That GCFEs Possess
- Digital Forensics Essentials
- Windows File System Basics
- Fundamental Forensic Methodology
- Evidence Acquisition Tools and Techniques
- Law Enforcement Bag and Tag
- Evidence Integrity
- Presentation and Reporting of Evidence and Analysis
- Windows XP, VISTA, and Windows 7 Investigation and Analysis
- Windows In-Depth Registry Forensics
- Tracking User Activity
- USB Device Tracking and Analysis
- Memory, Pagefile, and Unallocated Artifact Carving
- Facebook, Gmail, Hotmail, Yahoo Chat, and Webmail Analysis
- E-mail Forensics (Host, Server, Web)
- Microsoft Office Document Analysis
- Windows Link File Investigation
- Windows Recycle Bin Analysis
- File and Picture Metadata Tracking and Examination
- Prefetch Analysis
- Firefox and Internet Explorer Browser Forensics
- InPrivate Browsing Recover
- Deleted File Recovery
- String Searching and Data Carving
- Fully Updated to include full Windows 7 and Server 2008 Examinations
- Examine cases involving Windows XP, VISTA, and Windows 7

To learn more about the GCFE and the SANS Institute, visit their web site at http://computer-forensics.sans.org/certification/gcfe.

Malware Analyst
GIAC Malware Analysis Certification: GREM
The GIAC Reverse Engineering Malware (GREM) certification is designed for technologists who protect the organization from malicious code.

GREM-certified technologists possess the knowledge and skills to reverse-engineer malicious software (malware) that targets common platforms, such as Microsoft Windows and web browsers. These individuals know how to examine inner-workings of malware in the context of forensic investigations, incident response, and Windows system administration.

Certified Skills That GREM Certified Professionals Possess
- Assemble the toolkit for malware forensics
- Perform behavioral analysis of malicious Windows executables
- Perform static and dynamic code analysis of malicious Windows executables
- Intercept system and network-level activities in the analysis lab
- Patch compiled malicious Windows executables
- Shortcuts for speeding up malware analysis
- Core concepts for reverse-engineering malware at the code level
- x86 Intel assembly language understanding
- Identify key x86 assembly logic structures with a disassembler
- Patterns of common malware characteristics at the Windows API level
- Work with PE headers of malicious Windows executables
- Handle DLL interactions and API hooking
- Manual unpacking of protected malicious Windows executables
- Capability to subvert anti-analysis mechanisms built into malware
- Analyze protected malicious browser scripts written in JavaScript and VBScript
- Reverse-engineer malicious Flash programs
- Analyze malicious Microsoft Office (Word, Excel, PowerPoint) and Adobe PDF documents
- Examine shellcode in the context of malicious files
- Analyze memory to assess malware characteristics and reconstruct infection artifacts
- Use memory forensics to analyze rootkit infections

To learn more about the GREM and the SANS Institute, visit their web site at http://computer-forensics.sans.org/certification/grem.

Digital Forensics Certified Practitioner or Digital Forensics Certified Associate
DFCB certification requires a number of steps. It is the applicant's responsibility to complete each of these steps in a timely manner. Note that significant experience, training and education are required. Note also that a background check will be conducted. References will also be required to verify experience.

The Digital Forensics Certified Practitioner (DFCP) certification must demonstrate 2 or more years of "practical experience" in the last 3 years. Those seeking the Digital Forensics Certified Associate (DFCA) certification are not required to demonstrate practical experience over the last 3 years. Candidates for both certifications must have a minimum of 5 years' digital forensics experience overall. When we say "practical experience," we are referring to hands-on digital imaging/capturing of digital evidence and digital analysis (from evidence collection to reporting and if necessary, testifying to the evidence).

This certification will not test your knowledge of any particular forensic software. We believe a digital forensics certification should go much further than testing a candidate's knowledge of forensic software. This certification will cover all the aspects of digital forensics—the collection of digital forensics, the legal components, the validation of forensic tools, the reporting, etc. We want to be able to ensure a successful candidate is able to be fully versed in the entire digital forensics profession.

To learn more about the DCFP, DCFA, and the DCFB, visit their web site at www.DFCB.ORG.

Certified Digital Forensics Examiner

The Certified Digital Forensics Examiner (CDFE) certification from Mile2 is intended to represent a candidate's knowledge of a broad range of knowledge of computer forensics, eDiscovery, digital evidence, and related technologies.

CDFE certification is achieved by completing a 100-question exam over 2 h and with a passing score of 75%. The objectives of the CDFE exam are based on the modules of the Mile2 CDFE training program. However, attending the CDFE training program, or purchasing the Mile2 training materials, are not requirements for CDFE certification. Additional information can be found on the CDFE course outline and Certification Exams at Mile2 page.

Certified eDiscovery Specialist

The Certified eDiscovery Specialist (CEDS) certification from the Association of Certified eDiscovery Specialists (ACEDS) is a new certification for Electronic Discovery examiners. The CEDS designation is intended to validate the competency, knowledge, and expertise of an eDiscovery professional. ACEDS itself is a membership-based organization for aiding and promoting the professional interests of the eDiscovery community.

The CEDS is administered as a 4-h, proctored exam. Objectives on the exam include information management, legal framework, project planning data culling, international discovery, ethics, and technology.

Prior to taking the CEDS exam, candidates must provide proof of having at least 40 credits in eDiscovery (or closely related training, education, certification, or experience), two professional references, and have submitted a completed exam application and fee. Attending ACEDS training or a CEDS preparation seminar is optional. Membership in ACEDS is also optional but results in a reduced exam fee.

Additional details about the CEDS certification can be found on the ACEDS web site in the CEDS Examination Candidate Handbook.

Vendor Specific Certifications
EnCase Certified Examiner

This is a certification offered industry-wide through Guidance Software, the developers of EnCase forensic software to those qualified applicants completing the certification process. To learn more about the EnCase Certified Examiner (EnCE) and EnCase, visit their web site at www.encase.com.

Probably the most well known of all computer forensic software packages available commercially is the EnCase® software from Guidance Software. The EnCase Certified Examiner (EnCE®) is a training program for learning the use of Guidance Software's EnCase computer forensic software. Computer forensics examiners with the EnCE certification are generally considered experts in the use of EnCase.

A prerequisite for the EnCE certification is having 64 h of authorized computer forensic training (online or classroom), or having at least 12 months of verifiable computer forensic experience. It is also necessary to submit an EnCE application for approval to attempt the EnCE certification.

The EnCE certification is divided into a written exam and a practical exam. The written portion contains 180 computer-based questions that must be answered in 2 h, and covers much of the information found in the Official EnCE Study Guide from Sybex. The practical exam includes an exam-licensed copy of EnCase 6 and EnCase evidence files. The EnCE candidate has 60 days to analyze the evidence and answer a dozen or so questions about procedures, methodology, and report on the findings.

To take the practical exam, the written exam must be passed with a minimum score of 80%. Passing the practical exam require a score of 85%. Certification renewal is every 3 years, but collecting a few CPEs each year will satisfy the renewal requirements. There is currently no annual maintenance fee.

If the EnCE certification sounds interesting, have a look at the EnCE Study Guide for more details or contact certification@guidancesoftware.com.

EnCase Certified eDiscovery Practitioner

The EnCase® Certified eDiscovery Practitioner (EnCEP) program provides certification in the use of Guidance Software's EnCase eDiscovery software. EnCase eDiscovery is the leading eDiscovery solution for the search, collection, preservation, and processing of electronically stored information (ESI). Earning the EnCEP certification illustrates that a practitioner is skilled in the application of the solution to manage and successfully complete all sizes of eDiscovery matters in accordance with the Federal Rules of Civil Procedure.

Requirements for the EnCEP certification include attendance of an EnCase eDiscovery training course (live or online), or completion of the on-site EnCase eDiscovery implementation training, or the Advanced EnCase eDiscovery Certification training course. Three months experience in eDiscovery collection, processing, and/or project management is also required.

Testing for the EnCEP certification is a 100-question written exam and an online scenario exam. Both exams have a passing score of 80%. The EnCEP certification is valid for 3 years and is renewed by attending a minimum of 32 credit hours of eDiscovery education, or attending one CEIC conference and at least 10 eDiscovery laboratory sessions. Additional information can be found in the EnCEP FAQ.

AccessData Certified Examiner

This is a certification offered industry-wide through AccessData, the developers of forensic software products, including Forensic Toolkit (FTK), to those qualified applicants completing the certification process. To learn more about the AccessData Certified Examiner (ACE) and AccessData, visit their web site at www.accessdata.com.

The ACE certification from AccessData Group, LLC validates an exam candidate's proficiency with using AccessData's FTK, Password Recovery Toolkit (PRTK), FTK Imager, and Registry Viewer products. FTK is one of the more recognized tools in computer forensics. AccessData recommends that anyone needing to demonstrate proficiency with FTK acquires the ACE certification.

The ACE exam is a 90-min, multiple choice exam that is free to take either online or at the conclusion of an AccessData training class. The exam contains both written and practical assignments based on a case that is created and processed from an image file provided to the exam candidate. ACE Credential Maintenance requires that a renewal exam be taken every 1 or 2 years.

There are free preparation videos and an exam study guide available on the AccessData web site. AccessData recommends that the certification be taken in conjunction with their AccessData Boot Camp and Windows Forensics courses, but it is not required. You can find out more about the ACE certification process at the AccessData web site.

Forensics Team Policies and Procedures

The forensics team should always follow a structured documented process, wherein the content of the items to be investigated needs to be preserved, validated, and documented. Any investigation must be understood at the onset as to its dimensions, scope, and investigative methods which are best based upon proven techniques, such as proper and legal collection of evidence and obtaining proper bit-stream "hash encrypted" copies of evidence. The linear nature of investigation always needs documentation and supporting evidence, for technology can give unexpected results. So, always document everything and report all of it.

In additional to the incident response policies mentioned in Section 7, the following forensics-based policies need to be developed and implemented by the Security Incident Response and Forensics Team (SIR&FT) manager for the forensics activities to be conducted by the corporate forensics team. Forensics policies and procedures must cover the various activities that are performed by the analysts, investigators, and examiners, as well as the expert witness events when the assigned staff testifies in court cases at the end of the forensics investigations. The basic setup for policies must follow the same type of criteria as explained in Section 7 in that they have some general structure requirements to ensure user compliance and utilization. These include:

i. If too complicated, no one will follow
ii. If affecting productivity, they will fail and not be followed
iii. Clear and general as possible, but still cover why they are needed
iv. Always have consequences of actions
v. Keep current with technologies and corporate goals
vi. Align with regulatory and statutory needs.

The basic criteria for the forensics team policies and procedures are laid in the corporate security strategy, the corporate security policy documents, and the corporate-level security procedures of the organization. Each forensics team member needs to have awareness of these documents in light of the requirements that the following areas are covered in these documents:

- Ensure that incident response policies integrate with enterprise security plan.
- Have thorough knowledge of assets, risks, impact, and likelihood.

121

- Practice incident response policies and procedures in mock events.
- Stay current on vulnerabilities and threats.
- Have detection systems in place and monitor attacks.
- Understand asset controls.
- Enact mitigation based on evidence collected.
- Practice evidence collection procedures and techniques to identify the vulnerabilities.
- Know the documentation requirements for evidence.
- Know notification and reporting requirements.
- Know recovery procedures.
- Understand the analysis process during and after the incident.
- Have a framework for communications, both within the team and external to the team.

So, the basic kinds of forensics policies and procedures the team manager will be responsible to develop and implement include the following.

FORENSICS ANALYSIS PROCESS

The basic forensics process to be implemented by the organization and its staff is defined in this policy. An example would be the process as defined in Section 10. The staff needs to adhere to the documented process to ensure repeatability and validity of the forensics results and reports that follow the investigation and subsequent analysis for each event and examination. The policy itself and procedures which follow from this policy will define the methods and basic techniques for forensics activities in three or more types of event response.

a. One type will be the normal follow-on activities from a Security Incident Response Team (SIRT) response effort as found in the first part of this book.
b. The second type would be the stand-alone forensics response as requested by some manager or corporate entity for administrative or legal purposes.
c. The third type is the response efforts based upon external, possibly law enforcement, requests for legal or other governmental reasons.

DATA COLLECTION

The forensics analyst/specialist conducts the capture of the data at the scene of the incident utilizing various methods and techniques which include search and seizure of the hardware storage devices and machines, "live" data capture of volatile components of the system which disappear when the machine is powered down, and other data retrieval activities. Each of these "on-the-scene" actions needs to be documented and recorded during the time on scene for proper identification of the data, hardware, software, and circumstances surrounding the event. These collection processes need process guidance and this is the policy document for those processes. The policy for data collection is a critical one for the forensics team as it sets the standard for all further activities of the team during any examination or investigation. This policy with its attendant procedures needs to focus on the various methods and techniques expected to be used in the customer locations that the forensics team supports and provides their services for to their customers.

CHAIN OF CUSTODY

Each investigator needs to record every single activity with each piece of evidence gathered by the data analyst/incident responder. The process for this effort should be defined in this policy. When the chain of custody starts, when evidence is handed off to the investigator, when the evidence is transported, where it is stored, etc. should all be recorded and maintained in accordance with this policy. The primary criteria for the chain of custody would include the steps required to set it up and maintain it, as found in Section 13 and the chain of custody log usage as found in Appendix C.

EVIDENCE HANDLING AND CONTROL

Chain of custody practices and procedures for documentation for each piece of evidence are critical to ensure the evidence is not tampered with, stays pristine in its quality, and available to all examiners and other legitimate personnel who need access to it during the investigation and subsequent court activities. This process involves documenting the place and time of evidence gathering, who handles it at what point and why they are examining it. This evidence log sheet stays with the piece of evidence throughout the life of the evidence until it is no longer retained, stored, and otherwise needed. The handling of evidence is explained in detail in Section 13, so the policy would follow the basic needs as defined in that section.

EVIDENCE "HAND-OVER" TO EXTERNAL PARTIES, LEO

Maintaining the chain of custody for evidence in any case is vital, but especially so when the case involves handing the data over to local or federal law enforcement personnel. There will times when the forensics evidence collected will need to be delivered to law enforcement and court-appointed personnel. The criteria for this policy should delineate the actual logging processes for each individual piece of evidence to be transferred, the case it is associated with, and the LEO badge or ID number of the person receiving the evidence.

This process is known in the LEO community as "Silver Platter" evidence gathering, wherein the evidence is given to the LEO on a "silver platter" and they do not have to capture or seize the data. The documentation that goes with this evidence needs to be handling and delivered in accordance with the organizational team's chain of custody forms and evidence transfer policy.

HARDWARE SPECIFIC ACQUISITION—SIM CARDS, CELL PHONE, USB STORAGE, ETC.

Selection of the correct tool to examine and evaluate the particular device, the data stored on that device and the meta-data associated with the device, and the data are all important for each event. The primary purpose of this policy is to ensure the proper data handling for the specific component is followed and repeatable. Each type of storage device has hardware parameters, vendor recommendations for use, and technical characteristics which all affect the retrieval of the data stored on the device. Whether the storage device is a SIM card from some "smart-phone" or cell phone, or a USB external storage stick, or some other device or hard drive, each item must have its requirements, characteristics, and specifications available to the examiner to keep the device secure, safe, and functioning during the data retrieval and examination processes. This policy creates the requirement for any examiner, investigator, or analyst on the forensics team to research and obtain all the particular hardware characteristics of the equipment they are reviewing or examining. It is important that the exact size, parameters, and characteristics of each device is known to ensure full and complete examination is performed without missing any potential hidden or missing data structures. See the policy below about research for further understanding and explanation.

DATA TYPE ACQUISITION—AUDIO FILES, VIDEO FILES, IMAGE FILES, NETWORK FILES, LOG FILES

The various file types for data use and storage provide many varying methods for suspect data to be storage and retrieved from each data location. Each file type has particular data about the data, "meta-data," as well as file storage parameters associated with it. Audio files are stored in several different formats which have various CODEC formats; the same is true for video files. There is a long history of image files having data stored within the image files that is unassociated with the original image or picture. Each of these file types needs specific tools, techniques, and approaches for data examination and investigation.

There are many types of digital evidence which could be encountered by digital forensic analyst in dealing with forensics investigations and examinations. Not only files, videos, digital images, encrypted items, unallocated clusters, slacks, and so forth, but also digital audio files and digital image files might have to be captured and analyzed.

Digital image files may contain internal alterations to the pixel data wherein other data is stored within the image. This process is known under the heading of Steganography. These various files need special examination tools designed for examination of the storage parameters of the files to determine if additional data is within the file. Therefore, it is important to have the policies in place to guide the practice of examining these types of data files during the investigation.

In certain cases, the audio files become significant evidence to show the involvement of the suspects in the investigation. Usually an audio file contains speech records between two or more people talking about a plan to commit a crime; therefore, the analyst should be able to reveal this conversation to the investigator. Audio forensics is comprised of five steps, namely *acquisition*, *authentication*, *audio enhancement*, *decoding*, and *voice recognition*.

So there are requirements for each type of data set retrieved and each retrieval activity which all fall under this capture policy for the forensics team.

INVESTIGATION PROCESS

The repeatability of the investigation is defined to allow the investigation and its results to be evaluated for applicability, validity, and relevance to the case both during and after the investigation. This policy sets up the criteria for the process to be conducted by the investigator during the fourth step, selection, of the forensics process as mentioned in Section 10. The selection step is critical to the overall process and provides the basis for starting the investigation of data by selecting potential evidence files, datasets, and locations data could be stored and isolating event-specific data from normal system data for further examination. This process is documented in the policy, of course, accounting for the particular case events and parameters, to allow the manager, lawyers, and other interested parties to ability to review and understand the investigation and its logical flow as the process is followed.

EXAMINATION PROCESS

The validity of the examination is defined to allow the examination and its results to be evaluated for repeatability, significance, and relevance to the case both during and after the examination. This policy sets up the criteria for the process to be conducted by the investigator during the fifth step, examine, of the forensics process as mentioned in Section 10. This examination process requires the examiner to look for potential hidden storage locations of data such as slack space, unallocated space, and in front of File Allocation Table (FAT) space on hard drives. The examiner must remember to look in registry entries or root directories for additional potential indicators of data storage activity. This policy documents the examination methodology for reviewing the storage locations, hard drives, and other devices for potential hidden data locations, changed data locations, or other methods used for confusing the locations of the suspect data.

DATA REVIEW

This policy sets up the criteria for the process to be conducted by the investigator during the sixth step, classify, of the forensics process as mentioned in Section 10. This classification of the data process shows the need for evaluating the data in potential locations for relevance to current investigation. The critical question to be answered in this step: Is the data directly related to case, or does it support events of the case, or is it unrelated to the case? Data found in unallocated space can be overwritten with files or by automated processes. In many situations, unallocated space contains vast quantities of data, including deleted files. Forensic examiners must identify and extract data and files from unallocated space and review it to determine if it is of evidentiary significance.

RESEARCH REQUIREMENTS

Each device, component or storage location where the data is retained, has particular technical parameters, hardware criteria, and equipment specification for its use and activities. These all require the examiner to understand the use and specifics of each device used to store the data. The actual size, speed, and capacity of the suspect hard drive or network device under examination is needed to gather the "meta-data" around the device to make sure the full data volume is reviewed and evaluated; to review the entire dataset so no potential evidence is missed, erased, or missed. This policy focuses on ensuring all hardware and software is specified and researched prior to or during the examination for full coverage during the investigation.

FORENSICS REPORTING

This policy sets up the criteria for the process to be conducted by the investigator during the eighth step, present, of the forensics process as mentioned in Section 10. The presentation step is the reporting phase of the forensics activity that every case, investigator, analyst, and examiner are required to follow as the case and evidence is processed during the investigation. During the course of a forensics activity, the analysts, investigators, and examiners are required to document every event as they perform it. This process is often extremely critical to the outcome of the investigation and potential litigation of the case.

The Forensics Reporting Policy needs to include the various industry-specific criteria, the statutory and regulatory requirements for the jurisdiction they are operating in, and the organizational needs and guidance for the specific agency or organization they are providing this service to. Section 10 provides some of the criteria for the team manager to utilize during the performance of the reporting step, but here we provide some of the policy needs in reporting.

Reporting needs should include:

A. Name and background of person providing documentation
B. General case data such as investigation justification, dates, locations, and timeframes.
C. Evidence retrieved and examined for its relevance to case
D. Chain of custody of evidence highlights
E. Technical procedures used and when approved
F. Operational procedures used and when approved
G. Factual results of investigation
H. When allowed, interpretation of results by SME (Subject Matter Expert) under the expert witness mechanism
I. Outlining of the analysis process and the approved procedures used
J. Outlining of the investigative process and approved procedures used
K. Outlining of the examination process and approved procedures used
L. Report criteria of precision, truthfulness, and accuracy.

ANALYSIS OF RESULTS

The final analysis reviews the data from relevant location to ensure data is readable, legible, and relevant to investigation. The manager evaluates it for type of evidence: Is it direct evidence of alleged issue or is it related to issue? Typically, the manager knows there are two major types of evidence that guide arguments in court and legal cases:

A. Circumstantial evidence requires inference to reach a desired conclusion.
B. True direct evidence, in contrast, leaves little or no possibility of a different conclusion.

The legal parameters around the case, location, and jurisdiction of the courts to be involved in the case, and the particular evidence handling criteria are all part of this policy guideline. Where the evidence was seized from, when and how the evidence was obtained, under what legal circumstance was the evidence retrieved all are areas for the manager to focus this policy on.

EXPERT WITNESS PROCESS

Each investigation may have a need for one of the senior examiners to provide testimony in court about the evidence gathered and evaluated for the case. This policy will provide the general corporate guidance to the examiner while they are preparing for and providing this testimony. From a legal standpoint, the guidance and instructions should come from the corporate council, company lawyers, and outside retained legal advisors. This policy should allow for such advice to the expert witness as cases can be very long, involved, and detailed. This policy does NOT provide general legal advice since that is the purview of the legal profession, but it should cover the forensics particulars for the expert witness to testify to in the court system, or possibly in written documentation for administrative actions of the suspect and the evidence in the case.

See the Section 15 explanation for further understanding about this policy and what it should contain.

A good forensics policy should not contain or mention name of hardware/software; it just contains the steps of examination/analysis. How to apply the analysis and examination by using types of hardware/software is usually determined by the analyst/investigator when choosing which hardware/software will get the best results.

One of the ways to ensure the proper policies and procedures are in place for the forensics team is to use national and internal standards promulgated by organizations designated to provide guidance and direction in these types of activities. One such organization is the International Standards Organization, ISO. This organization has produced the ISO/IEC 27037:2012, Information technology—Security techniques—Guidelines for identification, collection, acquisition, and preservation of digital evidence standard. This ISO standard is designed to provide a harmonized and globally accepted methodology to safeguard digital evidence integrity and authenticity.

Since digital evidence is inherently fragile, as it may be easily altered, tampered with, or destroyed through improper handling or examination, the ISO/IEC 27037 provides guidance to individuals involved in the identification, collection, acquisition, and preservation of potential digital evidence such as:

- Digital evidence first responders (DEFR)
- Digital evidence specialists (DES)
- Incident response specialists
- Forensic laboratory managers.

Decision-makers can rely on the standard to determine the credibility of digital evidence. It can also be used by organizations involved in protecting, analyzing, and presenting digital evidence, as well as policy-making bodies creating and evaluating related procedures. The standard does not replace specific legal requirements of any jurisdiction, but is rather intended to serve as practical guidance in DEFR and DES investigations.

Management of Forensics Evidence Handling

The Security Incident Response and Forensics Team (SIR&FT) Manager is responsible for the control, management, and guidance in the use of, storage or and handling of all evidence gathered during any investigation, incident response, and examination under his control. This requires him to place strong controls in place for the gathering of evidence, storage of evidence, maintaining the chain of custody documents of the evidence, and the general handling of evidence as it is reviewed, analyzed, investigated, and examined during the normal course of events surrounding the evidence and its attendant case.

The chain of custody is the first rule for all investigations and it is paramount for the Team Manager to ensure each investigator, analyst, and examiner maintains this chain by logging onto an evidence log every time they touch, examine, review, or otherwise interchange with the piece of evidence. During the evidence collection phase of any investigation, the less people who handle the evidence, the better it is for control and ownership of the evidence. The evidence will undergo an evaluation itself as to who handled it, at what point in time did they have access to it and why did that person review and handle the evidence. This process will, most likely, be reviewed during any potential court case which involves the evidence, so it is important that each step, each access, and each action taken with the evidence is identified, documented, and reviewed by the Team Manager. The various parts of this process are defined below and the methods are explained.

CHAIN OF EVIDENCE

Initial Evidence Gathering

When an analyst or responder access the scene of an incident, they must first identify the potential evidence to be collected and gathered for further review in the forensics laboratory later. This activity of identifying the evidence requires them to document the process as they collect the hard drives, computers, external storage devices, and all the other pieces of evidence which could contain digital data which will be later classified as digital evidence during the investigative process. The analyst will identify the component which contains the digital data and write it down in their evidence log as to location, time, and the state of the evidence when collected. This evidence log for each piece of evidence then will stay with the evidence throughout the examination and investigational process all the way until it is either retained by the authorities or returned to the owner at the completion of the case. An evidence log will contain multiple fields for data entry by the analyst.

Image Control

Within the arena of forensic evidence is the primary and first activity of capturing the bit image of the data to be investigated. As this process is performed, each investigator conducts an encryption technique known as "hashing" wherein the image itself is run through an encryption program to produce a fixed-length output for integrity to be used later during the process for proof of replication of the image. This fixed-length output file is used to show mathematically the copy produced during capture is mathematically identical to the original. These images are controlled via the standard "chain of custody" process previously discussed. This process of image control provides the investigator with the ability to review and examine a copy of the original evidence rather than the actual original evidence. This precludes the potential "corruption" and/or inadvertent alteration of the evidence which could cause the evidence to be deemed inadmissible in court.

Multiple Devices

The Team Manager must ensure all evidence is properly identified, captured, reviewed, and examined during any investigation. In making sure all evidence is categorized and reviewed, the Manager reviews the data capture activities of the analyst, the investigator steps and the examiner's reports to check whether each and every possible device which contains data relevant to the case is examined. There are a multitude of data retention devices available and used in today's world; anything from external hard drives, flash drive, and standard DVD devices to smartphones, digital cameras, and music players all of which have data storage capabilities.

The author participated in a data capture/initial response event where the "suspect" lived in a single family home with a "southwestern" motif, where he had adobe rocks and cacti as living room decor, etc. The capture personnel were troubled at the end of the search and seizure activities because they had not found the large retention of images that they had expected to find. They were sure the data was around, but they could not find it. We then examined the home for further methods for data retention which were not so obvious. I walked around the house looking at the general decor and furniture used in the various rooms, looking for some signs of hidden and obscured data storage. I walked through the living room and looked at the bookshelves. Each bookshelf has a set of bookends made out of rocks from the desert. I picked up one of the bookend rocks and found a USB connection hidden in the bottom of the rock. As it turned out, each bookend was actually a modified storage device with TBs of storage capacity inside of it. The suspect data was stored in the home, just not in the usual locations. Once we got the data, the suspect confessed to the offenses which caused the search to be conducted.

So always be aware of multiple storage devices, locations, and methods which are available and used by people trying to hide what they are doing from examination and investigation.

Research Requirements

When examining a data storage mechanism, a device, a hard drive, a flash drive, or SDD, etc. always research the full dimensions, size, capacity, and system parameters for each device. The manufacturer's technical specifications help determine the full capacity of any mechanism during an examination of the evidence captured. The actual device size and data dimensions are frequently different from what the operating system uses and formats the device for, such as an 80 GB HD is often formatted for 77 or 78 GB of storage space by an operating system. The extra space is then typically used to store hidden data by potential suspects.

Using this data allows an investigator to review the full disk or storage media, looking for slack space, erased files, and potentially hidden data on the device or media. Network devices also can contain these types of data sections so review them in the same manner, with the technical specifications at hand. Watch for encrypted partitions within other controlled sections of the devices. This process is often used to hide data inside other data sets to obscure the actual potential evidence from the investigators.

Data Collection Criteria

There are two basic areas for the Team manager to oversee and review in this Evidence category. First, the process for review and collection must be followed during the collection and analysis phases of the investigation. The Team leader/manager needs to follow the standard audit and recovery techniques for proven methods and techniques of the analysts as they gather and collect the evidence. These processes allow for the review of the investigation even when the technology used may be new or different that previously used.

Second is Data Recovery. The term is used particularly in this manner because it is more a legal term of art than a scientific term. Further, there is a plethora of case law surrounding large-scale and typically expensive litigation costs to produce eDiscovery projects. Forensic examiners assist in the process of eDiscovery by determining locations where evidence relative to the civil litigation may exist, copying it, and producing it to litigators in some type of understandable form. Oftentimes there is contentious debate about the scope of what a party in litigation is or is not entitled to from the other party. Rule 26 and 34 of the Federal Rules of Civil Procedure (FRCP) now deal with electronically stored information (ESI). Private computer forensic practitioners, boutique firms, and the big five forensic consulting agencies all deal extensively with eDiscovery in civil litigation.

Some computer forensic consulting agencies have a data recovery division separate from their computer forensics division. Having a data recovery area can be incredibly useful for a computer forensic consulting firm because there are times when a suspect tries to destroy the hard drive or other digital media, knowing they are guilty and fearing that information will be found during a forensic examination. In these cases, data recovery specialists try to recover the damaged media before they turn it over to the forensic analysis department.

I recently completed a data recovery project wherein the client needed to recover pictures and brochures completed during normal business for her organization. She had no data backup mechanism in place and was in a panic since she had an organizational meeting with this missing data to be displayed prominently during the presentation. This recovery process actually took very little time to conduct, but the recovery mechanism was the key to accomplish the task quickly and easily.

Log Reviews

In today's digital world, especially in a corporate environment, network components, devices, and activities are monitored and recording all actions being conducted on the network. Any device which has a CPU can, be design, record any and all events that are processed by the CPU. So always look for the network devices and their logging and event capture mechanisms. These logs can be a great source of background data on the events under question, or even the logs could become evidence itself of potential suspicious activities or events.

With the devices used on the network, watch for time stamps on each event, correlating the event recorded with other records of activities, such as events from the suspect's computer, other network device logs, communications records, etc. The Team Manager's requirements here include requiring a log review for each potential device, correlation matrix of events and evidence records for each event, and an overall composite description of the log events tied to the digital evidence step by step, where possible.

eDiscovery

eDiscovery is a term that is sometimes used interchangeably with the terms computer forensics or digital forensics, however, to use them interchangeably is inaccurate. eDiscovery, short for electronic discovery, is the term used to refer to any type of electronic evidence produced during the course of civil litigation. In essence, the difference between eDiscovery and computer forensics is a question of order, and in its most fundamental sense, the distinguishing characteristic is volume. Typically, large eDiscovery projects involve the reconstruction of massive quantities of documents, e-mails, and other information from systems, servers, and backup media to large databases and searchable formats. These items are then reviewed by legal document review experts that will decide whether or not the information is relevant to the case. Software developers continue to produce programs that are capable of organizing and managing these massive discovery projects to make review more efficient and simple. These programs can cost thousands of dollars to purchase.

The term is used particularly in this manner because it is more a legal term of art than a scientific term. Further, there is a plethora of case law surrounding large-scale and typically expensive litigation costs to produce eDiscovery projects. Forensic examiners assist in the process of eDiscovery by determining locations where evidence relative to the civil litigation may exist, copying it, and producing it to litigators in some type of understandable form. Oftentimes there is contentious debate about the scope of what a party in litigation is or is not entitled to from the other party. Rule 26 and 34 of the FRCP now deal with ESI. Private computer forensic practitioners, boutique firms, and the big five forensic consulting agencies all deal extensively with eDiscovery in civil litigation.

In US law, discovery is the pretrial phase in a lawsuit in which each party, through the rules of civil procedure, can obtain evidence from the opposing party by means of discovery devices including requests for answers to interrogatories, requests for production of documents, requests for admissions, and depositions. Discovery can be obtained from nonparties using subpoenas. eDiscovery is concerned with the identification, Preservation, collection, processing, review and production of electronic documents that exist across a system or corporate network. The term eDiscovery was initially a US term, and in the United Kingdom this process is known as Disclosure.

In the discovery process, data are identified as potentially relevant by attorneys and the data is placed on legal hold. A legal hold refers to a process which an organization uses to preserve all forms of relevant information when it reasonably anticipates some type of litigation against it. It is a restriction on a record that exists as a result of current or anticipated litigation, audit, government investigation or other such matter that suspends the normal disposition or processing of records. Evidence is then extracted and analyzed using digital forensic procedures, and is reviewed using a document review platform. A document review platform is useful for its ability to aggregate and search large quantities of similar type/formatted ESI. ESI is considered different from paper-based information because of its intangible form, volume, transience, and persistence. ESI is usually accompanied by Metadata that is not found in paper documents and that can play an important part as evidence (e.g., the date and time a document was written could be useful in a copyright case). The preservation of Metadata from electronic documents creates special challenges to prevent spoliation.

Electronic discovery reference model

The Electronic Discovery Reference Model (EDRM) diagram shown here represents a conceptual view of the eDiscovery process.

The EDRM[1] was developed in 2005 to help create best practices and guidelines for those working in the field of eDiscovery (lawyers, eDiscovery vendors, organizations preparing for litigation, and so on); and that it has become a standard of going through the eDiscovery process and aiding adherence to the US FRCP. The model as depicted in the figure above has nine phases as follows:

1. Information Management
2. Identification
3. Preservation
4. Collection
5. Processing
6. Review
7. Analysis
8. Production
9. Presentation.

---

[1] Electronic Discovery Reference Model, http://www.edrm.net.

Information Management

The way an organization manages its data and information is very crucial for eDiscovery when the need for eDiscovery arises. A good information management policy ensures that whenever discovery becomes necessary, data and information can be readily and easily made available in a forensically sound manner without unnecessary delay. Laws pertaining to eDiscovery (like the US FRCP) require digital evidence (ESI) to be prepared and presented quickly when request for and in an acceptable manner. Good information management policies, like document retention policies and forensic readiness policies, go a long way in ensuring ESI is available in a timely and forensically sound manner.

Identification

In this phase, ESI that will be relevant to a case and its location are determined. The location could be e-mail, hard drives, backup tapes, and so on. Identification of relevant ESI begins once litigation is reasonably anticipated. Prior to discovery, the lawyers of the two parties in a case usually have a meet and confer session or scheduling conference, where they agree on what ESI would be relevant, and the methods of identifying such ESI. The location of identified ESI is assessed to determine what needs to be preserved.

Preservation

Preservation begins immediately and relevant ESI is identified. Once there is a reasonable anticipation of litigation, identified ESI have to be preserved by the organization. The duty to preserve evidence is responsibility of which the organization may be held account for. Employees who have relevant information in their custody (custodians) and IT departments need to be informed that their ESI has become subject to discovery; hence they have to be issued a litigation hold. The litigation hold is to ensure that custodians do not tamper with the ESI that has become relevant evidence from then on, avoiding risk of modification or loss; the IT department is to ensure that such ESI are isolated from access by the custodians and properly safeguarded. Maintaining a proper chain of custody ensures proper documentation of how the digital evidence was collected, stored, handled, and analyzed—this can prove that ESI was properly preserved. In the *AMD v. Intel* case, part of Intel's errors was a failure to properly communicate litigation hold to employees (relevant custodians of ESI).

Collection

This phase involves acquiring ESI that had been identified and preserved. Oftentimes, preservation and collection may take place simultaneously. The ESI is required to be collected in a forensically sound manner, should be proportionate, efficient, and targeted. The ESI could be collected by self-collection or forensic imaging.

Self-collection of ESI involves manual copying of files and/or forwarding e-mails by information custodians, the ESI having been identified as relevant to the case at hand and notice of litigation hold having been sent to the custodians and IT department. This method is risky in that employees may intentionally or unintentionally modify ESI during the collection process.

Forensic imaging involves making bit by bit copies of information storage media in a bid to preserve the ESI from alteration or contamination. This can also capture deleted items; hence there might be a need to review such images to ensure privileged information is not included (in the review process).

Processing

Collected ESI needs to be processed before moving it to the review stage. Processing involves indexing, searching, and de-duplicating the collected ESI to reduce nonrelevant material, while fulfilling the requirements of the requesting party as well as the court. Some ESI may have to be extracted from files like compressed folders (e.g., zip files); there may also be need to convert some files form native format where such format is outdated and no longer in use, or the software required to view it is not available to the requesting party and the court. The files in such cases may be converted to formats that can be easily accessed by the other party.

Review

ESI is reviewed after having been processed. The review tries to determine if there is any privileged information contained in the ESI, and to ensure the ESI is relevant and meets the necessary requirements of the case. The review can be done using a native file review or using a TIFF-/PDF-based review.

In native file review, the files are reviewed in their native (original) format, usually in read-only mode so as to prevent contamination of the ESI arising from unintentional modification. That notwithstanding, the risk of modification is not eliminated. E-mails are, however, normally converted to HTML format for native file review.

Files are reviewed in an image format (like PDF or TIFF) in a TIFF/PDF review. Here, the files are converted or saved in such image format to prevent alteration or contamination. The downside is some data cannot be viewed; for example, if the native format was Excel, formulas would not be available for review, only the output would be available in the image format.

Analysis

Analysis is the next phase in the eDiscovery process, although in reality it normally takes place along with review. The ESI is further examined to ensure it is in line with the requirements of the requesting party and the litigation as a whole. Content of ESI are analyzed and the review could be enhanced using tools like concept searching tools. Concept searching tools extract content from ESI by using key concepts and subject matter to examine the ESI based on meaning of phrases and subject matter, as opposed to using keywords.

Production

In this phase, how, what, where and when ESI is produced to an opposing party is covered. The US FRCP Rule 34(b) gives the party requesting for ESI the right to determine what ESI should be produced, in what form and when. ESI could be produced on paper, in native form or image form. Paper production requires printing out the ESI on paper, which could be cumbersome and expensive (printouts could end up being stacked several meters high). Native form production requires the ESI be produced in its original state, while image form requires production of the ESI in a duplicated form which could be in the form of TIFF/PDF or forensic images. Image form production is easier to handle without altering the ESI and is more commonly requested.

The produced data could be delivered to the requesting party either as a final production or a rolling production. The final production involves delivery of data at once after all previous phases have been carried out. A rolling production involves delivery of the data to the requesting party in phases.

Presentation

The final stage in the eDiscovery process from the EDRM model is the presentation of ESI at a trial or in settlement negotiations. ESI has to be presented in a way that nontechnical people (usually lawyers, judges, and jury members tend not to be tech savvy) can easily comprehend and appreciate the e-evidence. The e-evidence also has to be presented in a way that is professional and convincing in a bid to prove or disprove a claim. The chain of custody may also need to be confirmed during the presentation to support the fact that ESI is authentic and forensically sound. A presentation should look appealing, not too flashy, and should not be too technical such as to lose the judge or jury.

US FEDERAL RULES OF CIVIL PROCEDURE

The FRCP governs civil litigation within the United States. They came into effect on December 1, 2006, and there are rule changes being proposed around proportionality and reasonable search.

Some of the key rules regarding eDiscovery and ESI are:

Rule 16(b): This covers preparation for litigation. You need to address the handling of ESI with all parties at the earliest possible moment.

It also gives the court discretion in adopting agreements between parties on claims of privilege or protection over inadvertent production. This would also be the time to bring up any issues around meeting the request for disclosure, for example, the data is held in another jurisdiction with strict data protection policies that prevent moving the data to a jurisdiction with weak data protection laws or prevent using the data for litigation in another jurisdiction.

Rule 26(a)(b)(f)(g): This group of rules is there to provide protection from excessive of expensive eDiscovery request. It outlines the schedule of meetings that must take place between parties (f), timetables for disclosure (a), and defines what can be determined as *not reasonably accessible* (b). Also within this rule is the need for an attorney to sign every eDiscovery request, response or objection (g).

Rule 33: This defines business records created or kept electronically as discoverable, giving the requesting party access to them.

Rule 34: This creates a dispute resolution structure for document production. It allows the requesting party to specify the format of the document production. Typically there will be some degree of negotiation as to the formats and metadata.

Rule 37: This gives the judge the power to impose sanctions on parties that fail to permit or provide disclosure. It also creates a "safe harbor" to protect the party from adverse sanctions for failure to disclosure due to inadvertent loss. The key to claiming safe harbor is to be able to show that you took all the necessary steps to ensure that responsive data was not lost or deleted.

UK CIVIL PROCEDURE RULES

Civil litigation in the United Kingdom is governed by the Civil Procedure Rules (CPR), eDisclosure is covered under Practice Directive 31.

April 1, 2013, saw a major shakeup in the CPR under reforms recommended by Judge Jackson. The reforms run deep and cover a number of aspects of UK law. The key changes effecting eDiscovery center on budgeting and case management and encourage cooperation between parties at the earliest possible moment. The aim is for eDiscovery to be reasonable and proportionate to the importance, complexity, and sums involved in the case.

No more than 14 days before the first Case Management Conference (these are used by the courts for considering the issues in dispute and whether they can be narrowed before trial, for exercising their broad case management powers and for giving directions for the management of the proceedings up to trial) parties need to have completed a document listing all the documents potentially relevant to the matter, their location, and an estimate of costs to retrieve.

The menu options are as follows:

- An order dispensing with disclosure
- An order that a party disclose the documents on which it relies, and at the same time requests any specific disclosure it requires from any other party
- An order that (where practical) directs, on an issue by issue basis, the disclosure to be given by a party on the material issues in the case
- An order that a party give standard disclosure
- An order that a party disclose any documents which it is reasonable to suppose may contain information which may (i) enable the party applying for disclosure either to advance his own case or to damage that of the party giving disclosure or (ii) lead to a train of enquiry which has either of those consequences
- Any other order in relation to disclosure that, having regard to the overriding objective, the court considers appropriate.

No more than 7 days before the Case Management Conference both parties need to have submitted their budgets. These budgets are expected to be detailed and accurate, not "finger in the air" or "back of a cigarette" calculations. They must be accompanied by a signed statement of truth by an authorized representative of the party. The budget is expected to be reasonable and proportionate to the matter, otherwise the court will not approve them. Failure to submit budgets on time will mean that the parties have a minimal budget, just the court fees with no recoverable costs.

Digital Evidence Layers

Some of the areas to include in the management of digital evidence include the various components and data segments found during the investigational activities conducted by the investigator and the examiner. As each layer of the data evidence is examined, its criteria for data handling changes due to the nature of the location, type, and size of the data element being investigated.[2]

A quick review of the components of an investigation will show the needs are different at each layer of the evidence. These layers are:

1. Bottom Layer where system construction is examined

   This is the foundational layer for any examination. The core components of the computer are found here and the examination process starts with this area. This area sets up the norm for this computer, with determining the standard OS and files loaded on it.

---

[2]Volonino L, Anzaldua R, Godwin J. Computer forensics: principles and practices. Pearson; 2007. p. 139.

a. File system details

The primary details of the operating system, the version of the operating system, and the computer are determined and documented for further use. The standard software and hardware configurations are defined here.

b. Directory system structure

The type of file structure and directory system is determined at this layer. The file attribute mechanism is defined with time stamps, cluster allocations, and normal locations for all files.

c. Operating system parameters

The operating system parameters are found at this level. Where do the print files get stored is defined along with temporary file locations and sizes and default file storage locations.

d. Partition(s) information

Additional partitions are always available on today's computing systems and this is where those are examined. Always look for large portions of the hard drive/storage location that are not recognized by the operating system. This is a good indication there are additional partitions and maybe even additional operating systems loaded.

e. Dual-/Multiboot system

If there are additional operating systems loaded, then they are discovered during this level of examination. If these exist, look for additional storage locations, file structures, and storage mechanisms.

2. Second layer where the file header and extension analysis is performed

Examination, sorting, initial file analysis are all conducted during this layer of the inspection and investigation.

a. Exclusion of known files by hash analysis

Standard file structures for operating systems are well defined and available for hashing. Obtain a current copy of these hashes for the operating system under review and compare to determine areas of differences for further examination and potential evidence gathering.

b. File header information

Comparison of file header data to file type is conducted at this point. If different, then the file needs further analysis.

c. File extension information

Comparison of file extension data to file type is conducted at this point. If different, then the file needs further analysis.

d. Obvious files of interest (i.e., pictures in child porn case or e-mail communications in an espionage case)

This is an extraction of the file data activity being conducted, therefore only identifying the suspect file is performed here.

3. Third layer where password-protected files, encrypted files, compressed files, and previously deleted files are extracted, evaluated, and examined

    a. Extraction of password-protected files

    Always perform password-protected file extraction when these types of files are identified. They may be perfectly alright, but the potential for important data contained within these files is large, so always extract them.

    b. Extraction of encrypted files

    Always perform decryption on encrypted files when these types of files are identified. The best method is usually to determine the type of encryption to help determine the keys before attempting brute force decryption.

    c. Extraction of compressed files (especially e-mail)

    The compressed files are usually in this type of format for space saving reasons, so most toolsets have decompression mechanisms built-in to perform this type of extraction.

    d. Extraction of deleted files

    Always evaluate all deleted files to ensure the validity and relevancy to the case when extracting them.

    e. Link analysis

    Link file records the device to which a file is saved, time it occurred, and date last accessed.

4. Fourth layer wherein the unallocated hard drive space and the slack space between files are discovered, extracted, evaluated, and examined.

    a. Extraction of unallocated space files

    Now you are looking for files which were recorded to the device then erased. Most all operating systems simply remove the file pointers and allocation data when "delete" is performed; the actual data is not actually removed from the device. This process identifies these types of files still resident on the device.

    b. Extraction of file slack space files

    The space from the end of the file to the end of the memory allocated cluster is called slack space. Fragments of data can be identified and retrieved from these locations.

5. The fifth layer of evidence is where the file content itself is examined and evaluated

    a. File content

    What is the actual file content is identified and delineated during this step.

    b. Metadata

    The data about the files, images or other data structures is called metadata and is used to help define the actual file data.

    c. Application files

    Using the application as a guide, you identify the files associated with that application to determine if there are missing or moved files.

This process helps determine if there are other devices to be seized or other storage locations to be identified.

d. User configurations

What has the user customized on the computer for their own use that can lead you to other evidence, files, or other data structures and other locations of data?

e. Patterns

The ways files are named and stored is often patterned so the investigator can find the suspect's pattern of use and help determine methods and locations of suspect files.

Forensics Tools

The kinds of tools necessary for any forensics investigation always depend on the type of data, files, sources, and operating systems being reviewed. Each operating system has its own particulars of drivers, software libraries, and specific kernel code to be examined. Data refers to distinct pieces of digital information that have been formatted in a specific way. All the various data types have specific code and structure parameters associated with the actual bits and bytes of the data on the storage mechanism. Each dataset can have hidden and metadata tied to it which needs to be identified and reviewed by the analyst or examiner.

The Forensics Team Manager must make sure the actual tools needed for the investigator are available for use, licensed correctly, approved, and certified for use by the laboratory staff. Each tool must be obtained legitimately by the organization through the normal procurement system and then the staff needs to be trained in its proper use and application. There are many kinds of tools available, but one location to start reviewing the available tool market is the Computer Forensics Tool Testing program run by the US National Institute of Justice under the auspices of NIST. This location: www.cftt.nist. gov contains listings for each forensics tool tested to determine how well they perform core forensics functions such as imaging drive, extracting information, and the actual testing specifications used to test the tool, testing software used, and the complete testing methodology.

The site contains the tests organized by functional area tested with the full results documented and available for download. The functional areas defined include disk imaging, forensics media preparation, software-based write blockers, hardware-based write blockers, string search tools, deleted file recovery, and mobile device tools.

Forensic tools are valuable not only for acquiring disk images but also for automating much of the analysis process, such as:

- Identifying and recovering file fragments and hidden and deleted files and directories from any location (e.g., used space, free space, slack space)

- Examining file structures, headers, and other characteristics to determine what type of data each file contains, instead of relying on file extensions (e.g., .doc, .jpg, .mp3)
- Displaying the contents of all graphics files
- Performing complex searches
- Graphically displaying the acquired drive's directory structure
- Generating reports.

During evidence acquisition, it is often important to acquire copies of supporting log files from other resources—for example, firewall logs that show what IP address an attacker used. As with hard drive and other media acquisition, logs should be copied to sanitized write-protectable or write-once media. One copy of the logs should be stored as evidence, whereas a second copy could be restored to another system for further analysis.

Organizations have an ever-increasing amount of data from many sources. For example, data can be stored or transferred by standard computer systems, networking equipment, computing peripherals, cell and "smart" phones, personal digital assistants (PDAs), consumer electronic devices, and various types of media, among other sources. Always keep in mind as the Forensics process is conducted, the four main sources of data within any network or computer:

1. Files
2. Operating systems
3. Network traffic
4. Applications.

The NIST Guide for Forensics use in Incident Response, SP 800-86, offers the explanations of these four areas of data to explore and evaluate during investigations and examinations:

a. Files: As the SP 800-86 explains: "A data file (also called a file) is a collection of information logically grouped into a single entity and referenced by a unique name, such as a filename. A file can be of many data types, including a document, an image, a video, or an application. Successful forensic processing of computer media depends on the ability to collect, examine, and analyze the files that reside on the media.

Before media can be used to store files, the media must usually be partitioned and formatted into logical volumes. Partitioning is the act of logically dividing a media into portions that function as physically separate units. A logical volume is a partition or a collection of partitions acting as a single entity that has been formatted with a filesystem. Some media types, such as floppy disks, can contain at most one partition (and consequently, one logical volume). The format of the logical volumes is determined by the selected filesystem.

A filesystem defines the way that files are named, stored, organized, and accessed on logical volumes. Many different filesystems exist, each providing unique features and data structures. However, all filesystems share some common traits. First, they use the concepts of directories and files to organize and store data. Directories are organizational structures that are used to group files together. In addition to files, directories may contain other directories called subdirectories. Second, filesystems use some data structure to point to the location of files on media. In addition, they store each data file written to media in one or more file allocation units. These are referred to as clusters by some filesystems (e.g., File Allocation Table [FAT], NT File System [NTFS]) and as blocks by other filesystems (e.g., UNIX and Linux). A file allocation unit is simply a group of sectors, which are the smallest units that can be accessed on media."

b. OS: As the SP 800-86 explains: "An operating system (OS) is a program that runs on a computer and provides a software platform on which other programs can run. In addition, an OS is responsible for processing input commands from a user, sending output to a display, interacting with storage devices to store and retrieve data, and controlling peripheral devices such as printers and modems. Some common OSs for workstations or servers include various versions of Windows, Linux, UNIX, and Mac OS. Some network devices, such as routers, have their own proprietary OSs (e.g., Cisco Internetwork Operating System [IOS]). PDAs often run specialized OSs, including PalmOS and Windows CE. Many embedded systems, such as cellular phones, digital cameras, and audio players, also use OSs.

OS data exists in both nonvolatile and volatile states. Non-volatile data refers to data that persists even after a computer is powered down, such as a filesystem stored on a hard drive. Volatile data refers to data on a live system that is lost after a computer is powered down, such as the current network connections to and from the system. Many types of non-volatile and volatile data may be of interest from a forensics perspective.

The primary source of non-volatile data within an OS is the filesystem. The filesystem is also usually the largest and richest source of data within the OS, containing most of the information recovered during a typical forensic event. The filesystem provides storage for the OS on one or more media. A filesystem typically contains many types of files, each of which may be of value to analysts in different situations.

OSs execute within the RAM of a system. While the OS is functioning, the contents of RAM are constantly changing. At any given time, RAM might contain many types of data and information that could be of interest. For example, RAM often contains frequently and recently accessed data, such as data files, password hashes, and recent commands."

    c. Network: As the SP 800-86 explains: "Analysts can use data from network traffic to reconstruct and analyze network-based attacks and inappropriate network usage, as well as to troubleshoot various types of operational problems. The content of communications carried over networks, such as e-mail messages or audio, might also be collected in support of an investigation. The term network traffic refers to computer network communications that are carried over wired or wireless networks between hosts. This section provides an introduction to network traffic, including descriptions of major sources of network traffic data (e.g., intrusion detection software, firewalls).

Organizations typically have several types of information sources concerning network traffic that might be useful for network forensics. These sources collectively capture important data from all four TCP/IP layers. The following subsections highlight the major categories of network traffic data sources, firewalls and routers, packet sniffers and protocol analyzers, IDSs, remote access, security event management software, and network forensic analysis tools; as well as several other types of data sources."

    d. Applications: As the SP 800-86 explains: "Applications such as e-mail, Web browsers, and word processors are what make computers valuable to users. OSs, files, and networks are all needed to support applications: OSs to run the applications, networks to send application data between systems, and files to store application data, configuration settings, and logs. From a forensic perspective, applications bring together files, OSs, and networks. This section describes application architectures, the components that typically make up applications, and provides insights into the types of applications that are most often the focus of forensics. All applications contain code in the form of executable files (and related files, such as shared code libraries) or scripts. In addition to code, many applications have one or more of the following components: configuration settings, authentication, logs, data, and supporting files."

TYPES OF FORENSICS TOOLS

Different kinds and types of tools are needed by the analyst, examiner or investigator as they begin to look at, review and analyze the various data sources during their investigation. Here is a listing of suggested tool types available today, but please understand this list is by NO means all inclusive. There are many other areas being discovered each day with new tools coming to the workplace all the time, so do NOT view this as covering all areas.

- File System Navigation tool
  Many operating systems come with an embedded file navigation mechanism. There are also many external third-party tools available for use during

investigations. Each has features and components which allow searching for specific file extensions, metadata about files, and other file parameters. These tools provide quick identification of files which meet the needed criteria.

- Hashing tool

  Each and every time an evidence component is captured, it is to be cryptographically signed to ensure its integrity. This process is known as "hashing." It is called that because the process of one-way encryption of the file structure to a fixed-length output utilizes encryption algorithms known as hashes. These processes are of two primary encryption types: Message Digest (MD) outputs and Secure Hash Algorithm (SHA) outputs. The MD output depends upon the type of algorithm used with the most common one known as MD5. SHA output is slightly longer but its algorithm is more secure when it is used for confidentiality. Remember, the primary purpose is for integrity, to scientifically prove the data has been unaltered when reviewing and examining it. The integrity hash does not indicate where in the data the alteration has occurred. By recalculating the integrity hash at a later time, one can determine if the data in the disk image has been changed.

- Binary Search tool

  The tools used for binary search have the purpose of examining files to reveal bit patterns within. These tools look for specific patterns and types of data sequences found in known and maybe unknown types of files. Expecting data to be altered during storage and transmittal is a common mechanism the examiner must be aware of and look for when performing the evaluation of the files and data components so these types of tools assist in that endeavor.

- Imaging tool

  One of the basic requirements for any forensics investigation is to capture the data in a format that allows for examination of the complete dataset being retrieved. This process is called disk imaging. There are two primary areas where this process is applied in forensics. Bit copy image which covers the entire media where the data is found and filesystem imaging where the data structures are defined and stored.

  - Bit Copy

    Disk imaging is the process of making a bit-by-bit copy of a disk. Imaging (in more general terms) can apply to anything that can be considered as a bit-stream, e.g., a physical or logical volume, network streams, file directories. There are many tools and programs available to conduct these bit-stream image activities and I have listed several within this section. Always ensure your organization has tested and validated the tools before usage in a real-time capture event.

  - File System

    Within the UNIX and Linux operating systems, there is the concept of capturing an image of the filesystem as a copy of the entire state of the computer in a nonvolatile form such as a file. The operating system then can use this system image if it is shut down and later restored to exactly the same state as original. In these cases, system file images can and often are used for full system backups. Laptop computer hibernation is an example that uses an image of the entire machine's RAM.

- Deep Retrieval tool

  A forensics-based tool designed to retrieve data that has been deleted or "erased" for long periods of time, as well as the more recent material. Most current Data Recovery tools are also known as deep retrieval tools and provide the mechanisms to obtain and retrieve data from past uses, deletions and hiding of files and folders, so long as the drive has not been reformatted. Some of these tools allow for the hardware recovery of damaged drive utilizing various aspects of the physics of the media, the actual data magnetic platters, etc. The recovery for deep retrieval can also involve addition of or replacement of physical components on the drives, then retrieval of the data for use in evidence recovery efforts.

- File Chain Navigation tool

  A tool designed to trace dependencies and linking of files as they are found in the directories throughout the computer. This tool assists in determining possible alternate data streams and binding of files and libraries to executables.

- Case Management Systems

  There are many forensics case management software packages available in the industry. Several of these packages are well known, such as EnCase the Sleuth Toolkit and Forensics Tool Kit (FTK), and others are not so well known but just as functional. Always make sure the investigators are utilizing the organizational-approved case management system during each event and examination. If possible, obtain certifications for the investigators on each system used by the organization. The actual systems available cover end-to-end requirements for forensics investigations including case tracking of individual evidence components, data carving of evidence, found and identified evidence components, etc. Each case management system performs these activities in a little bit different manner which is usually what makes them unique, so always ensure the case tools match the case needs and criteria.

- Specific Examination Tools

  There are many specific forensics tools that have evolved to cover specific areas of investigations they include:

  - Steganography

    This class of tools assists in identifying images and files which have had data hidden inside other files. There are a number of steganographic tools available in the marketplace and for free on the Internet.

  - Internet history

    This class of tool is used for examining the cookies and Internet history files found in the use of browsers. Internet Evidence Finder (IEF) is just one of toolsets available. Each browser creates and stores cookies in its own format, so always ensure the tools used are related to the browser used.

■ Log Management Tools

The arena of log management tools has exploded over the past few years. Most implementations are included in the entire class of toolsets known as Security Event and Identification Monitor (SEIM) systems. There are many such tools available which receive log files from various devices on the network and correlate them by time and event and allow dashboard review, detailed analysis and deep data search capabilities within the package.

■ Volatile Data Capture Tools

There are a number of new data capture tools available today which allow capture of data from storage devices in "real-time" to retrieve and retain the data from the areas of machines which either cease to exist or are removed when a device or machine is powered down and turned off.

One such tool is Helix First Response developed by e-fense. This is a USB tool with its own method of enablement which does not interfere with the operating system running on the suspect device at the time of capture; therefore, there is no alteration of the system processes or memory when retrieving data.

TOOLS FOR SPECIFIC OPERATING SYSTEMS AND PLATFORMS

Note that data listed here is from commercial vendors and websites for products listed. This is NOT a comprehensive listing of tools. Also review and evaluate each tool for use in your environment and circumstances. Remember, Computer Forensics Tools are always being evaluated by National Institute of Justice (NIJ) and NIST, and current ratings and evaluations are available at www.cftt.nist.gov.

Windows tools include:

A. Log Parser

Log parser is a powerful, versatile tool that provides universal query access to text-based data such as log files, XML files, and CSV files, as well as key data sources on the Windows® operating system such as the Event Log, the Registry, the filesystem, and Active Directory.

B. EnCase

EnCase® Forensic, the industry-standard computer investigation solution, is for forensic practitioners who need to conduct efficient, forensically sound data collection and investigations using a repeatable and defensible process. The proven, powerful, and trusted EnCase® Forensic solution, lets examiners acquire data from a wide variety of devices, unearth potential evidence with disk-level forensic analysis, and craft comprehensive reports on their findings, all while maintaining the integrity of their evidence.

EnCase is a suite digital forensics products by Guidance Software. The software comes in several forms designed for forensic, cyber security, and eDiscovery use.

EnCase contains tools for several areas of the digital forensic process; acquisition, analysis, and reporting. The software also includes a scripting facility called EnScript with various APIs for interacting with evidence. EnCase contains functionality to create forensic images of suspect media. Images are stored in proprietary *EnCase Evidence File Format*; the compressible file format is prefixed with case data information and consists of a bit-by-bit (i.e., exact) copy of the media interspaced with hashes (usually MD5 or SHA1) for every 64 KB of data. The file format also appends an MD5 hash of the entire drive as a footer onto the image file. EnCase is available for use on most major operating systems but is primarily a Windows-based deployment.

C. ILook (LEO only)

The ILook Investigator © Forensic Software is a comprehensive suite of computer forensics tools used to acquire and analyze digital media. ILook Investigator © products include ILook v8 forensic application and the IXimager which are both designed to follow forensics best practices. They meet the computer forensics needs of Law Enforcement and Government. ILook Investigator © Forensic Software will continue to be provided FREE to law enforcement.

ILook is a powerful multithreaded, Unicode compliant, fast and efficient forensic analysis tool designed to examine digital media from seized computer systems and/or other digital media. ILook has robust processing capabilities including advanced e-mail deconstruction and analysis, thorough and comprehensive indexing capabilities, a wealth of reporting features, and advanced unallocated space data salvaging capability. ILook runs on Windows XP/Server platforms, both 32- and 64-bit versions.

ILook is an all-in-one computer forensics suite originally created by Elliot Spencer and currently maintained by the US Department of Treasury Internal Revenue Service Criminal Investigation Division (IRS-CI) Electronic Crimes Program. It was made available at no cost to law enforcement agencies and US government agencies at the discretion of the IRS-CI but is not available to the general public.

There is a commercial version available, *ILooKIX*, at Perlustro.com, home of the ILook developer, where it supports current versions of ILook for LEO and ILooKIX.

D. Paraben

Paraben quickly established itself as a leader in specialized computer forensic software with its release of PDA Seizure in early 2002. Paraben then released Cell Seizure, the first commercial tool for performing cell phone forensics. The handheld forensics line has culminated with the combination of these two tools into Device Seizure which supports more cell phones and PDAs than ever before.

P2 Commander is the forensics tool from the hard drive/media division of the company. A comprehensive digital forensic examination tool, P2 Commander incorporates E-mail Examiner, Network E-mail Examiner, Chat Examiner, Registry Analyzer, Forensic Sorter, and Text Searcher along with many other features into one comprehensive forensic analysis tool.

P2 Commander is a forensic tool from Paraben Corporation that is built to process large volumes of data in a fast and efficient manner. This tool can be used for a wide range of forensics analysis of systems like disk, chat, e-mail, registry, Internet files, and pornographic detection. One unique feature of P2 Commander which sets it apart from other forensics tools is the ability of P2 Commander to store its case files in what it calls forensic containers that are encrypted and write protected such that the digital evidence can be stored securely and makes it easier for third parties to review the evidence. This helps to ensure a proper chain of custody and to show that the evidence was not tampered with or contaminated during storage.

Paraben has been a leader in handheld digital forensics since early 2002 when Paraben's PDA Seizure 1.0 released followed by the release of the first commercially available tool for cellular forensics—Paraben's Cell Seizure. Device Seizure supports PDAs using the following Operating Systems: Palm through 6, Windows CE/Pocket PC/Mobile 4.x and earlier, BlackBerry 4.x and earlier, and Symbian 6.0. It also supports Garmin GPS devices. Combine this with support for thousands of cell phone models and you can see why Device Seizure moves mountains when it comes to digital forensics for handheld devices. With full physical data acquisitions, advanced analysis features, improved manufacturer support, and new cables added to the accompanying toolbox, the Device Seizure software is moving to new levels in handheld forensics.

E. ProDiscover

ProDiscover® *Forensics* is a powerful computer security tool that enables computer professionals to find all the data on a computer disk while protecting evidence and creating evidentiary quality reports for use in legal proceedings. ProDiscover includes the following features and components:

- Create Bit-Stream copy of disk to be analyzed, including hidden Hyper Patch Archive (HPA) section (patent pending), to keep original evidence safe.
- Search files or entire disk including slack space, HPA section, and Windows NT/2000/XP Alternate Data Streams for complete disk forensic analysis.
- Preview all files, even if hidden or deleted, without altering data on disk, including file Metadata.

- Maintain multitool compatibility by reading and writing images in the pervasive UNIX® dd format and reading images in E01 format.
- Support for VMware to run a captured image.
- Examine and cross reference data at the file or cluster level to insure nothing is hidden, even in slack space.
- Automatically generate and record MD5, SHA1, or SHA256 hashes to prove data integrity.
- Utilize user provided or National Drug Intelligence Center Hashkeeper database information to positively identify files.
- Examine FAT12, FAT16, FAT 32, and all NTFS including Dynamic Disk and Software RAID for maximum flexibility.
- Examine Sun Solaris UFS filesystem and Linux ext2/ext3 filesystems.
- Integrated thumbnail graphics, internet history, event log file, and registry viewers to facilitate investigation process.
- Integrated viewer to examine .pst/.ost and .dbx e-mail files.
- Utilize Perl scripts to automate investigation tasks.
- Extracts EXIF information from JPEG files to identify file creators.
- Automated report generation in XML format saves time, improves accuracy, and compatibility.
- Graphical user interface (GUI) and integrated help function assure quick start and ease of use.
- Designed to NIST Disk Imaging Tool Specification 3.1.6 to insure high quality.

F. TCPView

TCPView is a Windows program that will show you detailed listings of all TCP and User Datagram Protocol (UDP) endpoints on your system, including the local and remote addresses and state of TCP connections. On Windows Server 2008, Vista, and XP, TCPView also reports the name of the process that owns the endpoint. TCPView provides a more informative and conveniently presented subset of the Netstat program that comes with Windows. The TCPView download includes Tcpvcon, a command-line version with the same functionality.

G. AccessData

AccessData digital forensics solutions deliver unsurpassed forensic analysis of computers, network communications and mobile devices. We not only enable digital investigations of any kind, but we offer solutions for organizations of any size. From portable triage solutions to large-scale, enterprise-class investigation and incident response, AccessData technology has been recognized by industry media, analysts and real-world users as the most innovative, robust and user friendly.

FTK is a court-accepted digital investigations platform that is built for speed, analytics, and enterprise-class scalability. Known for its intuitive interface, e-mail analysis, customizable data views and stability, FTK lays the framework for seamless expansion, so your computer forensics solution can grow with your organization's needs.

In addition, AccessData offers new expansion modules delivering an industry-first malware analysis capability and state-of-the-art visualization. These modules integrate with FTK to create the most comprehensive computer forensics platform on the market.

H. COFEE (LEO only)

Computer Online Forensic Evidence Extractor (COFEE) is a toolkit, developed by Microsoft, to help computer forensic investigators extract evidence from a Windows computer. Installed on a USB flash drive or other external disk drive, it acts as an automated forensic tool during a live analysis. Microsoft provides COFEE devices and online technical support free to law enforcement agencies. COFEE was developed by Anthony Fung, a former Hong Kong police officer, who now works as a senior investigator on Microsoft's Internet Safety Enforcement Team. Fung conceived the device following discussions he had at a 2006 law enforcement technology conference sponsored by Microsoft. The device is used by more than 2000 officers in at least 15 countries.

The device is activated by being plugged into a USB port. It contains 150 tools and a GUI to help investigators collect data. The software is reported to be made up of three sections. First COFEE is configured in advance with an investigator selecting the data they wish to export; this is then saved to a USB device for plugging into the target computer. A further interface generates reports from the collected data. Estimates cited by Microsoft state jobs that previously took 3–4 h can be done with COFEE in as little as 20 min. COFEE includes tools for password decryption, Internet history recovery, and other data extraction. It also recovers data stored in volatile memory which could be lost if the computer were shut down.

I. Sysinternals.com tools

The Sysinternals website was created in 1996 by Mark Russinovich and Bryce Cogswell to host their advanced system utilities and technical information. Whether you're an IT Pro or a developer, you'll find Sysinternals utilities to help you manage, troubleshoot, and diagnose your Windows systems and applications.

The Sysinternals Troubleshooting Utilities have been rolled up into a single Suite of tools. This file contains the individual troubleshooting tools and help files. It does not contain nontroubleshooting tools like the BSOD Screen Saver or NotMyFault.

This suite of tools is available at: http://technet.microsoft.com/en-us/sysinternals/default

J. Foundstone.com tools

The Foundstone practice is one of the world's foremost authorities on information security. Whether through strategic consulting, technology consulting, education, or a combination of all three, McAfee Foundstone delivers strategic solutions to security challenges, going well beyond a short-term fix. Our security experts make sure you have the right processes and procedures in place, the most effective tools to support those processes and procedures, and the education to make it all work together effectively and seamlessly.

Foundstone was founded in 1999 by George Kurtz, Chris Prosise, Gary Bahadur, and William Chan. The company primarily provided information security consulting services then later created the Foundstone Enterprise Vulnerability Management product. Foundstone was acquired by McAfee in 2004. After the acquisition, the product team was integrated into McAfee's product development group and the services team was separated out into the Foundstone Division. Later the various service divisions of McAfee all merged under a single new division, called McAfee Professional Services and Foundstone became a group within it. Although Foundstone is owned by McAfee, it stays vendor neutral in order to remain impartial in its services.

The company's services are divided into four categories: Incident Response and Forensics, Strategic, Tactical, and Training with core services in the following:

- *Incident Response and Forensics*: The investigation, assessment, and containment of computer attacks and malware outbreaks.
- *Infrastructure Assessments*: The security evaluation of networks and systems to identify software and configuration vulnerabilities.
- *Software Security Assessments*: The identification of hardware and software vulnerabilities through black box, white box, and gray box testing.
- *Program Development and Risk*: The development of information security programs, policies, and procedure. Also included within these services are information security risk assessments.
- *Training*: Public and private classes on ethical hacking, incident response and forensics, and software security.

Free software such as Superscan and Hacme Bank have been released by Foundstone since its early inception. The security-centric tools provide aid to penetration testers in ethical hacking and teach software developers security fundamentals. Some of the basic Foundstone tools available are listed at the end of this section.

K. WinHex

WinHex is in its core a universal hexadecimal editor, particularly helpful in the realm of computer forensics, data recovery, low-level data processing, and IT security. An advanced tool for everyday and emergency use: inspect and edit all kinds of files, recover deleted files or lost data from hard drives with corrupt filesystems or from digital camera cards. Features include:

- Disk editor for hard disks, floppy disks, CD-ROM and DVD, ZIP, Smart Media, Compact Flash, …
- Native support for FAT12/16/32, exFAT, NTFS, Ext2/3/4, Next3®, CDFS, Universal Disk Format (UDF)
- Built-in interpretation of RAID systems and dynamic disks
- Various data recovery techniques
- RAM editor, providing access to physical RAM and other processes' virtual memory
- Data interpreter, knowing 20 data types
- Editing data structures using templates (e.g., to repair partition table/ boot sector)
- Concatenating and splitting files, unifying, and dividing odd and even bytes/words
- Analyzing and comparing files
- Particularly flexible search and replace functions
- Disk cloning (under DOS with X-Ways Replica)
- Drive images and backups (optionally compressed or split into 650 MB archives)
- Programming interface (API) and scripting
- 256-bit Advanced Encryption Standard (AES) encryption, checksums, CRC32, hashes (MD5, SHA1, …)
- Erase (wipe) confidential files securely, hard drive cleansing to protect your privacy
- Import all clipboard formats, including ASCII hex values
- Convert between binary, hex ASCII, Intel Hex, and Motorola S
- Character sets: ANSI ASCII, IBM ASCII, EBCDIC (Unicode)
- Instant window switching. Printing. Random-number generator
- Supports files >4 GB.

L. X-Way Forensics

All the features of WinHex plus:

- Ability to read and write .e01 evidence files (a.k.a. EnCase images), optionally with real encryption (256-bit AES, i.e., not mere "password protection")
- Ability to create skeleton images and cleansed images
- Ability to copy relevant files to evidence file containers, where they retain almost all their original filesystem metadata, as a means to selectively acquire data in the first place or to exchange selected files with investigators, prosecution, lawyers, etc.
- Complete case management
- Automated activity logging (audit logs)

- Write protection to ensure data authenticity
- Remote analysis capability for drives in network can be added optionally
- Additional support for the filesystems HFS, HFS + /HFSJ/HFSX, ReiserFS, Reiser4, XFS, many variants of UFS1 and UFS2
- Ability to include files from all volume shadow copies in the analysis (but exclude duplicates), filter for such files, find the snapshot properties, etc.
- The basis for a listed file is practically just a mouse click away. Easily navigate to the filesystem data structure where it is defined, e.g., FILE record, index record, $LogFile, volume shadow copy, FAT directory entry, Ext* inode, containing file if embedded
- Supported partitioning types: Apple supported in addition to MBR, GUID partitioning (GPT), Windows dynamic disks (both MBR and GPT style), LVM2 (both MBR and GPT style), and unpartitioned (Superfloppy)
- Very powerful main memory analysis for local RAM or memory dumps of Windows 2000, XP, Vista, 2003 Server, 2008 Server, Windows 7
- Shows owners of files, NTFS file permissions, object IDs/GUIDs, special attributes
- Compensation for NTFS compression effects and Ext2/Ext3 block allocation logic in file carving
- Convenient back and forward navigation from one directory to another, multiple steps, restoring sort criteria, filter (de)activation, selection
- Gallery view for pictures
- Calendar view
- File preview, seamlessly integrated viewer component for 270+ file types
- Ability to print the same file types directly from within the program with all metadata on a cover page
- Internal viewer for Windows Registry files (all Windows versions); automated and configurable powerful Registry report
- Viewer for Windows event log files (.evt, .evtx), Windows shortcut (.lnk) files, Windows Prefetch files, $LogFile, $UsnJrnl, restore point change.log, Windows Task Scheduler (.job), $EFS LUS, INFO2, wtmp/utmp/btmp log-in records, Mac OS X kcpassword, AOL PFC, Outlook NK2 autocomplete, Outlook Windows Address Book (WAB), Internet Explorer travelog (aka RecoveryStore), SQLite databases such as Firefox history, Firefox downloads, Firefox form history, Firefox sign-ons, Chrome cookies, Chrome archived history, Chrome history, Chrome log-in data, Chrome web data, Safari cache, Safari feeds, Skype's main.db database with contacts and file transfers, …

- Ability to collect Internet Explorer history and browser cache index. dat records that are floating around in free space or slack space in a virtual single file
- Extracts metadata and internal creation timestamps from various file types and allows to filter by that, e.g., MS Office, OpenOffice, StarOffice, HTML, MDI, PDF, RTF, WRI, AOL PFC, ASF, WMV, WMA, MOV, AVI, WAV, MP4, 3GP, M4V, M4A, JPEG, BMP, THM, TIFF, GIF, PNG, GZ, ZIP, PF, IE cookies, DMP memory dumps, hiberfil.sys, PNF, SHD and SPL printer spool, tracking.log, .mdb MS Access database, manifest.mbdx/.mbdb iPhone backup
- Keeps track of which files were already viewed during the investigation
- Include external files, e.g., translations or decrypted or converted versions of original files, and connect them to the files they belong with
- Ability to examine e-mail extracted from Outlook (PST, OST), Exchange EDB, Outlook Express (DBX), AOL PFC, Mozilla (including Thunderbird), generic mailbox (mbox, UNIX), MSG, EML.

UNIX tools include:

- File control utilities—DD, etc.

DD and the other standard UNIX utilities allow for use as forensics tools, especially in the areas of data capture and file examination. The dd="Dump Data" command is standard in all UNIX distributions. It can be used to read and write data from a media device and a data file. The dd command creates a raw format file that most computer forensics analysis tools can read. The issues with the use of dd include it requires advanced skill to use in a forensics setting and it does not automatically encrypt the output. One of the advantages of the dd command is that it can be combined with the split command segments output into separate volumes. The dd command is intended to be used as a data management tool; it's not designed for forensics applications and acquisitions but can be used adequately for investigative and imaging purposes.

The command under dd to create a duplicate copy of a disk drive is:

    # dd if = /dev/sda0 of = /case1/fdisk

The following command is to copy this file to another disk for review:

    # dd if = /case1/fdimage of = /dev/sda0 md5sum fdisk.dd > fdisk.md5

However, the enhanced version, known as the "dcfldd" command offers additional capabilities, including:

a. Specify hexadecimal patterns or text for clearing disk space
b. Log errors to an output file for analysis and review
c. Use several hashing options

    d. Refer to a status display indicating the progress of the acquisition in bytes

    e. Split data acquisitions into segmented volumes with numeric extensions

    f. Verify the acquired data with the original disk or media data.

So to create a duplicate copy of a disk using the enhanced dcfldd program the command would be:

\# dcfldd if = /dev/sda0 of = /case/case1/fdisk.dd hashwindow = 0
    hashlog = /case1/fdisk.dd

- **Wireshark—Ethereal (packet sniffer)**

Wireshark is the world's foremost network protocol analyzer. It lets you capture and interactively browse the traffic running on a computer network. It is the *de facto* (and often *de jure*) standard across many industries and educational institutions. Wireshark development thrives thanks to the contributions of networking experts across the globe. It is the continuation of a project that started in 1998.

Wireshark's most powerful feature is its vast array of display filters (over 114,000 fields in 1300 protocols). They let you drill down to the exact traffic you want to see and are the basis of many of Wireshark's other features, such as the coloring rules. Wireshark has a rich feature set which includes the following:

- Deep inspection of hundreds of protocols, with more being added all the time
- Live capture and offline analysis
- Standard three-pane packet browser
- Multiplatform: Runs on Windows, Linux, OS X, Solaris, FreeBSD, NetBSD, and many others
- Captured network data can be browsed via a GUI, or via the TTY-mode TShark utility
- The most powerful display filters in the industry
- Rich VoIP analysis
- Read/write many different capture file formats: tcpdump (libpcap), Pcap NG, Catapult DCT2000, Cisco Secure IDS iplog, Microsoft Network Monitor, Network General Sniffer® (compressed and uncompressed), Sniffer® Pro, and NetXray®, Network Instruments Observer, NetScreen snoop, Novell LANalyzer, RADCOM WAN/LAN Analyzer, Shomiti/Finisar Surveyor, Tektronix K12xx, Visual Networks Visual UpTime, WildPackets EtherPeek/TokenPeek/AiroPeek, and many others
- Capture files compressed with gzip can be decompressed on the fly
- Live data can be read from Ethernet, IEEE 802.11, PPP/HDLC, ATM, Bluetooth, USB, Token Ring, Frame Relay, FDDI, and others (depending on your platform)

- Decryption support for many protocols, including IPSec, ISAKMP, Kerberos, Simple Network Management Protocol (SNMP)v3, SSL/TLS, WEP, and WPA/WPA2
- Coloring rules can be applied to the packet list for quick, intuitive analysis
- Output can be exported to XML, PostScript®, CSV, or plain text

- Dsniff—Dug Song—author

  Dsniff is a collection of tools for network auditing and penetration testing. The tools dsniff, filesnarf, mailsnarf, msgsnarf, urlsnarf, and webspy passively monitor a network for interesting data (passwords, e-mail, files, etc.). The tools arpspoof, dnsspoof, and macof facilitate the interception of network traffic normally unavailable to an attacker (e.g., due to layer-2 switching). The tools sshmitm and webmitm implement active monkey-in-the-middle attacks against redirected SSH and HTTPS sessions by exploiting weak bindings in *ad hoc* PKI. Dsniff and its associated tools appear to have been abandoned by their original author, but there is a series of patches from Debian that seem to be applied by most Linux distributions before installing. These patches allow, among other features, to read from a PCAP file instead of listening for packets on a network interface.

- UNIX Operating System embedded tools

  GREP: Using the GREP command we can search through a variety of information sources. For the forensic analyst or incident handler, this tool provides a simplified method of searching for information. GREP is a UNIX command that allows you to search for a pattern in a list of files. Coupled with the use of regular expressions grep is a powerful tool for the investigator. Regular Expressions (RegEx): A regular expression (regex or regexp for short) is a special text string for describing a search pattern. You can think of regular expressions as wildcards on steroids.

- Nmap (security) Open Source

  Nmap ("Network Mapper") is a free and open source utility for network discovery and security auditing. Many systems and network administrators also find it useful for tasks such as network inventory, managing service upgrade schedules, and monitoring host or service uptime. Nmap uses raw IP packets in novel ways to determine what hosts are available on the network, what services (application name and version) those hosts are offering, what operating systems (and OS versions) they are running, what type of packet filters/firewalls are in use, and dozens of other characteristics. It was designed to rapidly scan large networks but works fine against single hosts. Nmap runs on all major computer operating systems, and official binary packages are available for Linux, Windows, and Mac OS X. In addition to the classic command-line Nmap executable, the Nmap suite includes an advanced GUI and results viewer (Zenmap), a flexible data transfer, redirection, and debugging tool (Ncat), a utility for comparing scan results (Ndiff), and a packet generation and response analysis tool (Nping).

NMAP is available for all of the following operating systems:

A. Linux (all distributions)
B. Microsoft Windows
C. Mac OS X
D. FreeBSD, OpenBSD, and NetBSD
E. Sun Solaris
F. Amiga, HP-UX, and Other Platforms

- DEFT (Digital Evidence and Forensics Toolkit) Linux Distribution—Open Source

  DEFT is a LINUX-based Live DVD-based distribution of multiple tools for Forensics and Evidence Capture activities. It is designed to assist the investigator in the acquisition and preservation of mass storage devices (hard drives, USB sticks, MP3 players, smartphones, etc.) or telematic traffic over IP networks; and case analysis and their management. Included in the kit is the DART (Digital Advanced Response Toolkit) with freeware Windows Computer Forensic tools.

  Macintosh tools include:

- CanOpener—Abbott Systems

  CanOpener is a Macintosh-based data recovery software package. Our universal file opener lets you read any file—and extract what you need including text, icons, PICS, and more. It's perfect for browsing all types of files, including old files, foreign files and files your Mac can't open, and it's indispensable for recovering text from damaged files. CanOpener lets you view virus infected files without launching the virus. So you can safely check suspect files and recover text from them—a powerful way to avoid virus infections.

- BlackLight—BlackBag Technologies

  BlackLight is a multiplatform forensic analysis tool that allows examiners to quickly and intuitively analyze digital forensic media. BlackLight is capable of analyzing data from Mac OS X computers, iOS devices (iPhone, iPad, iPod Touch) and Windows computers. It is compatible with all leading logical and physical forensic image formats. Examiners may use BlackLight as a time-saving data triage tool, or as an advanced forensic examination tool depending on the circumstance.

  BlackLight acquires logical iOS device data and imports a number of third-party and industry-standard forensic image formats:

  - UNIX/Apple image formats: dd, .dmg
  - Third-party image formats: EnCase® (EWF-E01), (EWF-L01), and SMART (EWF-S01) image files, ElcomSoft toolkit, Jonathan Zdziarski's Method, Cellebrite, and iXAM
  - VMware® virtual machine files

- Automatic iOS backup folder recovery and import
- Time Machine and Time Capsule
- Individual files and folders.

BlackLight supports a number of iOS and OS X messaging applications and message types including:

- iChat
- SMS
- MMS
- Skype
- iMessage.

BlackLight has built-in support for many picture and video file types, and includes several helpful and unique media processing and analysis features such as:

- Video Frame Analysis: Triage multiple video files, displayed as 4 × 4 frame sequences, to quickly separate contraband from benign media.
- Proprietary Skin Tone Analysis Algorithm: Sort pictures and video by the skin tone percentage contained in the file.
- Built-in GPS Mapping: Media files containing GPS data display with a placemark badge. View media file geolocation data on a Mercator map (offline) or using Google Maps (online) directly from the built-in GPS view.

BlackLight parses and displays Mac Mail application e-mail accounts, several Internet log types, and chat logs.

- Full Safari, Firefox, and Chrome web browser support. View visited URLs and URL names stored by the web browser. View bookmarked websites, dates, time, and cookie contents (text strings and URLs).
- Full iChat and Skype chat application support. Display active chat files with text content, dates, names, and file sizes. Export searchable chat conversations with examiner reports.
- Traverse the Mac Mail application directory structure for each user, and display all mail account names and e-mail addresses associated with specific e-mail message headers and content.

- Expert Witness—ASR Data

  ASR Data publishes a series of forensics tool software packages for multiple operating systems, starting with Macintosh-based packages. These are listed below:

  1. *SMART Linux*: Multiple versions of Live CDs customized for forensic work
  2. *SMART for Linux*: Integrated acquisition, authentication, and analysis in an intuitive GUI
  3. *SmartMount (Windows/Linux/Macintosh)*: Very flexible image mounting and virtualization engine

4. *Grok-NTFS (Windows/Linux/Macintosh)*: NTFS analysis tool with data visualization
5. *Grok-LNK (Windows/Linux/Macintosh)*: NTFS link analysis tool *(beta)*
6. *SAW (Windows/Linux/Macintosh)*: Data Acquisition and optimization framework
7. *SMART Enterprise Response (Linux)*: Enterprise scalable eDiscovery and document production suite.

Foundstone Tools

Tool Name	Tool Use
Clipcaptcha	Foundstone's clipcaptcha is an extensible and signature-based CAPTCHA provider impersonation tool
CredDigger v2.1	Foundstone CredDigger™ is a tool that attempts to gather data to assist with penetration testing on a corporate network
Fpipe v2.1	FPipe v2.1—Port redirector
FSCrack v1.0.1	GUI for John the Ripper
Night Dragon Vulnerability Detection Tool	Free utility that helps identify systems affected by the "Night Dragon" malware
Proxbrute v0.3	ProxBrute is a custom firmware written for the proxmark3. It extends the currently available firmware (revision 465) to support brute force attacks against proximity card access control systems
ShareScan v1.0.0.2	ShareScan is a free utility that enables IT security personnel to identify open Windows file shares available on the internal network
TesserCap v1.0	Foundstone's TesserCap is a GUI-based, highly flexible, interactive, point and shoot CAPTCHA analysis tool
VIDigger v1.0	Check the configuration of ESX server and the virtual machines hosted on ESX server against the VMware Infrastructure Hardening guide and other best practices
BinText 3.03	Finds ASCII, Unicode, and Resource strings in a file
DumpAutoComplete v0.7	Dump Firefox AutoComplete files into XML
Forensic Toolkit v2.0	Tools to help examine NTFS for unauthorized activity
Galleta v1.0	An Internet Explorer Cookie Forensic Analysis Tool
Pasco v1.0	An Internet Explorer activity forensic analysis tool
PatchIt v2.0	A binary file byte-patching program
Rifiuti v1.0	A Recycle Bin Forensic Analysis Tool
ShoWin v2.0	Show information about Windows, reveal passwords, and more
Vision v1.0	Reports all open TCP and UDP ports and maps them to the owning process or application
CookieDigger v1.0	CookieDigger helps identify weak cookie generation and insecure implementations of session management by web applications
HackPack v1.0	Foundstone HackPack™ is a tool designed to aid security professionals in keeping up with changes and updates to security software. The tool offers a simple interface to a large variety of security tools

(Continued)

Foundstone Tools (Continued)

Tool Name	Tool Use
Hacme Bank—Android v1.0	Hacme Bank™ Android is designed to teach mobile application developers, programmers, architects, and security professionals how to create secure software and evaluate their own software to identify vulnerabilities
Hacme Bank v2.0	Hacme Bank™ is designed to teach application developers, programmers, architects, and security professionals how to create secure software
Hacme Books	Foundstone Hacme Books is a learning platform for secure software development
Hacme Casino v1.0	Foundstone Hacme Casino™ is a learning platform for secure software development
Hacme Shipping	Hacme Shipping is a web-based shipping application developed to demonstrate common web application hacking techniques
Hacme Travel	Hacme Travel is designed to create secure software
Hash Calculator v1.0	Foundstone Hash Calculator is a Fiddler Extension that allows you to calculate hashes for input strings
SiteDigger v3.0	SiteDigger 3.0 searches Google's cache to look for vulnerabilities, errors, configuration issues, proprietary information, and interesting security nuggets on websites
SiteScope v1.0	Foundstone's SiteScope creates a site map and gathers metrics for a given web-based application
Socket Security Auditor v1.0	Foundstone Socket Security Auditor identifies the insecurely bound sockets on the local system preventing hackers from stealing valuable information
SSLDigger v1.02	SSLDigger v1.02 is a tool to assess the strength of SSL servers by testing the ciphers supported
SSLSmart	SSLSmart is a highly flexible and interactive tool aimed at improving efficiency and reducing false positives during SSL testing
WSDigger	WSDigger v1.0—Web services testing framework
BOPing	A scanner for the infamous Back Orifice program
Conficker Detection	Conficker Detection vulnerability in Microsoft Windows Server Service
CSniffer v1.0.0.3	Scan your infrastructure to discover if you have unencrypted Perforce passwords which could be stolen and used to penetrate your source code library
DDosPing	A network admin utility for remotely detecting the most common DDoS programs
DIRE	DIRE (Detecting Insecurely Registered Executables)
DSScan	Local Security Authority Subsystem Service (LSASS) scanner
FileInsight	A handy integrated tool environment for website and file analysis
MydoomScanner	Mydoom worm scanner
NetSchedScan	Remote Task Scheduler scanner
ScanLine	Command-line port scanner
SNScan	SNMP Detection Utility
SuperScan	Powerful TCP port scanner, pinger, resolver
SuperScan v3.0	Powerful TCP port scanner, pinger, resolver
Trout	Traceroute and Whois program

Legalities of Forensics

Some of the legal requirements for forensics were covered in Section 9 on the legal requirements for Incident Response; however, there are specific legal needs and parameters within the forensics arena which the Team Manager must keep in mind as investigations and examinations take place. There are guidelines for investigations, examinations, and captures which answer the following questions: What are the requirements for forensics investigations within both the public and private sectors? What are the laws and regulations for search and seizure of data and evidence, both in the United States and outside the United States? What data can be captured under a search warrant and what cannot be retained? and so on.

The criteria for forensics investigation testimony are wide and varied. The investigator or examiner will need to consult with legal personnel as well as management and media relations personnel when preparing to testify in a court case. Each case is different and will have areas of focus which are unique to the case and may not be in focus during a standard investigation which requires the potential testimony of the facts found out during the investigation to be presented in context of the case.

REASONS FOR LEGAL, STATUTORY, AND REGULATORY COMPLIANCE

In the United States, the laws and regulations that provide the legal framework for actual and perceived compliance and performance for all employees when they act on behalf of the organization they are employed by and work for. These laws provide for employer rights and privileges during the course of normal everyday events and actions performed by the workers and employees. As an example, when valuable or key personnel leave an organization, the employer will have the need and desire to ensure there are no potential "departures" of electronic versions of the company data and trade secrets, such as confidential customer data, source code, business plans, or technical documents. When a valuable employee departs to a competitor, or leaves to start an unspecified "new venture," or even leaves for some "time off," there is always

167

a concern that this scenario will result in trade secret litigation in civil court or even criminal theft of sensitive data which can lead to trade secret litigation. As a special agent has said: "For the prosecutor, the challenge is to have the data translated into a form that is acceptable as evidence to the courts…. Assuming that the fragile and elusive evidence can be gathered together, the prosecutor must keep in mind that he or she will one day need to be able to prove the chain of evidence. All processes will need to be appropriately documented in a way that can be understood by the layman and the prosecutor must be prepared if necessary to demonstrate that the 'original' digital material has not been changed or tampered with in any way."[1]

US CRITERIA, LAWS, AND REGULATIONS

- US Constitution Fourth Amendment
  The US Constitution's Fourth Amendment states "The right of the people to be secure in their persons, houses, papers, and effects, against unreasonable searches and seizures, shall not be violated, and no warrants shall issue, but upon probable cause, supported by oath or affirmation, and particularly describing the place to be searched, and the persons or things to be seized." Therefore, any evidence secured outside of a search warrant is considered excluded evidence, and no search warrant can be given without probable cause. This extends to the requirement of the search warrant needing a judicial approval before its execution. Determination of reasonableness depends on the judicial balancing of the individual interest, generally regarded as a privacy interest, against the governmental interest, including law and order, national security, internal security, and the proper administration of the laws. Reasonableness generally entails a predicate of probable cause and, with many exceptions, the issuance of a warrant.
  The Fourth Amendment "is wholly inapplicable to a search or seizure, even an unreasonable one, affected by a private individual not acting as an agent of the Government or with the participation or knowledge of any governmental official." United States v. Jacobsen, 466 U.S. 109, 113 (1984). As a result, no violation of the Fourth Amendment occurs when a private individual acting on his own accord conducts a search and makes the results available to law enforcement.
  The Fourth Amendment rule is that an investigator executing a search warrant is able to look in any place listed on the warrant where evidence might conceivably be concealed. Traditionally, an investigator was precluded from looking into any location beyond the evidence they wish to seize. However, electronic evidence may be stored anywhere.

---

[1] Pallaras S. New technology: opportunities and challenges for prosecutors. Crime, Law Soc Change 2011;56(1):71–89.

The result is that an investigator can electronically look anywhere in search of digital evidence. *Katz v. United States* stated that *"the Fourth Amendment protects people, not places."* The result is that the Fourth Amendment continues to be deeply tied to physical places.

- Wiretaps and Intercepts Laws

  Accordingly, investigators must consider two issues when asking whether a government search or a private search of a computer requires a warrant. First, does the search violate a reasonable expectation of privacy? And if so, is the search nonetheless permissible because it falls within an exception to the warrant requirement? Since the vast majority of computers are networked and communications is the main objective behind networking computers, the Wiretap laws become involved. The purpose of these laws is to protect voice and electronic communications from illegal interception. As an example, network sniffing is illegal unless one of the numerous exceptions applies. There are three key exceptions:

  1. The first exception allows for the protection of the owner's property or systems under attack.
  2. The next exception is the consent exception, if you have the consent of the user to monitor the communications. This is usually accomplished by the use of banners stating, "Using the computer constitutes your permission to be monitored." In most of the cases where this exception is used, the system owner must prove that the user received the banner notification before monitoring began.
  3. The third exception is the computer trespasser exception. This allows the system owner to monitor the attacker while the system is being attacked. Of course, it is legal to monitor in support of a court order or law enforcement. These exceptions do not authorize the system owner or operator to perform unlimited monitoring.

- ECPA Provisions

  The Electronic Communications and Privacy Act protects the right of the customers or subscribers of Service Provider services. This statute restricts the rights of the Service Provider to provide information concerning a customer's communications, or revealing the content of a customer's communications or information concerning a customer's network activity. Normally, this law is involved with undelivered e-mail and network activity by customers. Again, there are several exceptions to this law:

  a. The first exception states that the recipient of the communications can authorize the disclosure of the communications.
  b. The second exception states that a court order or Search Warrant can authorize the disclosure of this communications information.
  c. The third exception involves the Service Provider inadvertently obtaining the content of communications that involves criminal activity. This information can be provided to Law Enforcement.

    d. The fourth exception is the Service Provider's right to protect his property or service.

    e. The fifth exception states the Service Provider can provide the contents of communications to government agencies when the Service Provider inadvertently obtained the contents of a communication and the Service Provider believes that an emergency situation exists and a person may be seriously injured.

- Privacy Law provisions

The US Privacy Act of 1974 was originally passed as a result of the Watergate scandal and the apparent abuses of governmental power performed during that period. The primary features of the Privacy Act are as follows:

  - Restricts disclosure of personal information from systems of records
  - Requires Federal agencies to comply with the law for collecting, maintaining, using, and disseminating information from personal records
  - Provides individuals with access to records about themselves
  - Allows individuals to request amendments to records which are inaccurate, irrelevant, untimely, and incomplete
  - Addresses the collection, maintenance, use, and dissemination of Social Security Numbers
  - Provides legal remedies, both civil and criminal, for violations of the Privacy Act

Over the past 30 years this Act has been slightly modified to now encompass what is known as Personally Identifiable Information (PII) which includes:

  - Name
  - Social Security Number
  - Date and place of birth
  - Photo
  - Biometric records, etc., including any other personal information which is linked or linkable to an individual
  - Education
  - Financial transactions
  - Medical history
  - Criminal or employment history and information which can be used to distinguish or trace an individual's identity.

The use and storage of PII is considered one of the primary security safeguard requirements for all US Governmental agencies during the normal course of activities conducted by each agency.

- Federal Rules of Civil Procedure (FRCP) provisions for eDiscovery

Electronically stored information that is admitted as evidence at a trial or hearing is electronic evidence; it may include electronic communications, such as e-mails, text messages, and chat room communications; digital photographs; website content, including social media postings; computer-generated data; and computer-stored records, therefore subject to the requirements for discovery in an electronic format, otherwise known as "eDiscovery."

Under the Federal Rules of Evidence (FRE), relevant evidence is generally admissible, and irrelevant evidence is not. "Relevant evidence" is defined as evidence that has "*any* tendency to make the existence of *any* fact that is of consequence to the determination of the action more probable or less probable than it would be without the evidence." Rules 401 and 402 of the FRE address this fundamental question of "logical relevance." The major decision addressing the admissibility of electronic evidence is Judge Grimm's 51-page opinion in *Lorraine v. Markel American Insurance Company*, which reads as a comprehensive guide to the admission of electronic evidence. In *Lorraine*, Judge Grimm describes a decision model for addressing the admission of electronic evidence, which, unsurprisingly, is nearly identical to the one many proponents apply to the admission of more traditional forms of evidence.

a. The *Lorraine* model suggests that the proponent of electronic evidence focus first on relevance, asking whether the electronic evidence has any tendency to make some fact that is of consequence to the litigation more or less probable than it would be otherwise.

b. Second, the proponent should address authenticity, asking if he can present evidence demonstrating that the electronic evidence is what it purports to be.

c. Third, the proponent must address any hearsay concerns associated with the electronic evidence, asking if it is a statement by the declarant, other than one made by the declarant while testifying at the trial or hearing, offered for the truth of the matter asserted, and, if the electronic information is hearsay, whether an exclusion or exception to the hearsay rule applies.

d. Fourth, the proponent must address the application of the original documents rule.

e. Fifth, and finally, the proponent should consider "whether the probative value of the [electronic] evidence is substantially outweighed by the danger of unfair prejudice [,]" confusion, or waste of time. Careful consideration of these traditional evidentiary principles will permit a proponent to successfully admit electronic evidence.

- CFAA Provisions

The purpose of the Computer Fraud and Abuse Act is to establish the conditions under which a person can be prosecuted for causing damage to computers, computer information, or violating a person's privacy.

Damages must exceed $5000 in 1 year. However, there is a very liberal interpretation as to how the costs of damages are interpreted: cost of the damage and cost to repair the damage. Plus multiple incidents can be combined to meet the $5000 threshold. The law applies to any "protected" computer; any government computer, any computer involved in interstate or foreign commerce, or any computer used by the banking industry. The definition for damage is very liberal also: damage or alteration of medical records, anything affecting our national defense or security, anything that causes physical injury to anyone, or causes a threat to the public health and safety. The penalties range from 1 to 10 years in prison and a fine for the first offense. The punishment is determined by the hacker's "state of mind" or his intentions. In other words, was the damage caused by the hacker's reckless behavior, or did the hacker intentionally cause the damage, or did damage occur inadvertently by his actions?

EU CRITERIA, LAWS, AND REGULATIONS

NOTE: Data comes from European Union (EU) sites, as noted in links shown in text and from various online legal sites discussing the privacy and data security requirements for the EU.

The right to privacy is a highly developed area of law in Europe. All the member states of the EU are also signatories of the European Convention on Human Rights (ECHR). Article 8 of the ECHR provides a right to respect for one's "private and family life, his home and his correspondence," subject to certain restrictions. The European Court of Human Rights has given this article a very broad interpretation in its jurisprudence. Protection of personal data is a right which is separate but closely linked to the right to privacy.

Respect for private life was established in 1950 with the adoption of the ECHR—in the framework of the Council of Europe. Put in short terms, the right to privacy may be described as a right which prevents public authorities from measures which are privacy invasive, unless certain conditions have been met.

The right to data protection was introduced in the 1980s as a consequence of technical developments. Put in short terms, data protection principles aim to establish conditions under which it is legitimate and lawful to process personal data. Data protection legislation obliges those responsible to respect a set of rules and empowers the people concerned by granting them rights. Finally, it provides for supervision by independent authorities.

The four basic legal areas within the EU which cover forensics and privacy are:

1. Privacy—Directive 95/46/EC of Parliament and of the Council of October 24, 1995
2. Article 8 of the Convention of Human Rights, which provides for the protection of personal data
3. Article 10 of the Convention of Human Rights, which provides for the protection of personal expression
4. Article 7 of the Fundamental Freedoms and the Charter of Fundamental Rights of the European Union, which ensures the protection of private and family life, home, and communication.

In 1980, in an effort to create a comprehensive data protection system throughout Europe, the Organization for Economic Cooperation and Development (OECD) issued its "Recommendations of the Council Concerning Guidelines Governing the Protection of Privacy and Trans-Border Flows of Personal Data." The seven principles governing the OECD's recommendations for protection of personal data were:

1. Notice—data subjects should be given notice when their data is being collected
2. Purpose—data should only be used for the purpose stated and not for any other purposes
3. Consent—data should not be disclosed without the data subject's consent
4. Security—collected data should be kept secure from any potential abuses
5. Disclosure—data subjects should be informed as to who is collecting their data
6. Access—data subjects should be allowed to access their data and make corrections to any inaccurate data
7. Accountability—data subjects should have a method available to them to hold data collectors accountable for following the above principles.

The OECD Guidelines, however, were nonbinding, and data privacy laws still varied widely across Europe. The United States, meanwhile, while endorsing the OECD's recommendations, did nothing to implement them within the United States. However, all seven principles were incorporated into the EU Directive.

Australia

The Cybercrime Act 2001 No. 161, Items 12 and 28 grant police with a magistrate's order the wide-ranging power to require "a specified person to provide any information or assistance that is reasonable and necessary to allow the officer to" access computer data that is "evidential material"; this is understood to include mandatory decryption. Failing to comply carries a penalty of 6 months imprisonment. This covers most forensics activities, as well as mandatory key escrow and turnover of encryption keys to Law Enforcement Officer

(LEO) during the course of an investigation. This law gives LEO wide-ranging power to compel assistance in decrypting data from any party.

The Australian Privacy Act of 1988 deals with the protection of individual privacy, using the OECD Privacy Principles from the 1980s to set up a broad, principles-based regulatory model. Section 6 has the relevant definition where the critical detail is that the definition of "personal information" also applies to where the individual can be indirectly identified:

> "personal information" means information or an opinion (including information or an opinion forming part of a database), whether true or not, and whether recorded in a material form or not, about an individual whose identity is apparent, *or can reasonably be ascertained*, from the information or opinion.

The OECD guidelines mentioned above are the basic driving criteria for the use and practice of forensics and privacy in Australia. The Australian national government defers most forensics investigative criteria to each of its states and the laws which govern each location.

Canada

Canada started out very progressive in its legal treatment of computer crime and digital forensics. In 1985, Canada passed the *Criminal Law Amendment Act*. As an amendment to Section 342.1 to the *Criminal Code of Canada* (hereafter referred to as the *Code*) as well as adding Subsection (1.1) to Section 430 of the *Code*. The *Criminal Law Improvement Act 1997* added Subsection (d) to Section 342.1(1). The most relevant sections of the Code as they pertain to forensics and computer crime evidence and investigations are as follows:

> 342.1 (1) Every one who, fraudulently and without colour of right, *(a)* obtains, directly or indirectly, any computer service, *(b)* by means of an electro-magnetic, acoustic, mechanical or other device, intercepts or causes to be intercepted, directly or indirectly, any function of a computer system, *(c)* uses or causes to be used, directly or indirectly, a computer system with intent to commit an offence under paragraph (*a*) or (*b*) or an offence under section 430 in relation to data or a computer system, or *(d)* uses, possesses, traffics in or permits another person to have access to a computer password that would enable a person to commit an offence under paragraph (*a*), (*b*) or (*c*) is guilty of an indictable offence and liable to imprisonment for a term not exceeding ten years, or is guilty of an offence punishable on summary conviction.
>
> (2) In this section, "computer password" means any data by which a computer service or computer system is capable of being obtained or used; "computer program" means data representing instructions

or statements that, when executed in a computer system, causes the computer system to perform a function; "computer service" includes data processing and the storage or retrieval of data; "computer system" means a device that, or a group of interconnected or related devices one or more of which, *(a)* contains computer programs or other data, and *(b)* pursuant to computer programs, (i) performs logic and control, and (ii) may perform any other function; "data" means representations of information or of concepts that are being prepared or have been prepared in a form suitable for use in a computer system; "electro-magnetic, acoustic, mechanical or other device" means any device or apparatus that is used or is capable of being used to intercept any function of a computer system, but does not include a hearing aid used to correct subnormal hearing of the user to not better than normal hearing; "function" includes logic, control, arithmetic, deletion, storage and retrieval and communication or telecommunication to, from or within a computer system; "intercept" includes listen to or record a function of a computer system, or acquire the substance, meaning or purport thereof. "traffic" means, in respect of a computer password, to sell, export from or import into Canada, distribute or deal with in any other way.

(Criminal Code of Canada, part IX)

430. (1) Every one commits mischief who willfully

(a) destroys or damages property;

(b) renders property dangerous, useless, inoperative or ineffective;

(c) obstructs, interrupts or interferes with the lawful use, enjoyment or operation of property; or

(d) obstructs, interrupts or interferes with any person in the lawful use, enjoyment or operation of property.

(1.1) Every one commits mischief who willfully

(a) destroys or alters data;

(b) renders data meaningless, useless or ineffective;

(c) obstructs, interrupts or interferes with the lawful use of data; or

(d) obstructs, interrupts or interferes with any person in the lawful use of data or denies access to data to any person who is entitled to access thereto.

(Criminal Code of Canada, part XI)

However, there has been little change in the legal structures since 1985, in spite of the Mafiaboy and other hacking events traced to Canadian origins. There is the clear definition of a jurisdictional boundary for computer crime. All computer crime falls under the jurisdiction of the Information Technology Security Branch (ITSB) of the Royal Canadian Mounted Police (RCMP), which is responsible for the information technology security of the country.

The Results of the Investigation—Investigator Expert Testimony

Within the framework of the investigation and examination activities conducted for forensics activities, there will derive the need for the analyst, the investigator, and/or the examiner to testify in a court of law about the discoveries revealed during the investigation. The Security Incident Response and Forensics Team (SIR&FT) Manager will need to advise and assist the potential "expert" witness as to the scope, procedures, and methods for testimony, data presentations, and other action to be performed in support of the case. The basic process needed for this activity will need to be explained to the testifying employee. The five standard procedures followed during a trial wherein the team employee will participate include:

1. Prosecuting attorney presents the employee as a competent expert in the field in question.
2. Opposing attorney might attempt to discredit the Security Incident Response Team (SIRT) Member through the use of questions about competence, training, certifications, and/or experience.
3. The results of the initial testimony are weighted by the presiding judge and he finds the witness credible or not and rules on if the witness (the team employee) shall be considered an expert witness for the court or not.
4. Prosecuting attorney leads the employee through the evidence discovered.
5. Opposing attorney cross-examines the SIRT Member about the evidence and the procedures utilized.

The above scenario is predicated upon the SIRT Member testifying for the Prosecution in a criminal case. If the SIRT member is testifying for the defense or is testifying in a civil case, the general requirements are the same, just the actors are different.

The following is standard advice to provide the testifying employee on methods to follow in the courtroom during the testimony portion of the trial:

1. **Testimony in Court**

a. Be conscious of the jury, judge, and attorneys
b. If asked something you cannot answer, respond by saying:
    i. That is beyond the scope of my expertise
    ii. I was not requested to investigate that

c. Be professional and polite

d. Avoid overreaching opinions

e. Always acknowledge the jury and direct your testimony to them

f. Place microphone six to eight inches from you

g. Use simple, direct language to help the jury understand you

h. Avoid humor

i. Build repetition into your explanations

j. Use chronological order to describe events

k. If you're using technical terms, identify and define these terms for the jury

l. Cite the source of the evidence the opinion is based on

m. Make sure the chair's height is comfortable, and turn the chair so that it faces the jury

n. Dress in a manner that conforms to the community's dress code

o. Don't memorize your testimony

p. For direct examination, state your opinions, identify evidence to support your opinions, relate the method used to arrive to that opinion, and restate your opinion

2. Direct Examination Testimony

a. Work with your attorney to get the right language

b. Be wary of your inclination to be helpful

c. Review the examination plan your attorney has prepared

d. Provide a clear overview of your findings

e. Use a systematic easy-to-follow plan for describing your methods

f. Practice testifying

g. Use your own words when answering questions

h. Present your background and qualifications

i. Avoid vagueness

j. When you're using graphics in a presentation, keep in mind that you're instructing the jury in what you did to collect evidence

3. Cross-examination Testimony

a. Use your own words

b. Keep in mind that certain words have additional meanings

c. Opposing attorneys sometimes use the trick of interrupting you

d. Be aware of leading questions

e. Never guess when you do not have an answer

f. Be prepared for challenging, preconstructed questions, such as: Did you use more than one tool?

g. Rapid-fire questions

h. Sometimes opposing attorneys declare that you aren't answering the questions

i. Keep eye contact with the jury
j. Sometimes opposing attorneys ask several questions inside one question
k. Attorneys make speeches and phrase them as questions
l. Attorneys might put words in your mouth
m. Be patient
n. Most jurisdictions now allow the judge and jurors to ask questions
o. Avoid feeling stressed and losing control
p. Never have unrealistically high self-expectations when testifying; everyone makes mistakes.

Forensics Team Oversight

The Forensics Team should always follow a structured documented process, wherein the content of the items to be investigated need to be preserved, validated, and documented. Any investigation must be understood at the onset as to its dimensions, scope, and investigative methods which are best based upon proven techniques, such as proper and legal collection of evidence and obtaining proper bit-stream "hash encrypted" copies of evidence. The linear nature of investigation always needs documentation and supporting evidence, for technology can give unexpected results. So, always document everything and report everything.

Oversight is paramount before, during and after an investigation to ensure all data is collected in accordance with standards and guidelines, data is retained in the correct and secure manner, and the investigation reports are generated such that they are usable and acceptable to the administrative and legal authorities for use in potential actions and activities once the investigation is completed.

INVESTIGATOR'S CODE OF CONDUCT

A code of conduct for an organization is a set of general rules indicating how to behave in a way that benefits and supports the intent of the organization's mission statement and the organization's character.

A sample code of conduct for investigators follows from the Council of International Investigators:

"A private investigator/private detective belonging to the Council of International Investigators (CII) agrees to adhere to our Code of Ethics at all times:

1. To conduct myself in my profession with honesty, sincerity, integrity, fidelity, morality, and good conscience in all dealings with my clients.
2. To preserve forever my clients' confidences under any and all circumstances except where the clients' interest is contrary to criminal law.

3. To conduct all my investigations within the bounds of legality, morality, and professional ethics.
4. To refuse to employ the methods of wiretapping in any form in those countries where it is unlawful.
5. To retain in the strictest confidence every facet of my clients' interest from inquiries by third parties especially in matters involving national notoriety or publicity.
6. To cooperate with all recognized and responsible law enforcement and governmental agencies in matters within the realm of their jurisdiction.
7. To counsel my clients against any illegal or unethical course of action.
8. To explain to the full satisfaction of my client all fees and charges in his case and to render a factual report.
9. To retain my own professional reputation and that of my fellow investigators and professional associates.
10. To insure that all my employees adhere to this code of ethics."

Digital and Computer Forensics industry has developed a specialized version of these types of codes of conduct and ethics over the past few years, especially due to the potential of data tampering and alteration of the evidence used in a court case which could have serious or even life-threatening consequences. Within the forensics community, there have been many instances where investigators focused their efforts on using the evidence to prove one side of the case or the other which is the attorney's job in the case, not the investigator. So these types of codes of conduct have been found necessary for the development and proof of impartiality of the examiner or investigator during the prosecution of the case. An example of the type of Code of Conduct for a forensics examiner, analyst or investigator from the Digital Forensics Certification Board (DFCB) is found below:

"A Certificant of the DFCB shall:

1. not engage in, or pressure others to engage in, any conduct that is harmful to the profession of digital forensics including, but not limited to, any illegal or unethical activity, any technical misrepresentation or distortion, any scholarly falsification or any material misrepresentation of education, training, credentials, experience, or area of expertise;
2. demonstrate, at all times, commitment, integrity, and professional diligence;
3. avoid any action that could appear to be a conflict of interest;
4. comply with all lawful orders of courts of competent jurisdiction;
5. show no bias with respect to findings or opinions;
6. express no opinion with respect to the guilt or innocence of any party;
7. not disclose or reveal any confidential or privileged information obtained during an engagement without proper authorization or otherwise ordered by a court of competent jurisdiction;

8. examine and consider thoroughly all information (unless specifically limited in scope by court order or other authority) and render opinions and conclusions strictly in accordance with the results and findings obtained using validated and appropriate procedures;
9. report or testify truthfully in all matters and not knowingly make any material misrepresentation of information or otherwise withhold any information that, in so doing, might tend to distort the truth;
10. accept only engagements for which there is a reasonable expectation of completion with professional competence."[1]

1. **Standards and Guidelines for Digital Evidence**
   The Team Manager must ensure all data is collected in accordance with the predefined team standards and guidelines and any and all statutory and regulatory requirements for digital evidence within the scope of the examination. As explained in previous sections the forensics team methodology for collection and capture of the data which could be used for evidence must follow prescribed and defined procedures. These methods, techniques, and activities all require documentation for capture of the data, collection, and definition of the chain of custody of each and every piece of potential evidence and the means and methods of transporting the evidence to ensure no break in the chain of custody and "potential alteration" of the data from the capture location to the forensics laboratory or storage area. The standards to capture "live" data, collect evidence, record evidence on chain of custody forms, and transport of evidence, as defined in the evidence section, all need to be defined, written, reviewed, and approved prior to any real activity for forensics. All of these standards and guidelines are the responsibility of the Team Manager and should be developed by and under his control through the proper configuration management procedures for the organizations.

2. **Oversight during Capture of Forensics Data**
   When the Forensics team deploys to a scene, they require many tools and possibly will need guidance on-site for out-of-the-ordinary situations. The Team Manager will need to go with the team for oversight of the forensics capture activities, for guidance in the proper use of the capture tools and techniques, and for general management of the scene while the technicians and analysts are performing their duties. The Team Manager should provide "buffering" for the team members with other personnel at the scene, with the outside interested parties and with the on-site management. Once the Team Manager has performed the oversight and review of the analysts several times and knows they are performing their activities correctly, he probably doesn't need to keep the oversight up, but should periodically check on them during capture events.

---

[1] DFCB_DFCB_Code_of_Ethics_and_Standards_of_Professional_Conduct_Version_1.1_Dec08.

Some of the areas the Team Manager needs to watch for during the capture activities as conducted by the analyst include:

1. Initial process to determine which actions are priorities during "live" capture of system volatile files and process while the machine is still on, before turning the machine off. The Team Manager should provide guidance for the junior members of the team during this critical phase of the process. He should observe the senior members occasionally to ensure the process and documented steps are aligned and being used to complete the processes, to provide support data for the capture, and to make sure the documentation of the volatile memory capture event steps taken are written down correctly and sequentially.

2. Analyst process for retrieving suspect data initially onto the external storage media. While the actual data is identified for capture, the Team Manager ensures the analyst has detailed notes of the reasons for the areas of data capture, and explanations of the process used to identify which devices and storage locations are being retrieved from and why these components and perhaps not others.

3. Analyst process for conducting the bit-stream image copy of suspect data. Depending upon which operating system is being used and which image capture tool is being utilized, the Team Manager should monitor the analyst "bit-stream" image activity to ensure it is conducted securely and safely.

4. Analyst process for conducting the hash encryption action upon the captured data. Once the data is copied unto the retention media, it needs to be cryptographically "hashed" to provide proof of integrity for future uses.

5. Analyst process for recording of the evidence during the capture unto the chain of custody forms. The Team Manager should make sure the analyst is documented each and every step correctly into the case log and onto the evidence forms as they are acquired and reviewed. This process is vital to the "Chain of Custody" requirements which will appear later during the case activities.

6. The method of storage for transfer of the various captured media, machines, and technical components seized during event. The Team Manager needs to monitor the capture analyst/technician during the movement of the seized data and equipment. The criteria for specialized transport of seized equipment is spelled out elsewhere in this book, but the Manager should oversee the activities to make sure all takes place in an acceptable fashion.

7. The logical process flow the analyst follows during the capture activities to watch for inclusion of all areas and components of potential evidence. The Team manager follows the capture and seizure activities to watch out for missed steps and possible data capture missteps during

the process. His role here is to make sure the logical sequence used to retrieve and capture the data is defendable and repeatable.

The Team Manager then reviews each of these activities and conducts an after-action review with the analyst to improve the actions for the next event and to provide guidance to better conduct forensics actions.

3. **The Investigation Reports are Usable and Acceptable**

One of the other areas of focus for the Team Manager is the investigative, examination, and analysis reports that are generated by the team during and at the conclusion of the investigation. The Team Manager needs to ensure the reports conform to the standards he has created and the corporation requires for the report format and then the reports meet the substance requirements for the examination with the results of the forensics defined, delineated, and prominently written up in the report. His job, once the report is submitted for review, then becomes to check on the logic of the findings, the methods and techniques of investigation are well documented, and to ensure the conclusions follow the evidence from the examination.

The reports become the basis for forensics testimony in court cases, therefore, it is paramount the results and the logic leading to the conclusions are explainable, logical, direct (where possible), and above all, accurate in their portrayal of the evidence and its resulting logical results. These reports are indeed evidentiary documents in court cases so they must be defined as such and utmost care must be taken during their creation. It is important the reports and the underlying scientific methods for the data in the reports are realistic and provable.

The US Supreme Court provides the following list of factors to consider before a court should rule on the admissibility of the scientifically generated evidence. This set of factors is known as the Daubert Rules which comes from the case *Daubert v. Merrell Dow Pharmaceuticals*, 113 S. Ct. 2786 (1993). The rules are:

1. Whether the theory or techniques has been reliably tested and verified by two or more sources
2. Whether the theory or technique has been subject to peer review and publication
3. What is the known or potential rate of error of the method used
4. Whether the theory or method has been generally accepted by the scientific community.

So the Team Manager needs to review all the data in each report to ensure it meets these criteria before sending to the legal activity supporting the investigation. Remember, 65–75% of the times, these cases end up in legal proceedings, so it is important to be accurate and forthcoming in each produced document and report.

USE OF TEMPLATES FOR INFORMATION RECORDING

Since most forensics investigations are dynamic in nature, it is and would be very inefficient to attempt to create and generate investigative documentation each and every time new information is discovered. So, the creation and generation standard template for recording forensics investigative information facilitates the accurate, direct, and timely recording of events, actions, steps taken, and information during the course of the investigation. These templates should be under the configuration control of the Forensics team Manager before and after the investigation and the manager should be the primary technical reference for their structure.

Templates to be developed by the Team Manager for use should include ones for chain of custody on each piece of evidence, capture parameters for location and time of initial capture of the evidence, initial review of evidence to include the hash parameters for the evidence, hard drive review template which includes data fields for the vendor and technical specifications for the hard drive, and an evidence log sheet wherein all pieces of evidence for the case are entered onto one form to ensure completeness of the reviews.

Suggested templates for use are included in Appendix C.

PART

3

General Management and Team

This part covers corporate oversight, management, and direction for the SIR&FT and its activities. One of the areas relevant to this activity is the utilizing the standards produced for Incident Response and Forensics. External statutory and regulatory requirements for the organization are another area of consideration.

EXTERNAL CONSIDERATIONS

There are numerous state, federal, and international compliance regulations affecting businesses around the globe which affect the corporate oversight, management, and legal standing of the organization. These requirements include:

- Payment Card Industry Data Security Standard (PCI DSS)
- Sarbanes–Oxley Act (SOX)
- Health Insurance Portability and Accountability Act (HIPAA)
- Health Information Technology for Economic and Clinical Health (HITECH) Act

- Gramm–Leach–Bliley Act (GLBA)
- US State Breach Notification Laws (46 out of 50 states)
- Canadian Personal Information Protection and Electronic Documents Act (PIPEDA)
- European Union (EU) Data Protection Directive
- Hong Kong's Personal Data (Privacy) Ordinance
- Japan's Personal Information Protection Act (JPIPA)

Unfortunately these regulatory and statutory needs and requirements are only increasing on a global scale, not reducing as most business leaders would hope. One of the areas to consider assisting the organization is to implement the international standards and guidelines available to position the corporation in a much more favorable posture with respect to these external factors. Two of these standards in the Incident Response and Forensics fields are the ISO 18044 and ISO 27037 with ISO 27042 pending final approval as of July 2013.

ISO/IEC 18044

ISO/IEC TR 18044:2004 *Information technology—Security techniques—Information security incident management* provides advice and guidance on information security incident management for information security managers and information systems managers. ISO/IEC TR 18044:2004 distinguishes between an information security event and an incident as follows:

- An information security event is an identified occurrence of a system, service, or network state indicating a possible breach of information security policy or failure of safeguards, or a previously unknown situation that may be security relevant.
- An information security incident is indicated by a single or a series of unwanted or unexpected information security events that have a significant probability of compromising business operations and threatening information security.

Incident management includes incident response. Incident management encompasses a variety of activities including proactive efforts to limit or prevent incidents, whereas incident response is the reactive element in the event of an incident.

The goals of incident management and response activities can be summarized as:

- Detect incidents quickly.
- Diagnose incidents accurately.
- Manage incidents properly.
- Contain and minimize damage.
- Restore affected services.

- Determine root causes.
- Implement improvements to prevent recurrence.

ISO 27037

ISO/IEC 27037:2012 *Information technology—Security techniques—Guidelines for identification, collection, acquisition and preservation of digital evidence* provides guidance on identifying, gathering/collecting/acquiring, handling, and protecting/preserving digital forensic evidence, that is, "digital data that may be of evidential value" for use in court.

One of the most critical issues in forensic investigations is the acquisition and preservation of evidence in such a way as to ensure its integrity. As with conventional physical evidence, it is crucial for the first and subsequent responders (defined as "Digital Evidence First Responders" and "Digital Evidence Specialists") to maintain the chain of custody of all digital forensic evidence, ensuring that it is gathered and protected through structured processes that are acceptable to the courts. More than simply providing integrity, the processes must provide assurance that nothing untoward can have occurred. This requires that a defined baseline level of information security controls is met or exceeded. Digital forensic evidence can come from any electronic storage or communications media such as cell phones, computers, iPods, video game consoles, and so on. By its nature, digital forensic evidence is fragile—it can be easily damaged or altered due to improper handling, whether by accident or on purpose. Prior to the release of ISO/IEC 27037, there were no globally accepted standards on acquiring digital evidence, the first step in the process. Police have developed their own national guidelines and procedures for the acquisition and protection of electronic evidence. However, this creates issues when cross-border crimes are committed since digital forensic evidence acquired in one country may need to be presented in the courts of another. Tainted evidence that *may* have been acquired or protected without the requisite level of security may be legally inadmissible.

The standard provides detailed guidance on the identification, collection, and/or acquisition, marking, storage, transport, and preservation of electronic evidence, particularly to maintain its integrity. It defines and describes the processes through which evidence is recognized and identified, documentation of the crime scene, collection and preservation of the evidence, and the packaging and transportation of evidence. The scope covers "traditional" IT systems and media rather than vehicle systems, cloud computing, etc. The guidance is aimed primarily at first responders.

Every country has its own unique legislative system. A crime committed in one jurisdiction may not even be regarded as a crime in another. The challenge is to harmonize processes across borders such that cybercriminals can be prosecuted accordingly. Therefore, a means to allow and facilitate the exchange and use of reliable evidence (i.e., an international standard on acquiring digital evidence) is required.

"Digital evidence," meaning information from digital devices to be presented in court, is interpreted differently in different jurisdictions. For the widest applicability, the standard will avoid using jurisdiction-specific terminology. It will not cover analysis of digital evidence, nor its admissibility, weight, relevance, etc. It also will not mandate the use of particular tools or methods.

ISO 27042

ISO/IEC 27042 *Information technology—Security techniques—Guidelines for analysis and interpretation of digital evidence* provides guidance on guidelines for the analysis and interpretation of digital evidence.

The standard will "lay down certain fundamental principles which are intended to ensure that tools, techniques and methods can be selected appropriately and shown to be fit for purpose should the need arise. [It will also] inform decision-makers that need to determine the reliability of digital evidence presented to them. It is applicable to organizations needing to protect, analyze and present potential digital evidence. It is relevant to policy-making bodies that create and evaluate procedures relating to digital evidence, often as part of a larger body of evidence."

This standard is pending final approval and publishing by the ISO organization (as of July 1, 2013).

General Team Management

The Security Incident Response and Forensics teams (SIR&FT) both will need general corporate oversight and guidance from the highest sections of the corporation as they are daily exposed to and support directly related bottom-line efforts of the organization. Data privacy, corporate trade secrets, and personal information of employees and officers are all areas in which these team members will have dealings and visibility regularly, therefore, they will need understanding of the corporate culture and strategic objectives. These areas cause the team personnel to have to be considered some of the most trusted agents of the organization and demand they be treated as such, especially during an incident response event or forensics activity.

CORPORATE LEVEL MANAGEMENT CONSIDERATIONS

The corporate oversight requirements for SIR&FT Management need to focus on the general corporate culture for risk tolerance for the business activities. The corporate leadership, the officers and the board, have the requirement, under compliance needs and regulations (GRC domain: Governance, Risk, and Compliance), to set the risk appetite of the organization and portray to the rest of the organization via strategy documents, corporate guidance, general communications, and personal leadership. Each Line of Business (LOB) must have some guidance for what areas to address in their policies and procedures. This includes data privacy needs and requirements which can include external factors to be considered such as Health information if the unit deals with HIPAA or other health data, or personal information if the unit deals with Personal Identifiable Information (PII) in its daily actions. If the organization has Intellectual Property (IP) used in the organization, this needs to be clearly portrayed to the SIR&FT Manager before any occurrence dealing with the IP. The IP requirements are especially important if the organization is subject to or suspects industrial espionage, since that is not a criminal, but a civil offense.

The senior corporate management needs to have in place a method of risk review for all potential exposure points for the organization. This construct would include a Risk Review mechanism for threats to the organization and the potential vulnerabilities of the organization and its IT infrastructure. The first part of this methodology needs to look at the assets of the organization and their value to the group. What do they (the assets) cost to run, to replace, to redesign, to rebuild, and to retire all are questions to consider for the asset valuation portion of this process. The asset control requirements for the LOB also need to be defined and documented for proper consideration.

Following up the asset review are the three basic areas within any risk assessment process that the organization must perform in order to properly advise the SIR&FT during response events. These three areas (threat assessment, vulnerability assessment, and control analysis) are all areas which the SIR&FT Manager can advise on, participate in, or even help create options for during the assessment process at a corporate level. Often the Incident Response team members are extremely aware of the threat environment of the organization as they are often researching the current state of threats, malware analysis techniques, and other "hacker" type activities occurring in the community. The team members and manager can advise the risk assessment team on the validity and viability of the threats as defined during the assessment. The team members, both incident handlers and forensics analysts, can advise on the vulnerability assessment parts of the review. Both areas (Incident Response and Forensics) are often exposed to various vulnerabilities and have detailed understanding of operating systems, applications, databases, and equipment they have gathered during the normal course of their daily job performance. The control analysis portion of the assessment is often where the forensics investigators can excel in providing detailed analysis or inputs to the recommendations of the current and planned controls needed to properly meet the standard security objectives of confidentiality, integrity, and availability.

Once these parts are accomplished, then the organization conducts the business evaluation and impact analysis actions for each area of concern, piece of equipment or system under review. This process is important for the subsequent Incident Response Plan development, the Forensics Team training efforts, and the overall SIR&FT preparation step as discussed in Sections 3, 10, and 13. Then the corporate security staff, the corporate sponsor, and the IT staff come up with control recommendations and the overall risk determination for the system or network under review. This lays the foundation for the SIR&FT policies and procedures development efforts as the core strategy is now defined and the Incident Response and Forensics actions to prepare for are now documented.

Corporate reviews of risk assessments conducted by the regular security staff need visibility to the SIR&FT Manager and personnel. This allows for proper training of the team members during exercises which would focus on the most likely scenarios of data breach, insider threat, and external driven events before the actual response event occurs and the team has to respond. As part of this process, the corporate security plan and policies need to include the various incident response and forensics policies as defined elsewhere in this book. The integration of the team-specific policies allow for understanding by everyone possibly involved in an event during the response activity.

The SIR&FT needs this guidance from the corporate area in order to determine methods of response, priorities of response based on value to the LOB during an incident response or forensics investigation.

CORPORATE NEEDS TO SUPPORT THE TEAM ACTIVITIES

Integration of the SIR&FT into the corporate security and risk management structure ensures the organization can respond to an event before it becomes a disaster to the corporation, the LOB, and the customers/clients of the organization. As part of this integration several areas need inclusion to the team action.

The security detection and monitoring activities of the organization need visibility to the team and its daily activities. This provides a mechanism for possible early response to an active exploit or other suspect act. This also provides the SIR&FT members with the corporate and IT metrics and monitoring results to evaluate for potential risks and current trends in the organizational events, actions, and traffic. This allows the Team Manager to project areas for training and testing events which would be relevant to the goals of the corporation.

Another area in which the corporate activities need to align with the SIR&FT actions is the testing and exercise events for the recovery and the evaluation of the various IT components and systems within the corporate infrastructure. Test and evaluation actions are usually scheduled on an annual basis for most industry verticals, with additional exercises usually scheduled quarterly within the Disaster Recovery area. When these events are planned, designed and tested, the SIR&FT members should participate as Subject Matter Experts (SMEs) or as active responders to ensure close cooperation with the organization's IT and Business key personnel and staff. This provides additional information for the SIR&FT to adjust and modify the Response and Forensics policies and procedures so they align with the actual LOB and IT response policies and procedures to minimize the business disruption during a real event response. This testing effort also provides valuable interchange and lessons for the Team members on how and why the various LOB operate the way they do within the context of business objectives and critical system recovery actions.

These testing events are also a prime area for training for the team members to practice their evidence capture techniques, the evaluation of tools and their use in the field, and adjustment to procedures for investigation. Practice of evidence collection procedures and techniques in order to identify the vulnerabilities in procedures is just one goal of these kinds of efforts. Another advantage is the development of analytic skills of the team members to adjust their on-scene actions and efforts to properly read, evaluate and respond to various types of incidents and investigations. The lessons learned from these activities provide great insight into the actual knowledge, skills, and abilities of the team members and also provide a great learning experience for all team members and the supporting staff of the organization, without jeopardizing real data or production efforts.

This process also provides ability of the SIR&FT Manager to identify the required reporting needs of the various divisions and to know who should and who should not be notified during real response event. Each of these criteria can become important during a breach response event or during an insider forensics investigation so the correct parties are kept informed and other personnel are not inadvertently told information they should not have access to or knowledge of through this method.

The corporate standards for documentation, policy, and procedure development all need to be available to the SIR&FT Manager as he defines requirements for designs and produces these documents for inclusion within the corporate documentation system. Each form, policy, and procedure needs to meet the corporate criteria for content, format, and approval in order it is within the needs, requirements, and allowed usage by the team members as they respond to each event, investigation, and incident. Included in these criteria are the Incident Response and the Forensics specific needs for each document such as the Evidence Capture and Chain of Custody Log forms which could have applicability external to the organization.

The primary methods of communications within the organization for the Team Manager must be predefined before an event or incident to make sure all appropriate management and key personnel are aware of the status and progress of each activity or investigation. There will be many times when it is not appropriate to inform certain LOB managers of the surrounding event concerning an active investigation, whether it is because an insider may have perpetrated it or because the control of the results is paramount. So the predefined lines of communications become necessary and important from a senior management level. The Team Manager must be sensitive to the political and economic issues around these actions, therefore, the needed communication are kept to a minimum as the event unfolds.

THIRD-PARTY SUPPORT DURING AND AFTER EVENTS

When limitations are observed in the performance of special or specific areas of an investigation, there may arise a situation where the SIR&FT Manager has to bring in a third party. In that case, he needs to validate that the third party has acceptable processes and procedures established and active in their job performance. Additionally, validation requires that a nondisclosure agreement is in place. He needs to ensure that all of the processes established by the corporation are considered during the negotiations with the third party. Considerations and vendor selection should be established prior to the need arising. When time is of the essence, the Team manager is not going to want to prevent progress while a contract is negotiated, therefore many corporate managers of Incident Response and/or Forensics Teams preselect outside experts and corporations while setting up the team internally to the organization.

Outside consultants and organizations can provide needed and valuable expertise in select or specific areas that would not normally be required for standard incident handlers or forensics investigators. This preselection process is often conducted by the Team Manager in conjunction with the contracting staff of the organization and involves all the normal contractual activities such as requirements definitions, requests for information or proposals from contractors, and bid selection processes. So the SIR&FT Manager is not alone in this process and should use the organizational structures for these actions and activities.

Limitations may be imposed by many methods at any role within the forensics management team. It may be wise to identify more senior subject matter expert for each role in the event any form of limitations are imposed upon the process and establish relationships with them in the event they are needed. The Team Manager needs to investigate the background of persons and agencies that he proposes to utilize for consultation, making sure they are certified and have past experience in the areas of investigation pertinent to the individual case being examined. As defined above, this evaluation needs to take place prior to the pressure-packed situational issues that an expert can be exposed to during a crisis response or investigative action. The knowledge, integrity, and credibility of expert witnesses can be crucial to the outcome of a court case or successful resolution of an active exposure or incident. Integrity and confidence in the process and the person may be the determining factor in the success or failure of an investigation.

Corporate IT-Related Security Relationship with SIR&FT

The uniqueness of the relationship between the SIR&FT and the IT staff of the organization requires we look at it independently of any other external relationship for the SIR&FT. The relationship between the SIR&FT and the IT staff, which may include IT Security personnel, becomes paramount during an incident response effort or forensics investigation. The IT staff should be supportive of the SIR&FT members as they respond, as they test, as they decipher events, and as they produce update recommendation to the infrastructure based upon event resolutions. The IT staff focus is on the business objectives of the business units, whereas the SIR&FT focus is on the successful resolution of any incident or investigation, reporting of resolutions, and analysis of the root causes of the event in order to determine best corporate-level courses of action to ensure security of the organization and its information.

Corporate guidance and oversight, especially focused on the financial and continued operations of the corporation/department/agency as a result of some incident or investigation, provides general IT guidance to the IT staff in the areas of risk management, purchasing of IT, statutory and regulatory compliance, and general management of the IT support actions. But as we reviewed in Section 17, corporate oversight provides detailed guidance to the SIR&FT activities for the organization. So, the identification of the general IT policies is critical to the successful implementation and results of any incident response or investigation conducted by the SIR&FT members.

BASIC IT CONTROL AND SECURITY AREAS OF INTEREST

Some of the basic IT Control Areas and IT Security areas that Team members need awareness and understanding of in order to accomplish their job and conduct response and investigative efforts include:

- Recovery Framework
  The IT structure for Disaster Recovery is important to the successful resolution of incident response and determines the general results of

one of the major incident response steps: Successful Return to Normal operations for the affected Business Unit after an incident. The general Recovery method is usually based on the IT Backup mechanism instituted for each server or device as defined by the Recovery Time Objective and Recovery Point Objective time frames within the organization's Business Impact Analysis (BIA). The SIR&FT members need to know the rotation and sequencing for each backup, the location for the storage of the backup media (tapes, disks, etc.), and the methods of transporting the storage media to the alternate storage facility. Each area for backup actions should be documented for ease of use and recovery subsequent to any incident to facilitate recovery and return to normal operations.

- Training

  The IT and Security staff within the IT department each receive additional training beyond the normal user training which all personnel receive in the organization. Elevated privilege account activity needs additional security and authorization training for each user with these types of access to ensure they perform their actions in accordance with the corporate policies, procedures, and requirements. Additional training requirements are placed on personnel with these access rights when conducting their job performance if in several different industrial verticals, such as the governmental, energy, and financial sectors. With these additional training requirements, the SIR&FT members need to be aware of the training received by the privilege account holders, especially in light of insider threat issues and potential elevated account compromise issues.

- Testing

  There are many areas with the IT scope of activities which require testing and evaluation efforts. The SIR&FT needs awareness of each and every testing effort to ensure there are no compromises or inadvertent breaches during the testing. The testing of development of new or modified applications, infrastructure changes, installation of new equipment, standing up new capabilities, expansion of network capacities, new security components, and backup/recovery mechanisms are all areas which the potential exposure is of concern and the team should be monitoring the efforts during the event.

  Any exercise effort conducted by the IT organization needs coordination and cooperation efforts with the SIR&FT as there is always an exposure potential during the exercise wherein the corporate production information or machines could become compromised. All Disaster Recovery, Incident Response, Certification and Accreditation, and Business Continuity exercises are to be considered within this arena.

- Reporting Structure

  The business units provide a trove of data for the SIR&FT to review each day with respect to business activities, customer feedback, and interchange with the organization and websites, strategic alignment within the business community, internal user experiences with applications and the network, etc. Each report generated should be initially reviewed by a team member for relevance and trend status in case the report has a small or large critical data component to see if there are any business activities which could be an indicator of a compromise or other IR indicator.

The SIR&FT reporting efforts should always follow the corporate report requirements for form, substance, and format. The various types of reports being generated by the SIR&FT will require some external coordination and formatting as well, since these reports could end up being provided to Law Enforcement or other legal entities. All reports should be generated with this consideration for content and structure while being created and written.

- Jurisdiction

  At a corporate level, when an incident is discovered and declared, the SIR&FT Manager needs to be in charge of all response efforts and report directly to the most senior executive available at the time of discovery. The jurisdictional disputes which will inevitably come due to each business unit manager effected wanting their area to be returned to operations first need executive remediation and clearly defined guidance, which should be in the BIA, Business Continuity Plan (BCP), and the Incident Response Plan (IRP) documents. Each recovery effort needs corporate involvement to create an environment where the parties included and affected are communicated with, advised, and provided status information to help reduce these disputes.

  As the incident response progresses, each part of the corporate infrastructure may need to be tested and then cleared to return to operations, so the SIR&FT Manager, as the Response Manager, should be the only one executive allowed to authorize the systems and equipment to be connected and returned to service. This provides a clear and direct line of responsibility for control, containment and eradication of the issue which caused the incident and keeps the information secure for the organization. Otherwise, by allowing other managers to turn on their sections independently, the potential of the issue remaining or even expanding is large and possibly damaging to the corporation.

- Data and Media Control

  The basic control for all removable media is often a critical area for the IT department as this is often the primary way malicious software (Malware) is introduced into the corporate operating environment. There are many types and sizes of portable drives today and many have very large data storage capacities wherein the data can be placed and stored. Most all USB devices in today's world have storage capability and data can be retained on them without others knowing it is stored there. Control of the USB access is often a method for controlling this potential "way" into the network.

When data is transported on devices or storage media, the IT staff are often the primary personnel creating and moving the media. The method and means of the media storage needs to be identified and documented for the SIR&FT to allow the team to trace and follow the media in case there is an issue which develops around a possible data breach involving the storage of the data. The movement of the media to the alternate storage facility, the creation of the storage media during the backup activities, and the use of the media for recovery efforts within the organization all are potential areas where there are openings for issues and problems with the data.

- Privacy—Need to Know

  The IT Staff, especially the System and Network Administrators, are the point people in the area of privacy, access to data, and the corporate data that no one should know outside the organization. This basic security concept is known as the "need to know" and requires only those people who need the information for their daily work activities have an access to the critical data itself. Just because someone is a manager does not automatically dictate they have access to the data.

  There are many laws and regulations which cover the data, the information, and the personnel of the organization. We covered many of them in other sections of this book so I will not repeat them. The primary area is that each person involved with and each dataset to be reviewed or printed each has a privacy consideration which has to be performed with it as it is interchanged with and or printed. Always keep in mind the potential external data classification and compliance requirements for data handling and data manipulation.

- Audit Trail

  The various activities of the IT System Administrators and Network Administrators are usually recording in the audit logs of the device or system they are performing the work on. These log files are often the only mechanism which shows the actions and the results of the actions performed, such as account creations, Access Control List (ACL) changes, privilege changes, and elevations. The recording of these activities is commonly performed in an automatic fashion by the device or system and the records are considered the paramount means for performing network forensics investigations by the SIR&FT. Therefore, it is of primary importance to the SIR&FT activities that these logs be records, saved and moved off of the production machine intact, without alteration, to the audit log storage location as soon as possible after recording.

  A common method of hiding illegal or unauthorized actions is to alter the recording of these events in the audit logs themselves. So during investigations, the SIR&FT members are going to review these files looking for missing entries, missing time events, and changes with no explanation. If the entire log is missing could have significance, but if there are missing entries in the log, that indicates even higher significance as that would mean someone is trying to hide their actions.

- Documentation and Version Control

  The various machines, devices, and applications supported by the IT staff throughout the organization all need to be identified, documented, and have baseline configurations for operational and security considerations. The documentation produced by the vendor for the system, application, or device should always be under documentation control to ensure the current version is the one which is available to all, including the SIR&FT members so they can research the appropriate manual when performing an incident response or investigation.

  The versioning of the software and hardware as deployed within the organization is also of major importance so as to allow the SIR&FT as well as the other organizations within the corporation to act on, perform on, and conduct their business on the most current "approved" version of the system or application. Each version of software must be documented and go through the corporate configuration management system to provide a level of assurance that the output information has been produced by the system or application in its proper method and format. This normal corporate configuration management and version control system should itself be documented with Change Control Board (CCB) charters CC requests, etc.; all of which the SIR&FT must have availability to in case the change is the root cause of an incident or even a breach.

  Historically, this one area has created many data breaches and control failures by IT staff not informing security personnel of changes when they are being reviewed or even installed. The potential for control failure or bypass, increased vulnerabilities being intentionally or unintentionally introduced to the work environment are both major considerations that the SIR&FT and IT staffs must work together to prevent and/or resolve if there are current issues in the organization.

- Variations

  Corporate variations or exceptions must be documented to ensure the security controls as implemented have not been compromised and therefore cause an exploit to be conducted on the corporate system or network. There are three basic areas where these variations will occur in the IT arena that the SIR&FT Manager needs to be aware of:

  - Policy

    Variations in policies will often depend on local environmental conditions, regional requirement, or external factors for a particular line of business.

- Framework

  The security framework and the IT framework, which are developed together and part of enterprise architecture for the organization, can have certain variations based upon location or line of business which other parts of the organization would not implement or even allow.

- Established Procedures

  The corporate IT procedures for performance of the various IT functions are usually centralized, but there are often variations which come into play in a decentralized operational arena. If one part of the company has a method for handling tape backups because of customer requirements that does not follow the corporate norm, this would be an example of the procedure variation.

  As previously mentioned in other sections, there are many policies and procedures which IT departments put in place to help monitor and control the security and actions of the corporate users within the organizational guidance requirements for confidentiality, integrity, and availability for use and interaction with corporate assets and information. These types of corporate policies for general security support needed for SIR&FT activities include the following and are only briefing explained here (the detailed explanation for each policy is found in other sections):

- Acceptable Use Policy

  The Acceptable Use Policy (AUP) defines for each user of the corporate system, network, or application, what actions are allowed and what actions are Not allowed on the network, system, or application. This policy will cover corporate equipment, corporate premises, and corporate property.

- Privacy

  The Privacy policy sets the corporate level of privacy for each person interchanging with the corporate staff, using corporate equipment, and/ or utilizing corporate information. This policy is used as a supplement to statutory and regulatory guidance for privacy within the areas of operations for the corporation.

- Password

  The Password policy sets the requirements for password use by the user when logging into a network, system, or application of the corporation. The Password policy will define the password structure requirements, password reuse criteria, and other actions based on the password mechanism for authentication.

- Document Retention

  The requirements for document retention are often externally determined for the organization. If the document is required to be retained for a long period of time can be a compliance issue, a regulatory issue, or even a legal, statutory issue. So the retention period for each document should be individually defined at document creation time and this policy should cover those actions.

- Data Retention
  The retention policy for data should be developed in accordance with any external requirements, as well as corporate needs for data usage and storage. As an example, if the data to be retained is financial, then the external factors require the data to be stored and available for 10 years after use and submittal to the US Government.

- Change Control and Configuration Management
  The IT configuration management and change control policy is necessary to monitor and control the various application-, system-, and network-based changes which are inevitable within any corporation. Users are going to request changes to these various systems and application to either improve or modify the workflow and functions of the system or application and the security of the affected system is often altered or compromised by these "supposed" improvements. These policies are placed into effect to prevent this type of negative event.

- Disposal of Assets
  The disposal policy is designed to prevent sensitive but outdated printed or electronic data from becoming exposed to the outside world. Dumpster Diving is still very prevalent in today's digital world as one means of reconnaissance from external agents to obtain data about an organization.

- Data Classification
  Any organization should have a classification of data policy in practice. This process for labeling corporate data provides the users and administrators guidance as to the importance of the data they are handling and thereby provides resource use and handling mechanisms to these users. This policy should provide additional security from the techniques of Social Engineering and Information or Data Spillage.

- HR
  The HR policy set, although not IT specific, has many applications within the IT arena. This policy set covers employee hiring, termination, transfer, and background verifications. Personnel Security practices start with HR and are often critical to ensure the Insider Threat is minimized as best as possible.

- Public Relations
  Who can speak for the organization and under what circumstances are necessary in today's Internet-based communications world. Social media posted corporate information, Press Releases, and the direct SIR&FT-based incident reporting requirements are critical to the security, safety, and corporate reputational abilities and activities.

There are certainly other policies and procedures which a corporation or organization will develop and provide to the organization which cover additional areas of concern and focus for users which can and will affect the SIR&FT response actions. The SIR&FT Manager should ensure each of these corporate-level policies is in effect and active. These newer type of policies will include areas of interchange of users with outside organizations and social media outlets, utilizing current technology, and many other activities. Some of these policies would include but are not limited to:

1. **Appropriate Use of Social Media Policy**

   In today's work environment around the world, many organizations allow their users to access the various social media sites during work hours. The process for monitoring and controlling what is said on these sites and by whom needs to be covered in this policy. The individual sites are covered by their own policy document, but the general practices and procedures for allowable activities are covered in this document.

   The various governmental agencies and monitoring organizations watch these sites for insider data, inappropriate information posts, possible slanderous or malicious posts and information, etc. I have participated in an investigation of insider trading wherein the suspect posted inside information on future activities to his social media account to advise others about future corporate actions before the formal announcement. The others then took action to profit from this data before the normal public was aware of the impending action. The governmental agency found this to be classified as insider trading and the user was convicted and jailed for this illicit activity. So having a policy covering these social media events is critical to both the user and the corporate security. Individual Social media sites each have their unique criteria for use and activities. Some are very active locations and should have their own policy for content from corporate locations and users. Some of these sites are specific to corporate use and are actively used as follows:

   A. Corporate YouTube Policy

   The YouTube site is a place to put videos created by the organization for dissemination to its users and others interested in the company and its activities and products. Often corporations place promotional videos here about their products and or services as well as detailed training video seminars for the use of their products. The videos are placed onto the YouTube site in either a downloadable or nondownloadable format and can be controlled for updates and content. Much of today's training seminars are stored here by the content provider or author, so monitoring the use of and the content of the corporate videos needs to be conducted and covered by this policy.

B. Corporate Facebook Account Policy

The Facebook online social networking service, wherein users create a personal profile, add other users as friends, and exchange messages, including automatic notifications when they update their profile, has developed over the past few years into the primary mechanism for online communications for the newer Internet users and younger generational users. Users can create profiles with photos, lists of personal interests, contact information, and other personal information. Users can communicate with friends and other users through private or public messages and a chat feature. They can also create and join interest groups and "like pages," some of which are maintained by organizations as a means of advertising. Additionally, users may join common-interest user groups, organized by workplace, school or college, or other characteristics, and categorize their friends into lists such as "People from Work" or "Close Friends."

The corporate Public Relations staff will need to ensure the corporate Facebook page is maintained with acceptable and approved content at all times. Many outside organizations constantly monitor particular sites for content updates and automatically notify others when content is altered or updated. The current generation of users follows this site tremendously, as evidenced at this time of this writing; Facebook has over 1 Billion user accounts active. The corporate policy needs to be developed before a corporate-related Facebook page is created that is not under the control of the PR staff of the corporation.

C. Corporate LinkedIn Policy

LinkedIn has developed as a business-based corporate location for company data announcements, user activity, and exchange point for information about the company and its workers. It has provided the "networking" online ability usually found in the old face-to-face events and conferences. There are many corporations that provide company data on their LinkedIn site, post job openings, and post upcoming events, and announcements on their location. Each post needs to be reviewed for content and context to ensure it is the stance of the organization and follows the corporate public relations practices and policies.

2. Bring Your Own Device Corporate Policy

Today's corporate environment has developed a practice of allowing users and executives to utilize today's technological devices connectivity to the corporate network for work-related activities. This process is called Bring Your Own Device (BYOD) and provides the organization means to reduce the costs and overhead for purchasing and maintaining remote-connected devices (laptops, etc.).

The BYOD policy is the corporate policy covering these devices, their use, and their security for the users. The policy should cover the equipment allowed and the BYOD Authorization Process which should describe the required steps each staff member who chooses to connect his or her own device to the organization's systems or networks must take to remain compliant with the BYOD Policy. We have included a sample BYOD Policy in Appendix C.

3. **Company Telecommuting Policy**

The corporate Telecommuting Policy describes the organization's guidelines and process for requesting, obtaining, using, and terminating remote access to organization networks, systems, and data for the purpose of enabling staff members to regularly work from home on a formal basis. This policy will describe the means and methods for allowance of the practice of telecommuting by the corporate employees and users to access the corporate network and resources.

4. **Website Content Policy**

This policy is designed to be actively placed onto the corporate website and control the updating of the site's content. This policy defines a language used to declare a set of content restrictions for a web resource, and a mechanism for transmitting the policy from a server to a client where the policy is enforced. The W3 organization has this policy designed and defined on their location. They define as: "Content Security Policy, a mechanism that a web application can use to mitigate a broad class of content injection vulnerabilities, such as cross-site scripting (XSS). Content Security Policy is a declarative policy that lets the authors (or server administrators) of a web application inform the clients from where the application expects to load resources."[1]

5. **E-mail Use Policy**

The primary method of communications internal to the organization and for the most part, external to the organization is going to be conducted through e-mail. The e-mail policy will cover the use, the security, the archiving, the retention, and the complete parameters of the corporate e-mail system. All the criteria for controlling, setting up accounts, the data retention of the user's data, and the security of the e-mail system will be found here in this policy. This policy is probably going to be the longest one within the corporate policy construct, as it covers every user in the organization and all of their primary means of correspondence within the organization. The archiving and retention mechanisms need special coverage from a forensics and IR perspective as this one area is covered statutorily, regulatory and legally through eDiscovery and court-directed legal hold requirements.

---

[1] http://www.w3.org/TR/CSP/.

6. **File Sharing and File Transfer Policy**

   The corporate user often shares files with other corporate users and maybe even outside entities. This policy will cover the requirements for the practice of corporate file sharing and file transfers to others outside the organization. Security of sensitive information, Intellectual property use and rights, and legal requirements for this activity will all be covered in this policy. This area can be of vital importance to the organization and every user of this information needs to be made aware of the corporate policy and adhere to it to protect the confidentiality and integrity of the data shared and the data transferred in and out of the organization.

7. **Remote System Access Policy**

   The corporate Remote Access Policy describes the organization's guidelines and processes for requesting, obtaining, using, and terminating remote access to networks, systems, and data. Secure remote access to corporate resources enables the organization and its authorized staff and contractors to fulfill organizational goals and objectives more efficiently. Secure remote access also encourages healthier work/life balances by enabling staff to perform work-related tasks from alternative locations or after regular business hours and on weekends.

   This policy will be used to control, monitor, define, and create access for the organization's remote location users whenever they access the corporate network, and from whatever location they are attempting access from at the time.

8. **Wireless Usage Policy**

   This policy is the corporate definition of when and where Wireless devices, Access Points, and network components are to be allowed. Every unit in the corporate environment will have a possible use for wireless devices and access. Examples include the marketing unit may want to have a collaborative development of the new strategic marketing plan and want everyone to share the data as it is developed but only allow access to the marketing folks and no one else until it is finalized, or customers, clients, and guests may want Internet access while using their own laptops or mobile devices when visiting the corporate locations. Each type of access needs to be identified and defined in the corporate Wireless Use policy before the request for access is received.

Relationship Management

There are many situations within the Incident Response and Forensics domains where other internal corporate organizations and/or external agencies, organizations, and third-party corporations will need to or must participate in the response efforts. It is important to identify other groups within the organization that may be needed to participate in incident handling so that their cooperation can be solicited before it is needed. As the NIST SP 800-61 says, "Every incident response team relies on the expertise, judgment, and abilities of others, including—

- **Management.**
- **Information Security.**
- **Telecommunications.**
- **IT Support.**
- **Legal Department.**
- **Public Affairs and Media Relations.**
- **Human Resources.**
- **Business Continuity Planning.**
- **Physical Security and Facilities Management."**[1]

Some of the divisions, both internal to the corporation and external to the corporation that these types of working relationships are needed for, include the following components and personnel:

1. *Law Enforcement*
   Many organizations often fear turning over cases to law enforcement agencies, for fear of suffering publicity, relationship damage, reputational risk, or embarrassment. If an incident is reported to law enforcement, then it will be objectively investigated. Regardless of what some may say, there are many highly qualified and experienced individuals in the law enforcement community who take pride in the standard of work they perform, and who value their objectivity. In recent years, the law enforcement community has developed many training and certification

---

[1] NIST SP 800-61 rev.1, pp. 2–14, March 2008.

activities for search and seizure efforts which include forensics, imaging of machines and devices, search techniques for law violations, etc. The development of national standards in forensics tool evaluations and methods of hashing have greatly contributed to the development of very competent and professional law enforcement forensics analysts and investigators. As a matter of fact, the law enforcement community has produced some of the forensics community's thought leaders of today, such as Warren Kruse, forensics and incident response author and former NJ State Police officer, and Dan Mares, author of the Maresware Forensics Toolkit and former instructor at the Federal Law Enforcement Training Center (FLETC).

The primary relationship driver between any corporate forensics team and law enforcement is determined at the point of legal considerations by the corporate counsel, the SIR&FT manager, the corporate officers, and the law surrounding the jurisdiction of criminal behavior. The US legal system is designed to provide the criminal prosecution in the purview of the government (local, state, or federal) and not that of the corporation or the individual. Therefore, any criminal event will be investigated and evidence produced by the law enforcement agencies which support the judicial system. The US Constitution's Fourth Amendment on Search and Seizure is then the primary guidance for all investigative actions. One of the evaluation areas for the corporate counsel is the general fact that once the data is turned over to the law enforcement officials, the US Freedom of Information Act (FOIA) becomes applicable; therefore, the data surrounding the case will eventually become public information. The corporate officials will need to make a risk-based decision based upon reputational risk about criminal versus civil proceedings at this point.

Once data is found to be potentially involved in a criminal situation and the corporate executives decide to pursue the case, the appropriate contact should be made with the law enforcement agency responsible for the type of possible crime discovered. This process will probably include an interview with the alleged victim organization, transfer of the potential evidence through the use of the chain of custody forms discussed in the previous sections and in Appendix C, and then possible LEO review and capture of data onsite at the scene.

Some of the law enforcement organizations which provide information and guidance in the incident response and forensics arenas include the locations and websites listed below. There is a much longer and more detailed listing of locations and sites in Appendix A.

- U.S. Department of Justice: http://www.usdoj.gov
- Department of Justice Canada—Ministère de la justice Canada: http://canada.justice.gc.ca

- The European Union Ministry of Justice: http://europa.eu/pol/justice/index_en.htm
- The Internet Crime Complaint Center (IC3) http://www.ic3.gov
- Internet Fraud Complaint Center http://www1.ifccfbi.gov or http://www.ifccfbi.gov/index.asp

2. *Legal*

Legal experts should review incident response and forensics plans, policies, and procedures to ensure their compliance with both the local, regional, and federal laws and Federal guidance and regulations, including the right to privacy. The corporate counsel personnel are aware of the statutory and regulatory requirements for the organization in each area that there are operations and production. Each division of the corporation may have unique legal or regulatory situations which the corporate counsel will be involved in while they are occurring; therefore, they will be cognizant of the operating environment, the compliance environment, the physical environment, and the reporting environment. In fact, in many organizations, the corporate counsel is made responsible for the external reporting requirements for the entire organization. In addition, the guidance of the general counsel or legal department should be sought if there is reason to believe that an incident may have legal ramifications, including evidence collection, prosecution of a suspect, or a lawsuit. During any incident or investigation, the legal staff must be involved and aware of the actions, activities, and findings as they are determined by the SIR&FT members. The SIR&FT Manager is to keep the legal staff in the flow of the data and aware of the progress of the incident handling and/or the forensics investigation.

3. *LOB Management*

The management of each Line of Business (LOB) is always focused on the business unit's profit, input and output, people, and general activities to bring into the corporation more business, income, and opportunities. This focus on the business unit and its objectives requires most managers in these positions to not be aware of the requirements and needs of the SIR&FT and their normal operational methods when responding to events and during investigations. There are several areas within the relationship between the SIR&FT and the Operational managers that should be focused on by the SIR&FT Manager as these activities are conducted.

- *Set boundaries for activities*

  Each operational line unit manager is going to be focused on their unit's operational status and want their unit to be brought back to full normal operations as soon as it can after the event or incident. They need guidance from the SIR&FT Manager as to what actions are acceptable by their personnel during the event or investigation, what are the corporate expectations for the unit performance during these activities, and how the unit can and should support the team while these activities are being performed. Each affected unit always will want to be the first back to normal operations, so the priorities for recovery should be based in the Recovery documentation of the unit and the organization. The Business Impact Analysis (BIA) document previously developed during the Business Continuity efforts of the organization will serve as the guide for the SIR&FT as well as the Business Unit for the sequence and methods of recovery for each unit. This BIA sets the criteria for business unit, which the SIR&FT Manager then applies to the individual incident and then he (not the LOB Manager) sets the boundary of the activities allowed for the unit during and after the event or investigation. Using these corporate-driven and corporate-directed criteria allows for clear and direct guidance to be given to the unit managers so there are minimal conflicts to be resolved during the event. The SIR&FT Manager then can focus on the needs for the organization while the response is occurring and during the subsequent follow-up activities.

- *Ensure C-Level support in action and writing*
  C-Level Management invariably plays a pivotal role in incident response and forensics investigations. In the most fundamental sense, C-Level management establishes incident response policy, budget, and staffing. They are the corporate entity which assigns the SIR&FT Manager, gives him the authority to carry out the event resolution efforts and investigations, and provides the overarching senior management guidance to the full corporation when these activities are transpiring. Ultimately, the corporate executive management is held responsible for coordinating incident response among various stakeholders, minimizing damage, and reporting to outside regulatory and compliance agencies and other parties. Without this C-Level management support, the SIR&FT effort is unlikely to be successful in its endeavors. This C-Level support is always most valuable when dealing with the various corporate entities and with the outside agencies and organizations the SIR&FT often must interchange with during the normal course of an investigation or an incident response.

- *Maintain professional relationship*
  The operational line managers and LOB executives are usually going to have very little awareness or exposure to the standard SIR&FT methods, techniques, and activities. They will, invariably, want to know what is happening during the response or investigation, how the team members perform their actions, and want to know everything about the team and its members. This can cause distractions and may even impede the response or investigation. So, it is very important to maintain a strictly professional attitude and

relationship with the LOB management as these efforts are conducted to reduce the effects of interrupts and distractions.

■ *Don't become their friend/advisor—professional ethics*
Often the LOB managers want advice and understanding to better respond and prepare for future events. While this is commendable, I have seen this create a relationship of advisor or friend to the LOB manager which can impede decision-making on either side of the relationship with the result of bad decisions for the business being made based upon friendship rather than business objectives.

4. *Technical Staff*
IT technical experts (e.g., system administrators, network administrators, and software developers) not only have the needed technical skills to assist during an incident but also usually have the best understanding of the technology with which they deal on a daily basis. This understanding can facilitate response decisions such as whether to disconnect an attacked system from the network. The SIR&FT often employs the use of and may even retain members of the IT Staff as adjunct subject matter experts in certain response situations or investigations. Some of the major areas that the SIR&FT Manager should concentrate on with respect to the Technical Staff include:

a. *Work with, rather than against*
The Technical Staff have the day-to-day operational knowledge and expertise around the systems, applications, and the network activity for the organization. The SIR&FT members need this knowledge during and after an incident activity or investigation so they will need a knowledge transfer from the IT Staff while performing their duties. It is valuable to gain this information and knowledge so the team members don't have to investigate areas which are not relevant to the actual event.

i. *Unless they are also suspect*
Always keep in mind with the insider threat potential that the Technical Staff members themselves can be suspect in an event or the subject of an investigation; therefore, it is important that the SIR&FT Manager makes a determination as soon as possible during the initial response whether any of the internal staff are involved in the event and whether they should be part of the response or excluded from the response.

ii. *Review logs and procedures*
The IT Staff is usually in charge of monitoring, reviewing, and moving the various log files from the server and network devices. The moving of these files to the log server or storage location is usually, in today's environment, an automated process performed daily since log files can get very large quickly with many devices

providing inputs to SIEM systems. The process documents and procedures should be available for review by the SIR&FT members when needed during response events. In fact, a corporate security team member may be assigned to review these log files as a method of monitoring the events and traffic activity so as to determine if any suspicious activity or event maybe occurring on the various system. The SIR&FT Manager must assure availability of these files for both response and investigative needs during and subsequent to any event, which is especially significant for after-the-fact eDiscovery and Forensics Tracing requirements.

b. *Maintain working relationship*

The SIR&FT members and team Manager should attempt to maintain a good working relationship with the IT Staff of the organization. Since the IT staff focus is business operations, the Team Manager needs to keep this perspective in mind during the course of events, interchanges with the IT staff, and any requests for support or assistance while having the response and investigative activities performed. The IT Staff has many operational priorities and requirements which often take their entire focus during the daily activities, so requesting support can be problematic unless the staff has a good working relationship with the SIR&FT.

c. *Special relationship with the IT Security Staff*

Members of the corporate or LOB information security team are often the first to recognize that an incident has occurred or is occurring and may perform the initial analysis of incidents. Often the members of the corporate Information Security staff end up becoming members of the SIR&FT when an exceptionally large or critical incident is discovered or identified. As the SIR&FT Manager reviews the criteria for team members, he will often find the best qualified corporate personnel are the corporate or LOB security staff members and he will be tempted to pull them onto the team at various times and under various circumstances. This is a common practice today in the corporate environment and will provide a unique and valuable method of ensuring the communications between the LOB security staff and the SIR&FT are maintained and maybe even enhanced during incident response or investigative events.

Additionally, LOB or corporate information security staff members may be needed during other stages of incident handling—for example, altering network security controls (e.g., firewall rule-sets) to contain an incident or conduct an examination. Follow-on activities, after action report generation and Lessons Learned actions to be performed by the organization are commonly performed by the IT Security staff within each business unit or by the corporate security unit for the corporation to show oversight and compliance results after a breach or incident. In fact, some business sectors require this level over activity to provide outside organizations (regulators, auditors, etc.) assurance that the problems identified have been resolved and appropriately handled.

5. *Outside Consultants*

The SIR&FT often will experience situations, when responding to events and incidents, where the team members have little or no expertise or understanding of the breadth, depth, and scope of the problem encountered. In these types of situations, the Team Manager would then bring in to the situation an outside expert within the field of concern. The SIR&FT Manager should have a series of outside consultants and experts in the various fields that the organization conducts business and activities. There are multiple areas the Team Manager should address before any of these types of incidents are discovered. They include but are not limited to the following:

■ *Outside Agencies and Experts*

The SIR&FT Manager should review the industry and identify potential vendors within the areas of concern or little experience of the team members and then contact these external organizations to review and possibly contract with them before an incident occurs. The areas of possible focus for these outside contracts can be the technologies recently deployed within the organization that there are no resident subject matter experts for within the organization, specialized technology-driven forensics requirements (Cloud, Cell Phone, unique databases, Big Data, etc.), or possibly even operational focus points such as chemical or industrial PLC activities. The Manager should build a set of requirements for the third-party organizations/consultants and then solicit proposals from the vendors. Once received, the Manager then should review the inputs to see where there could be matches to internal needs and conduct selection activities in accordance with corporate practices and procedures. Some of the areas to include in the requests for information and requests for proposals are covered:

■ *Background reviews of third-party experts*

Each organization which provides inputs and data in response to the Team Manager's data call or RFI/RFP should include references for past work completed, possible corporate reference documents, capabilities statements of the services provided and products used. Some of the areas to be included in the requesting documents are:

- *Knowledge*
    - Knowledge, skills, and abilities of the third-party company and its staff.

- Areas of expertise and experience in past activities of similar nature and size.
- Types of events and incidents reviewed, responded to and assisted in mitigation for.
- *Integrity*
    - The integrity of the organization as relayed by references.
    - Full and complete results delivered to customers.
- *Credibility*
    - Organizational credentials and ratings.
    - Staff credentials and experience.
    - Reference checks.

■ *Past Performance actions and results*

The SIR&FT Team Manager should request at least three references from customers of the third-party company to contact and check on skills, completeness of work, investigative results, experience with staff, customer satisfaction, and other criteria as defined by the corporation's RFP process and procedures. This area also covers the needs for the SIR&FT Manager to ensure the third-party company can perform the needed actions in conformance with the corporate and industry requirements for the type of work expected and anticipated by the potential contract.

- *Rates and Services*
    - Solicitation rates based upon RFP/RFI requests
    - Rates for related unrequested services
    - Capabilities statements of services provided

6. **Human Resources**

When an employee is the apparent target of an incident or is suspected of causing an incident, the human resources department often becomes involved—for example, in assisting with disciplinary proceedings or employee counseling. Often, the human resources division will try to determine the results of a finding or action required from an investigative report that has resulted from the SIR&FT actions and activities. Especially in insider threat cases, the personnel department will be the primary administrative overseer of what will happen to the suspect. In most of these cases, the first activity to be conducted by the responders is to ensure the personnel policies and procedures employed cover the "suspected" offence in writing. Often I have seen where everyone thought the offense was covered, but in reality, it was not in the AUP or other employee signed document. These policies are administered by the HR unit and the signed documents are often found in the employee's personnel file. The SIR&FT Manager must work with the Human Resources department to ensure all the right forms and policy documents are signed by the right people when dealing with investigations, since, in my experience, 65% of the time these cases end up in court. Appropriate Non-Disclosure Agreements, Teaming Agreements, and even subcontracts for employment all need to be monitored and controlled by the Human Resources department, but verified by the Team Manager.

7. *Other Corporate Departments*

There are other divisions of the corporation where relationships are important depending upon the incident or investigation and its surrounding circumstances. These divisions include:

a. *Facilities*

Some computer security incidents occur through breaches of physical security or involve coordinated logical and physical attacks. Threats made against the organization may not indicate whether logical or physical resources are being targeted. The facilities support organization(s) are often the first to sense and respond to a potential network breach, if it is physically performed. The incident response team also may need access to facilities during incident handling—for example, to acquire a compromised workstation from a locked office. Thus, close coordination between physical security and facilities management and the incident response team is important. The component organizations within this realm include the physical plant unit (HVAC, Electrical, Engineering, Landscaping, etc.) and the physical security unit (guard force, gate monitors, etc.).

b. *Continuity/Recovery Staff*

Computer security incidents undermine the business resilience of an organization and act as a barometer of its level of vulnerabilities and the inherent risks. The Business Continuity unit within the corporation is often aware of the recovery and restitution requirements for each division and unit. Business continuity planning professionals should be made aware of incidents and events and their possible impacts so they can fine-tune and update the business impact assessments, disaster recovery plans, risk assessments, and continuity of operations plans.

Further, because business continuity planners have extensive expertise in minimizing operational disruption during severe circumstances, they may be valuable in planning responses to certain types of incidents, such as a denial of service (DoS). Organizations should also ensure that incident response policies, recovery procedures, and business continuity processes are in sync. These are the people within the organization who derive the critical infrastructure recovery plans after disasters and major disruptive events so they can lend a major level of support to the SIR&FT when responding to large-scale activities.

c. *PR/PA/Media relations/Corporate Communications*
Depending on the nature and impact of an incident, a need may exist to inform the media and, by extension, the public (within the constraints imposed by security and law enforcement interests). The Public Relations organization should be involved at all levels of response due to the current compliance needs of the organization, especially concerning data breach response requirements as this area often requires external communications with regulators, the shareholders, the stakeholders, and the public. The PR department can help the SIR&FT Manager formulate the proper reports and communications for release and response to these outside agencies. The PR department provides the guidance and expertise needed to properly project the corporate stances in certain situations when needed by the SIR&FT Manager.

d. *Telecommunications*
Some incidents involve unauthorized access to telephone lines, such as dialing into unsecured modems. Private Branch Exchange (PBX) compromises often are intertwined with break-ins into other systems. The telecommunications department can provide expertise and assistance to the SIR&FT during and after the response efforts as the telecommunications staff is aware of the current capabilities and the POCs and procedures for working with telecommunications carriers. Telephone lines, carriers, and access to the upstream equipment and providers are all areas within the domain of this department. Response needs and communications with carriers and upstream providers can be critical to the successful resolution of certain types of incidents perpetrated from outside of the organization in the DDOS and remote access attack arenas.

Conclusion

Security Incident Response is a dynamic, varied, and ever-changing field. This ability to respond to and compensate for the multiple sources of potential security incidents is vitally important to any organization. From the smallest to the largest organization, Security Incident Response is valuable, necessary and in many case, the highest priority for safety and security of all people involved. Proper security incident response requires dedication to proper procedures and attention to great detail which often yields great satisfaction.

Forensics is a growing, ever-expanding subfield of Security Incident Response with a lot of demanding precise requirements for investigators, examiners, and analysts. These fields combine in most organizations with corporate policies, procedures, and guidance from one executive office. The management and oversight for these response activities will continue to be in focus from both a corporate and governmental perspective for years to come.

THE INCIDENT RESPONSE TEAM

Understanding the requirements for an Incident Response team is the basic first step for any manager to set up the team and run the response activity for his organization. Once again, to incorporate and formalize a specialized Security Incident Response Team (SIRT) is critical to the organization. This specialized SIRT consists of a senior team leader, multiple team members, corporate legal counsel representative, and potentially other staff members based upon the extent and depth of the incident. As with any security program or activity, senior management-executive level support is paramount to the success of the effort and the response unit. The SIRT receives its authority directly from the highest levels of the organization, either the Board of Directors or the Corporate Office/Senior Executive/Senior Management. The SIRT is directly responsible for the entire incident investigation and response and has the authority to override all other corporate staff decisions and activities with respect to the incident. With the senior management support efforts come, the clearly defined corporate incident response policies and procedures which are important to ensure proper data and information handling during incident response and potentially any legal actions resulting from such an incident. SIRT roles and responsibilities, especially with respect to the other corporate staff, during the response efforts and subsequent investigations.

THE FORENSICS TEAM

The basic requirement for any forensics team is to capture and record the data and then review and examine the data to produce evidence of the issue or activity. The process is based on scientific principles and follows defined scientific methodologies. These process activities are repeatable, reviewable, refinable, and recordable. Full forensics activities usually require a laboratory setting for examination of the various devices and storage media in a secure and clean environment to avoid contamination. Forensics has often been implemented and supported as a subset of Incident Response once the IR steps get to the Eradication section. This is usually the point at which there is then two paths to follow:

1. Recovery, Rebuild, Return to Normal Operations
    This section covers fixing the issue to include restoring the machine from new purchase all the way to returning the organization to its normal operating state. This is the full Incident Response final step process as explained in "The Incident Response Team" section.
2. Examine, Investigation, Analyze, Report
    This section covers reviewing the data captured and recorded, analyzing it for anomalies and/or malicious software, determining the intent of the code, software, commands, and recorded activities, then producing a report of the events, data and logic behind them for potential use in a legal or administrative setting. This is the full Forensics final steps as explained in this section.
    Using Forensics as part of Incident Response is not a new concept as evidenced by the NIST SP 800-86 recommendations from 2006:

Implementing the following recommendations should facilitate efficient and effective digital forensic activities for departments and agencies.

1. **Organizations should ensure that their policies contain clear statements addressing all major forensic considerations, such as contacting law enforcement, performing monitoring, and conducting regular reviews of forensic policies and procedures.**
    At a high level, policies should allow authorized personnel to monitor systems and networks and perform investigations for legitimate reasons under appropriate circumstances. Organizations may also have a separate forensic policy for incident handlers and others with

forensic roles; this policy would provide more detailed rules concerning appropriate behavior. Forensic policy should clearly define the roles and responsibilities of all people and external organizations performing or assisting with the organization's forensic activities. The policy should clearly indicate who should contact which internal teams and external organizations under different circumstances.

2. **Organizations should create and maintain procedures and guidelines for performing forensic tasks, based on the organization's policies and all applicable laws and regulations.**
Guidelines should focus on general methodologies for investigating incidents using forensic techniques, since it is not feasible to develop comprehensive procedures tailored to every possible situation. However, organizations should consider developing step-by-step procedures for performing routine tasks. The guidelines and procedures should facilitate consistent, effective, and accurate actions, which is particularly important for incidents that may lead to prosecution or internal disciplinary actions; handling evidence in a forensically sound manner puts decision makers in a position where they can confidently take the necessary actions. The guidelines and procedures should support the admissibility of evidence into legal proceedings, including information on gathering and handling evidence properly, preserving the integrity of tools and equipment, maintaining the chain of custody, and storing evidence appropriately. Because electronic logs and other records can be altered or otherwise manipulated, organizations should be prepared, through their policies, guidelines, and procedures, to demonstrate the integrity of such records. The guidelines and procedures should be reviewed periodically, as well as when significant changes are made to the team's policies and procedures.

3. **Organizations should ensure that their policies and procedures support the reasonable and appropriate use of forensic tools.**
Organizations' policies and procedures should clearly explain what forensic actions should and should not be performed under various circumstances, as well as describing the necessary safeguards for sensitive information that might be recorded by forensic tools, such as passwords, personal data (e.g., Social Security numbers), and the contents of e-mails. Legal advisors should carefully review all forensic policy and high-level procedures.

4. **Organizations should ensure that their IT professionals are prepared to participate in forensic activities.**
IT professionals throughout an organization, especially incident handlers and other first responders to incidents, should understand their roles and responsibilities for forensics, receive training and education on forensic-related policies and procedures, and should be prepared to cooperate with and assist others when the technologies that they are responsible for are part of an incident or other event. IT professionals should also consult closely

with legal counsel both in general preparation for forensics activities, such as determining which actions IT professionals should and should not perform, and also on an as-needed basis to discuss specific forensics situations.

In addition, management should be responsible for supporting forensic capabilities, reviewing and approving forensic policy, and approving certain forensic actions, such as taking mission-critical systems off-line.[1]

FINAL WORDS

So when the opportunity is given for you to manage and/or set up an SIR&FT, expect a great adventure, challenge, and growth experienced for your career. As Peter Allor, FIRST[2] Steering Committee member and program manager for cyber incident and vulnerability handling for IBM said in an interview several years ago:

> AS a Manager of the SIR&FT activities in your organization make sure you have a good solid background in IT and your organization's uses of IT. You don't have to have be universal in your knowledge; you have to be conversant in what the issues are and how they impact. The key part of that is developing an understanding to the point that you can actually use the most important skill you have, communicating to the business owner what the problem is in plain, simple English.

> AS a Manager of the SIR&FT Team, look for incident handlers and forensics analysts that can communicate the essence of the problem: what it means to me and what my options are, do you have ways we can mitigate and what is that going to cost the business. It is not just a matter of cost in that it is going to take X number of dollars to remediate right now; it is a matter of what will it cost the business in the process. When can it be done? Do I have to do it immediately and therefore stop operations, or can I get through to a natural quiet period, whether it is the night, the weekend, at the end of a quarter or things of that nature.

> So you, as the SIRT Team Manager, have to really be in tune to that so understanding business is probably the next important part right behind communications. Notice I put the technical skills almost third then. That is kind of different from what most people look at in incident response because they are looking for the most technically adept, which we want in incident handlers, but when you start moving up in the career field the look that tends to rise to the surface is understanding business and communication skills.[3]

---

[1] NIST SP 800-86, 2006.

[2] Forum for Incident Response and Security Teams. www.first.org.

[3] Incident Response Essentials—Peter Allor, FIRST.org. Tom Field, Editorial Director, August 13, 2009. www.bankinfosecurity.com.

References

- Federal Information Processing Standards (FIPS) 199, *Standards for Security Categorization of Federal Information and Information Systems*, December 2003
- Federal Information Processing Standards (FIPS) 200, *Minimum Security Requirements for Federal Information and Information Systems*, March 2006
- Federal Information Security Management Act of 2002 (FISMA)
- National Institute of Standards and Technology Special Publication 800-53, rev. 4, *Recommended Security Controls for Federal Information Systems*
- National Institute of Standards and Technology Special Publication 800-61 rev. 1, *Computer Security Incident Handling Guide*, March 2008
- National Institute of Standards and Technology Special Publication 800-86, *Guide To Integrating Forensic Techniques into Incident Response*, August 2006
- Office of Management and Budget (OMB) Circular A-130, *Management of Federal Information Resources*, Appendix III, *Security of Federal Information Resources*, November 2000
- Office of Management and Budget M-06-15, *Safeguarding Personally Identifiable Information*
- Office of Management and Budget M-06-16, *Protection of Sensitive Agency Information*
- Office of Management and Budget M-06-19, *Reporting Incidents Involving Personally Identifiable Information and Incorporating the Cost for Security in Agency Information Technology Investments*
- The Privacy Act of 1974
- The Computer Fraud and Abuse Act of 1987
- *"Windows Forensics and Incident Recovery,"* Harlan Carvey, Addison-Wesley, New York, NY, 2005
- *"Incident Response: Computer Forensics Toolkit,"* Douglas Schweitzer, Wiley Publishing, Indianapolis, IN, 2003
- *"Computer Forensics: Computer Crime Scene Investigation,"* John Vacca, Charles River Media, Hingham, MA, 2002

- "Creating a CSIRT" 1 day training course, CERT/CC, Software Engineering Institute, Carnegie Mellon University, Pittsburgh, PA, 2009
- *"Intrusion Detection and Prevention,"* Carl Endorf, Eugene Schultz, Jim Mellander, McGraw-Hill, USA, 2004
- *Computer Security Incident Handling Guide: Recommendations of the National Institute of Standards and Technology,* NIST Publication 800-61 rev. 1, USA, 2008
- ISACA, *Certified Information Security Manager (CISM) Review Manual 2012,* Chapter 4, Information Security Incident Management, USA, 2012
- ISACA, *Security Incident Management Audit/Assurance Program,* USA, 2009
- *CSIRT Management,* Kabay, M.E., Self-Published, USA, 2009
- *Incident Response: A Strategic Guide to Handling System and Network Security Breaches,* Schultz, E., R. Shumway, New Riders, USA, 2002
- *"Creating a Computer Security Incident Response Team: A Process for Getting Started,"* Software Engineering Institute, CERT Coordination Center, Carnegie Mellon University, 2006
- *"Defining Incident Management Processes for CSIRTs: A Work in Progress,"* Software Engineering Institute, Carnegie Mellon University, USA, 2007
- *"Critical Incident Management,"* Sterneckert, Alan B., Auerbach, USA, 2004
- *"Managing Security Incidents in the Enterprise,"* Symantec, USA, 2003
- United States Computer Emergency Readiness Team (US-CERT)
- *"System Forensics, Investigation and Response,"* Vacca, John, K. Rudolph,
- *"Handbook for Computer Security Incident Response Teams,"* US-CERT: 2003-04-01, West-Brown, Moira J., Don Stikvoort, Klaus-Peter Kossakowski, Georgia Killcrece, Robin Ruefle, Mark Zajicek, Carnegie Mellon University, USA, 2003
- *"File System Forensic Analysis,"* Carrier, Brian, Addison-Wesley, 2005.
- *"Digital Evidence and Computer Crime,"* Casey, Eoghan, Academic Press, 2004.
- *"Computer Forensics: Incident Response Essentials,"* Kruse, Warren G., II, Jay G. Heiser, Addison-Wesley, 2001.
- *"Staffing Your Computer Security Incident Response Team—What Basic Skills Are Needed?,"* Software Engineering Institute, CERT Coordination Center, Carnegie Mellon University, 2003

INCIDENT RESPONSE ONLINE RESOURCES

Incident Detection

- US-CERT, Common Sense Guide to Prevention and Detection of Insider Threats (http://www.us-cert.gov/reading_room/prevent_detect_insiderthreat0504.pdf)
- MS-ISAC/US-CERT, Current Malware Threats and Mitigation Strategies (http://www.us-cert.gov/reading_room/malwarethreats-mitigation.pdf)

- CJCSM 6510.01 CH3: Defense-in-Depth—Information Assurance (IA) and Computer Network Defense (CND), August 14, 2006 (https://infosec. navy.mil/pub/docs/documents/dod/cjcs/cjcsm_6510_01_ch2_ch3.pdf)
- NCSD, Cyber Security Responses to Physical Security Breaches (http:// www.us-cert.gov/reading_room/cssp_cyberresponse0712.pdf)

Incident Response Team

- CERT/CC, Action List for Developing a Computer Security Incident Response Team (http://www.cert.org/csirts/action_list.html)
- CERT/CC, Staffing Your Computer Security Incident Response Team— What Basic Skills Are Needed? (http://www.cert.org/csirts/csirt-staffing. html)
- CERT/CC, Creating a Computer Security Incident Response Team: A Process for Getting Started (http://www.cert.org/csirts/Creating-A-CSIRT.html)
- Handbook for Computer Security Incident Response Teams (CSIRTs), CMU/SEI-2003-HB-002 (http://www.sei.cmu.edu/publications/ documents/03.reports/03hb002.html)

User Awareness

- US-CERT, Protect Your Workplace Campaign (http://www.uscert.gov/ reading_room/distributable.html)
- OnGuardOnline—A Consortium of the Department of Justice, Federal Trade Commission, Department of Homeland Security, US Postal Service, and Securities and Exchange Commission (www.onguardonline.gov)
- StaySafeOnline (http://www.staysafeonline.info/)

Incident Recovery

- US-CERT, Recovering from a Trojan Horse or Virus (http://www.us-cert. gov/reading_room/trojan-recovery.pdf)
- US-CERT, Computer Forensics (http://www.us-cert.gov/reading_room/ forensics.pdf)

Key Organization

- Department of Homeland Security, National Cyber Security Division, US Computer Emergency Readiness Team (US-CERT) http://www.us-cert.gov
- Multi-State Information and Analysis Center http://www.msisac.org
- Carnegie Mellon University/CERT Coordination Center http://www.cert. org/csirts/
- Information Security and Privacy Advisory Board http://csrc.nist.gov/ispab/
- National Institute of Standards and Technology, Computer Security Division http://csrc.nist.gov/
- Forum of International Response Security Teams http://www.first.org

Incident Response

- Defining Incident Management Processes: A Work in Progress (www.cert. org/archive/pdf/04tr015.pdf)
- CERT/CC, Avoiding the Trial-by-Fire Approach to Security Incidents (http://www.sei.cmu.edu/news-at-sei/columns/security_matters/1999/mar/security_matters.htm)
- NIST SP-800-86 "Guide to Integrating Forensic Techniques into Incident Response" (http://csrc.nist.gov/publications/nistpubs/800-86/SP800-86.pdf)
- National Information Assurance (IA) Approach to Incident Management (IM) (http://www.cnss.gov/Assets/pdf/CNSS-048-07.pdf)

Incident Reporting/Documentation

- NIST SP 800-61, Computer Security Incident Handling Guide (http://csrc.nist.gov/publications/nistpubs/800-61/sp800-61.pdf)
- NIST SP-800-92 "Guide to Computer Security Log Management" (http://csrc.nist.gov/publications/nistpubs/800-92/SP800-92.pdf)
- Incident Management articles (in particular CNDSP accreditation): (https://buildsecurityin.us-cert.gov/daisy/bsi/articles/best-practices/incident/223.html)
- CERT/CC, Incident Reporting Guidelines (http://www.cert.org/tech_tips/incident_reporting.html)

US Computer Emergency Readiness Team: The US-CERT, in coordination with the Office of Management and Budget (OMB), coordinates warnings among Federal departments and agencies. The US-CERT maintains a 24/7 operations center with connectivity to all major Federal cyber operations centers and private-sector Internet service providers, information-sharing mechanisms, and vendors. The US-CERT, in concert with the Homeland Security Operations Center (HSOC), acts as a focal point to collect and disseminate, to the appropriate audiences, information received from public- and private-sector sources. Also, US-CERT, as part of the Department of Homeland Security (DHS) provides technical and operational support to the IIMG, and interacts with private and public sectors on a continuous basis throughout the extent of the incident.

Department of Defense (DOD): DOD operates a network of Computer Emergency Response Teams which are staffed 24/7. These teams are coordinated by the US Cyber Command (CYBERCOM) to identify, mitigate, and, if necessary, respond to cyber-attacks. US Cyber Command (USCYBERCOM) provides continuous intelligence analysis of cyberthreats. Finally, the Law Enforcement/Counter Intelligence Center, located at the CYBERCOM, brings together DOD's law enforcement and counterintelligence organizations in response to cyber incidents.

Forensics and eDiscovery Online Resources

Computer Crime Research Center (http://www.crime-research.org/)

Computer Forensics Tool Testing (CFTT) Project (http://www.cftt.nist.gov/)

National Institute of Justice (NIJ) Electronic Crime Program (http://www.ojp.usdoj.gov/nij/topics/ecrime/welcome.html)

National Software Reference Library (NSRL) (http://www.nsrl.nist.gov/)

RFC 3227: Guidelines for Evidence Collection and Archiving (http://www.ietf.org/rfc/rfc3227.txt)

The Electronic Evidence Information Center (http://www.e-evidence.info/)

Computer Crime and Intellectual Property Section (CCIPS), US Department of Justice (http://www.cybercrime.gov/)

Federal Bureau of Investigation (FBI) (http://www.fbi.gov/)

International Association of Computer Investigative Specialists (IACIS) (http://www.cops.org/)

National White Collar Crime Center (NW3C) (http://www.nw3c.org/)

Regional Computer Forensics Laboratory (RCFL) (http://www.rcfl.gov/)

Relevant Incident Response and Forensics Publications from Governmental Agencies and Organizations

US

US Department of Commerce and National Institute of Standards and Technology (NIST) are designated as the single US governmental agency responsible for security procedures and standards development. NIST provides multiple computer security guidelines known as special publications (SP) for various computer security related requirements. NIST also provides recent research into the Forensics and Incident Response arenas through a series of publications known as Interagency Reports (IR).

NIST Special Publications

SP800-61—"Computer Security Incident Handling Guide"

The NIST SP 800-61 REV.2, entitled "Computer Security Incident Handling Guide," dated August 2012 is a very well developed and extremely well thought out document to start an incident response program development. This document covers developing an incident response capability, handling an incident, team management, and development of checklists and recommendations for various incident response requirements. This document is great for private organizations and corporations to adapt and utilize in their own environment. Always review local, national, and international organizational and governmental requirements for security policies, procedures, and guidelines.

Sections included in this volume include:

- Introduction
- Organizing a Computer Security Incident Response Capability
- Handling an Incident
- Handling Denial of Service Incidents
- Handling Malicious Code Incidents
- Handling Unauthorized Access Incidents
- Handling Inappropriate Usage Incidents
- Handling Multiple Component Incidents

SP800-72—"Guidelines on PDA Forensics"

This Special Publication was published in 2004 and provides guidance on the forensics investigative actions available for Personal Digital Assistant devices. The guide provides its summary as: "Personal Digital Assistants (PDAs) are a relatively recent phenomenon, not usually covered in classical computer forensics. This guide attempts to bridge that gap by providing an in-depth look into PDAs and explaining the technologies involved and their relationship to forensic procedures. It covers three families of devices – Pocket PC, Palm OS, and Linux-based PDAs – and the characteristics of their associated operating system. This guide also discusses procedures for the preservation, acquisition, examination, analysis, and reporting of digital information present on PDAs, as well as available forensic software tools that support those activities.

The objective of the guide is twofold: to help organizations evolve appropriate policies and procedures for dealing with PDAs, and to prepare forensic specialists to deal with new situations involving PDAs, when they are encountered. The guide is not all-inclusive nor is it a mandate for the law enforcement and incident response communities. However, from the principles outlined and other information provided, organizations should nevertheless find the guide helpful in setting policies and procedures."[1]

Sections included in this volume include:

- Introduction
- Background
- Forensics Tools
- Procedures and Principles
- Preservation
- Acquisition
- Examination and Analysis
- Reporting
- References

SP800-83—"Guide to Malware Incident Prevention and Handling for Desktops and Laptops"

NIST published SP 800-83 first in November 2005 to address the best business practices and guidance for how organizations should handle the malware (malicious software) currently being transmitted and exchanged across the Internet and found on local networks. They have recently, July 2012, published an updated revision, rev. 1, to this guide. This document covers the methods for determining malware presence, malware identification, and malware eradication from a network or computing device. Newer versions of malware are identified and discussed in the most recent revision.

---

[1] NIST SP800-72, "Guidelines on PDA Forensics," November 2004.

Sections included in this volume include:

- Introduction
- Understanding Malware Threats
- Malware Incident Prevention
- Malware Incident Response
  - Preparation
  - Detection and Analysis
  - Containment
  - Eradication
  - Recovery
  - Lessons Learned

SP800-86—"Guide to Integrating Forensic Techniques into Incident Response"

In August 2006, NIST provided a guidance document on integrating Forensics into Incident Response activities known as SP 800-86, "Guide to Integrating Forensic Techniques into Incident Response." This guidance document, as part of the NIST series of Computer Security documentation series on Best Business practices, provides detailed guides, technical analysis, and management practices for inclusion of the digital and network forensics actions into an organizational Incident Response activity. It leads off with basic ideas for how forensics and incident response work together.

"Because of the variety of data sources, digital forensic techniques can be used for many purposes, such as investigating crimes and internal policy violations, reconstructing computer security incidents, troubleshooting operational problems, and recovering from accidental system damage. Practically every organization needs to have the capability to perform digital forensics (referred to as forensics throughout the rest of the guide). Without such a capability, an organization will have difficulty determining what events have occurred within its systems and networks, such as exposures of protected, sensitive data. This guide provides detailed information on establishing a forensic capability, including the development of policies and procedures. Its focus is primarily on using forensic techniques to assist with computer security incident response, but much of the material is also applicable to other situations."

Sections included in this volume include:

- Establishing and Organizing a Forensics Capability
- Performing the Forensics Process
- Using Data from Data Files
- Using Data from Operating Systems
- Using Data from Network Traffic

- Using Data from Applications
- Using Data from Multiple Sources

SP800-88—"Guidelines for Media Sanitation"

NIST published SP 800-88 first in September 2006 to address the best business practices and guidance for how organizations should handle the media being utilized in the organization. They have recently, September 2012, published an updated draft revision, rev. 1, to this guide. This document covers the techniques and practices for ensuring media utilizing with the computing environment is monitored and controlled effectively and efficiently. Methodologies for removal, reuse, and destruction of media are included. Types of media and the best method for reuse (recycle) of the media are also included for organizations to reflect the economics of reusing media after cleaning, cleansing, and even degaussing of the particular type of media. Newer versions of media are identified and discussed in the draft revision, which should be published in its final form sometime in the next 6–12 months from the writing of this book, July 2013.

Sections included in this volume include:

- Introduction
- Background
- Roles and Responsibilities
- Information Sanitation and Disposition Decision Making
- Summary of Sanitation Techniques

SP800-92—"Guide to Computer Security Log Management"

The NIST guidance for computer log management was published in September 2006, but has remained very relevant and current since then. The guide identifies a log as a record of the events occurring within an organization's systems and networks. Logs are composed of log entries; each entry contains information related to a specific event that has occurred within a system or network. Many logs within an organization contain records related to computer security. These computer security logs are generated by many sources, including security software such as antivirus software, firewalls, and intrusion detection and prevention systems; operating systems on servers, workstations, and networking equipment; and applications. The guide provides general methods and techniques for identifying items to be logged, methods for logging of events, and mechanisms which allow for transfer, review, and reduction of log files after review. The guide recommends for organizations focusing on log management criteria to implement the following:

1. *Organizations should establish policies and procedures for log management.* Requirements and recommendations for logging should be created in conjunction with a detailed analysis of the technology and resources

needed to implement and maintain them, their security implications and value, and the regulations and laws to which the organization is subject (e.g., FISMA, HIPAA, SOX). Generally, organizations should require logging and analyzing the data that is of greatest importance, and also have nonmandatory recommendations for which other types and sources of data should be logged and analyzed if time and resources permit. The organization's policies and procedures should also address the preservation of original logs. Many organizations send copies of network traffic logs to centralized devices, as well as use tools that analyze and interpret network traffic. In cases where logs may be needed as evidence, organizations may wish to acquire copies of the original log files, the centralized log files, and interpreted log data, in case there are any questions regarding the fidelity of the copying and interpretation processes. Retaining logs for evidence may involve the use of different forms of storage and different processes, such as additional restrictions on access to the records.

2. *Organizations should prioritize log management appropriately throughout the organization.*
   The organization then should prioritize the requirements and goals based on the organization's perceived reduction of risk and the expected time and resources needed to perform log management functions. An organization should also define roles and responsibilities for log management for key personnel throughout the organization, including establishing log management duties at both the individual system level and the log management infrastructure level.

3. *Organizations should create and maintain a log management infrastructure.* A log management infrastructure consists of the hardware, software, networks, and media used to generate, transmit, store, analyze, and dispose of log data. Log management infrastructures typically perform several functions that support the analysis and security of log data. The current SIEM tools available today in the marketplace offer many options and features for log management and storage which should be investigated for the organizational applicability and use.

4. *Organizations should provide proper support for all staff with log management responsibilities.*
   To ensure that log management for individual systems is performed effectively throughout the organization, the administrators of those systems should receive adequate support. This should include disseminating information, providing training, designating points of contact to answer questions, providing specific technical guidance, and making tools and documentation available.

5. *Organizations should establish standard log management operational processes.* Major log management operational processes typically include configuring log sources, performing log analysis, initiating responses to

identified events, and managing long-term storage. These activities will include the following areas:

a. Monitoring the logging status of all log sources
b. Monitoring log rotation and archival processes
c. Checking for upgrades and patches to logging software, and acquiring, testing, and deploying them
d. Ensuring that each logging host's clock is synched to a common time source
e. Reconfiguring logging as needed based on policy changes, technology changes, and other factors
f. Documenting and reporting anomalies in log settings, configurations, and processes.

Sections included in this volume include:

- Introduction
- Introduction to Computer Security Log Management
- Log Management Infrastructure
- Log Management Planning
- Log Management Operational Processes
  - Configure Log Sources
  - Analyze Log Data
  - Respond to Identified Events
  - Manage Long-term Log Data Storage
  - Provide Other Operational Support
  - Perform Testing and Validation
  - Summary

SP800-101—"Guidelines on Cell Phone Forensics"

NIST produced this Cell Phone Forensics guide in May 2007. It states its purpose as "Mobile phone forensics is the science of recovering digital evidence from a mobile phone under forensically sound conditions using accepted methods. Mobile phones, especially those with advanced capabilities, are a relatively recent phenomenon, not usually covered in classical computer forensics. This guide attempts to bridge that gap by providing an in-depth look into mobile phones and explaining the technologies involved and their relationship to forensic procedures. It covers phones with features beyond simple voice communication and text messaging and their technical and operating characteristics. This guide also discusses procedures for the preservation, acquisition, examination, analysis, and reporting of digital information present on cell phones, as well as available forensic software tools that support those activities."[2]

---

[2] NIST SP 800-101, May 2007.

It provides guidance and techniques for cell phone and SIM Card forensics and has several organizational recommendations especially important for SIR&FT Managers:

A. **Organizations should ensure that their policies contain clear statements about forensic considerations involving cell phones.**
"The organizational cell phone forensics policy should allow authorized personnel to perform investigations of organizationally issued cell phones for legitimate reasons, under the appropriate circumstances. The forensic policy should clearly define the roles and responsibilities of the workforce and of any external organizations performing or assisting with the organization's forensic activities.

B. **Organizations should create and maintain procedures and guidelines for performing forensic tasks on cell phones.**
Guidelines should focus on general methodologies for investigating incidents using forensic techniques. While developing comprehensive procedures tailored to every possible situation is performing all routine activities in the preservation, acquisition, examination and analysis, and reporting of digital evidence found on cell phones and associated media. The guidelines and procedures should facilitate consistent, effective, accurate, and repeatable actions carried out in a forensically sound manner, suitable for legal prosecution or disciplinary actions. The guidelines and procedures should support the admissibility of evidence into legal proceedings, including seizing and handling evidence properly, maintaining the chain of custody, storing evidence appropriately, establishing and maintaining the integrity of forensic tools and equipment, and demonstrating the integrity of any electronic logs, records, and case files. The guidelines and procedures should be reviewed periodically, and also whenever significant changes in cell phone technology appear that affect them.

C. **Organizations should ensure that their policies and procedures support the reasonable and appropriate use of forensic tools for cell phones.**
Policies and procedures should clearly explain what actions are to be taken by a forensic unit under various circumstances commonly encountered with cell phones. They should also describe the quality measures to apply in verifying the proper functioning of any forensic tools used in examining cell phones and associated media. Procedures for handling sensitive information that might be recorded by forensic tools should also be addressed. Legal counsel should carefully review all forensic policy and high-level procedures for compliance with international, federal, state, and local laws and regulations, as appropriate.

D. Organizations should ensure that their forensic professionals are prepared to conduct activities in cell phone forensics.
Forensic professionals, especially first responders to incidents, should understand their roles and responsibilities for cell phone forensics and receive training and education on related forensic tools, policies, guidelines, and procedures. Forensic professionals should also consult closely with legal counsel both in general preparation for forensics activities, such as determining which actions should and should not be taken under various circumstances. In addition, management should be responsible for supporting forensic capabilities, reviewing and approving forensic policy, and examining and endorsing unusual forensic actions that may be needed in a particular situation."[3]

Sections included in this volume include:

- Introduction
- Background
- Forensics Tools
- Procedures and Principles
- Preservation
- Acquisition
- Examination and Analysis
- Reporting
- References

SP800-155—"BIOS Integrity Measurement Guidelines"

NIST produced the draft of this Special Publication in December 2001 to outline and define the security pieces, parts, and components needed to create and establish a secure Basic Input/Output System (BIOS) mechanism for integrity checking and reporting. Unauthorized modification of BIOS firmware creates a significant threat because of the BIOS's unique and privileged position within the PC architecture. SP 800-155 focuses on two scenarios: detecting changes to the system BIOS code stored on the system flash and detecting changes to the system BIOS configuration. This publication is intended for hardware and software vendors that develop products that can support secure BIOS integrity measurement mechanisms, and can be used by forensics personnel to assist in the methods and evaluations of BIOS-related issues and events discovered during response activities.

Sections included in this volume include:

- Introduction
- Background

---

[3] NIST SP 800-101, May 2007.

- BIM Functional Components
  - Roots of Trust (RoTs)
  - Integrity Attribute and Measurement Baselines
  - BIOS Integrity Reporting
  - BIOS Integrity Measurement Collection and Transmission
  - Measurement Assessment Authority
  - Remediation Activities
- Multiple Appendixes

NIST Interagency Reports

NIST Interagency or Internal Reports (NISTIRs) describe research of a technical nature of interest to a specialized audience. The series includes interim or final reports on work performed by NIST for outside sponsors (both government and nongovernment). NISTIRs may also report results of NIST projects of transitory or limited interest and are often published later on in other NIST documents in a more comprehensive form.

NIST IR 7100

This NISTIR, entitled: "PDA Forensic Tools: An Overview and Analysis," was published in August 2004 and provides an overview of current forensic software, designed for acquisition, analysis, reporting of data discovered on PDAs, and an understanding of their capabilities and limitations as of the technology level available in 2004. Additional areas were enhanced and updated when the SP 800-72 was published 2 years later.

Sections included in this volume include:

- Introduction
- Background
- Removable Media
- Synopsis of PDA Seizure
- Synopsis of Encase
- Synopsis of PDD
- Synopsis of Pilot-Link
- Synopsis of DD
- Analysis Overview
- PDA Seizure Outcome—Pocket PC
- PDA Seizure Outcome—Palm OS
- Encase Outcome—Palm OS
- Encase Outcome—Linux
- Summary
- Conclusions

NIST IR 7250

This NISTIR, entitled: "Cell Phone Forensic Tools: An Overview and Analysis," was published in October 2005 and provides an overview of current forensic software, designed for acquisition, examination, and reporting of data discovered on cellular handheld devices, and an understanding of their capabilities and limitations as of the available technology levels in 2005. Additional areas were enhanced and updated when the SP 800-101 was published 12 months later.

Sections included in this volume include:

- Introduction
- Background
- Forensics Toolkits
- Analysis Overview
- Synopsis of PDA Seizure
- Synopsis of Pilot-Link
- Synopsis of Cell Seizure
- Synopsis of GSM.XRY
- Synopsis of Oxygen Phone Manager
- Synopsis of Mobile Edit
- Synopsis of BITPIM
- Synopsis of TULP 2G
- Synopsis of SIMIS
- Synopsis of FORENSICSIM
- Synopsis of Forensic Card Reader
- Synopsis of SIMCON
- Conclusions
- Appendixes with Testing Results

NIST IR 7298 rev. 2

This NISTIR, entitled: "Glossary of Key Information Security Terms," was published at Revision 2 in May 2013 and is the compilation of the various governmental glossaries for security terms in use. This covers most of the major terms and helps define the terms in reference the US Governmental use of security terms.

NIST IR 7387

This NISTIR, entitled: "Cell Phone Forensic Tools: An Overview and Analysis," was published in March 2007 and provides an overview of current forensic software, designed for acquisition, examination, and reporting of data discovered on cellular handheld devices, and an understanding of their capabilities and limitations as of the available technology levels in 2007. It is a follow-on to *NISTIR 7250 Cell Phone Forensic Tools: An Overview and Analysis*, which focuses on tools that have undergone significant updates since that publication or were not covered previously.

Sections included in this volume include:

- Introduction
- Background
- Forensics Toolkits
- Analysis Overview
- Synopsis of Device Seizure
- Synopsis of Pilot-Link
- Synopsis of GSM.XRY
- Synopsis of Oxygen Phone Manager
- Synopsis of Mobile Edit!
- Synopsis of BITPIM
- Synopsis of TULP 2G
- Synopsis of SecureView
- Synopsis of Phonebase2
- Synopsis of CELLDEK
- Synopsis of SIMIS2
- Synopsis of FORENSICSIM
- Synopsis of Forensic Card Reader
- Synopsis of SIMCON
- Synopsis of USIMDETECTIVE
- Conclusions
- Appendixes with Testing Results

NIST IR 7490
This NISTIR, entitled: "Digital Forensics at the National Institute of Standards and Technology, Software Diagnostics and Conformance Testing," was published in April 2008 and provides an overview of three projects at NIST related to Forensics:

1. National Software Reference Library (NSRL),
2. Computer Forensic Tool Testing (CFTT),
3. Computer Forensic Reference Data Sets (CFReDS) which provides resources for the digital investigator.

These projects are supported by the US Department of Justice's National Institute of Justice (NIJ), federal, state, and local law enforcement, and the National Institute of Standards and Technology Office of Law Enforcement Standards (OLES) to promote efficient and effective use of computer technology in the investigation of crimes involving computers. Numerous other sponsoring organizations from law enforcement, government, and industry are also providing resources to accomplish these goals.

NIST IR 7516
This NISTIR, entitled: "Forensic Filtering of Cell Phone Protocols," was published in August 2008 and provides methods of usage for forensics filters on

cell phone call management systems. The NIST explanation is as follows: "Phone managers are non-forensic software tools designed to carry out a range of tasks for the user, such as reading and updating the contents of a phone, using one or more of the communications protocols supported by the phone. Phone managers are sometimes used by forensic investigators to recover data from a cell phone when no suitable forensic tool is available. While precautions can be taken to preserve the integrity of data on a cell phone, inherent risks exist. Applying a forensic filter to phone manager protocol exchanges with a device is proposed as a means to reduce risk."[4]

Sections included in this volume include:

- Introduction
- Background
- Filtering Considerations
- Phone Manager Protocol Considerations
- Nokia Phone Manager Filtering
- Motorola Phone Manager Filtering
- Conclusions
- References

NIST IR 7559

This NISTIR, entitled: "Forensics Web Services," was published in June 2010 and provided a propose to the design and architecture of a forensic web services (FWS) that would securely maintain transactional records between other web services. These secure records can be re-linked to reproduce the transactional history by an independent agency. In this report we show the necessary components of a forensic framework for web services and its success through a case study. These web services are in widespread use today and include WS-Security, SOAP, SOA, etc. Web services based on the eXtensible Markup Language (XML), Simple Object Access Protocol (SOAP), and related open standards, and deployed in Service Oriented Architectures (SOA) allow data and applications to interact without human intervention through dynamic and *ad hoc* connections.

Sections included in this volume include:

- Introduction
- Background on Web Services
- Web Service Attacks
- Challenges in Forensics of Web Services
- Overview of FWS
- Forensics Over Web Services

---

[4]NIST IR 7516, August 2008.

- Related Work
- Conclusion

NIST IR 7617

This NISTIR, entitled: "Mobile Forensic Reference Materials: A Methodology and Reification," was published in October 2009 and provides the theoretical and practical issues with automatically populating mobile devices with reference test data for use as reference materials in validation of forensic tools. It describes an application and data set developed to populate identity modules and highlights subtleties involved in the process. Intriguing results attained by recent versions of commonly used forensic tools when used to recover the populated data are also discussed. The results indicate that reference materials can be used to identify a variety of inaccuracies that exist in present-day forensic tools.

Sections included in this volume include:

- Introduction
- Background
- Forensics Reference Material
- Identity Modules
- Character Sets
- Data Structures
- Elementary Files
- Layers of Abstraction
- Application Design
- Reference Test Data
- Forensics Tool Assessments
- Handsets
- Summary
- References

NIST IR 7658

This NISTIR, entitled: "Guide to SIMfill Use and Development," was published in February 2010 and provides the following: "SIMfill is a proof-of-concept, open source, application developed by NIST to populate identity modules with test data, as a way to assess the recovery capability of mobile forensic tools. An initial set of test data is also provided with SIMfill as a baseline for creating other test cases. This report describes the design and organization of SIMfill in sufficient detail to allow informed use and experimentation with the software and test data provided, including the option to modify and extend the program and data provided to meet specific needs."[5]

---

[5] NIST IR 7658, February 2010.

Sections included in this volume include:

- Introduction
- Overview
- Installation and Operation
- Data and Schema Definitions
- Design and Implementation
- Code Modifications
- References

US-CERT Documents

Handbook for Computer Security Incident Response Teams (CSIRTs)

Carnegie Mellon University's Software Engineering Institute originally produced this document in December 1998 and last revised it in April 2003 as a guide to formulating Incident Response teams conducting Incident Response. The book states the following: "This document provides guidance on forming and operating a computer security incident response team (CSIRT). In particular, it helps an organization to define and document the nature and scope of a computer security incident handling service, which is the core service of a CSIRT. The document explains the functions that make up the service; how those functions interrelate; and the tools, procedures, and roles necessary to implement the service.

This document also describes how CSIRTs interact with other organizations and how to handle sensitive information. In addition, operational and technical issues are covered, such as equipment, security, and staffing considerations.

This document is intended to provide a valuable resource to both newly forming teams and existing teams whose services, policies, and procedures are not clearly defined or documented. The primary audience for this document is managers who are responsible for the creation or operation of a CSIRT or an incident handling service. It can also be used as a reference for all CSIRT staff, higher level managers, and others who interact with a CSIRT."[6]

Sections included in this volume include:

- **Introduction**
- **Basic Issues**
  - CSIRT Framework
  - CSIRT Services
  - Service Categories
  - Service Descriptions

---

[6] CMU/SEI-2003-HB-002 Software Engineering Institute. First release: December 1998, 2nd Edition: April 2003.

- Selection of Services
- Information Flow
- Policies
- Attributes
- Content
- Validation
- Implementation, Maintenance, and Enforcement
- Quality Assurance
- Definition of a Quality System
- Checks: Measurement of Quality Parameters
- Balances: Procedures to Assure Quality
- Constituents' View of Quality
- Adapting to Specific Needs
- The Need for Flexibility
- Legal Issues
- Institutional Regulations
- **Incident Handling Service**
  - Service Description
  - Objective
  - Definition
  - Function Descriptions
  - Availability
  - Quality Assurance
  - Interactions and Information Disclosure
  - Interfaces with Other Services
  - Priority
  - Service Functions Overview
  - Triage Function
  - Use of Tracking Numbers
  - Use of Standard Reporting Forms
  - Preregistration of Contact Information
  - Handling Function
  - Incident Life Cycle
  - Incident Analysis
  - Tracking of Incident Information
  - Announcement Function
  - Announcement Types
  - A Priori Considerations
  - Announcement Life Cycle
  - Feedback Function
  - Interactions
  - Points of Contact
  - Authentication

- Secure Communication
- Special Considerations
- Information Handling
- Information Collection
- Information Verification
- Information Categorization
- Information Storage
- Information Sanitizing and Disposal
- Prioritization Criteria
- Escalation Criteria
- Information Disclosure
- **Team Operations**
  - Fundamental Policies
  - Code of Conduct
  - Information Categorization Policy
  - Information Disclosure Policy
  - Media Policy
  - Security Policy
  - Human Error Policy
  - Continuity Assurance
  - Continuity Threats
  - Workflow Management
  - Out-Of-Hours Coverage
  - Off-Site Coverage
  - Security Management
  - Staff Issues
  - CSIRT Staff
  - Hiring Staff
  - Arrival and Exit Procedures
  - Training Staff
  - Retaining Staff
  - Extension of Staff

EU

ENISA
Good Practice Guide for Incident Management

European Network and Information Security Agency (ENISA) produced this document as guidance to the European community in 2010. This guide complements the existing set of ENISA guides that support Computer Emergency Response Teams (CERTs, also known as CSIRTs). It describes good practices and provides practical information and guidelines for the management of network and information security incidents with an emphasis on incident handling.

The main focus area of the guide is the incident handling process—the core service carried out by most CERTs—which involves the detection and registration of incidents, followed by triage (classifying, prioritizing, and assigning incidents), incident resolution, closing, and post-analysis.

The topics covered by the guide include the formal framework for a CERT, roles (who does what), workflows, basic CERT policies, cooperation, outsourcing, and reporting to management.

For a CERT in the set-up stage, this guide will provide very valuable input on how to actually shape incident management and especially the incident handling service. For existing CERTs, it can serve as a means to enhance their current services and to obtain input and ideas for improvement. The primary target audiences of this guide are CERT technical staff and management.

Sections included in this volume include:

- Management Summary
- Legal Notice
- Acknowledgements
- Introduction
- Framework

APCO—British Association of Chief Police Officers

The British Association of Chief Police Officers has produced a document entitled: "Good Practice Guide for Computer-Based Electronic Evidence," which covers the forensics guidance for the following areas within the law enforcement community:

The basic guidance provided for LEOs is well presented and straightforward in this document. Sections included in this volume include:

- The principles of computer-based electronic evidence
- Overview of computer-based electronic investigations
- Crime scenes
- Home networks & wireless technology
- Network forensics & volatile data
- Investigating personnel
- Evidence recovery
- Welfare in the workplace
- Control of paedophile images
- External consulting witnesses & forensic contractors
- Disclosure
- Retrieval of video & CCTV evidence
- Guide for mobile phone seizure & examination

Forensics Team Templates

The Forensics Team should always follow a structured documented process, wherein the content of the items to be investigated need to be preserved, validated, and documented.

Templates provide a standardized methodology to follow for each investigative event conducted by the Forensics and/or Incident Response team member. Template types include but are not limited to:

1. Evidence Capture Form

Computer Evidence Capture

Item Number(s): _____
Case: _____

To be completed by initial collector:

Evidence collected by (name): _____
Date/Time collected: _____
Evidence description: _____
_____

Describe Collection method (include operating system, utility, commands, arguments, etc): _____
_____

What application software/utility is required to view the file?: _____
_____

Where is evidence initially stored?: _____
How is evidence initially secured?: _____
Collector signature: _____ Date: _____

Copy History:

Date	Copied By	Copy Method	Disposition of original and all copies

Evidence Particulars

Evidence Hash (print name, sign & date): _____
Copy Hash (print name, sign & date): _____

Evidence Details - Type?: _____

Evidence Details - Make?: _____

Evidence Details - Model?: _____

Evidence Details – Serial Number?:_____

Were Photos Taken during Seizure?:_____

Notes on Evidence Seizure
_____
_____
_____
_____
_____
_____
_____

2. Chain of Custody Log

Incident Investigation: Chain of Custody Form

Department: _____

Use this form to record the transfer of evidence to another location and/or person.

Item _____

Incident _____

Transferred From: _____ Transferred To: _____

Date	Time	Location	Name	Signature	Organization	Location	Name	Signature	Organization

3. Device Research Form

Device Research Form			
Case Number:		Reference Number:	
Make:		Model:	
Serial #:		Size:	
Cylinders:		Heads:	
Sectors:		Jumpers:	
Volume Label:		# of Partitions:	
Mfg Datasheet	Yes/No	Mfg Date:	
Date Purchased:		Data Formatted:	
Format Type:		Format Size:	
Date Imaged:		Size Imaged:	
Hash Image		Hash Verification	
Notes			

4. Evidence Review Form

Evidence Review Form			
Case Number:		Reference Number:	
Make:		Model:	
Serial #:		Size:	
Cylinders:		Heads:	
Sectors:		Jumpers:	
Volume Label:		# of Partitions:	
Partition 1 Name:		Partition 2 Name:	
Partition 3 Name:		Partition 4 Name:	
Image SW Used:		Write Blocker Type Used:	
Time Collected:		Time Source:	
Hash Image		Hash Verification	
Notes			

There are certainly other forms which can be developed and utilized by the team members, so this is not an all-inclusive listing of possible templates for use. All templates are found on the publication website.

Attached is a sample version of a computer security BYOD policy, one of the many policies mentioned in the book.

Below is a sample BYOD policy template that organizations can adapt to suit their needs (include additional details when and where it is appropriate). Some companies may need to add sections that apply to different user groups with varying job requirements. Finally, be sure to have legal counsel review it.

Company XXX: BYOD Policy

Company XXX grants its employees the privilege of purchasing and using smartphones and tablets of their choosing at work for their convenience. Company XXX reserves the right to revoke this privilege if users do not abide by the policies and procedures outlined below.

This policy is intended to protect the security and integrity of Company XXX's data and technology infrastructure. Limited exceptions to the policy may occur due to variations in devices and platforms.

XXX employees must agree to the terms and conditions set forth in this policy in order to be able to connect their devices to the company network.

Acceptable Use

- The company defines acceptable business use as activities that directly or indirectly support the business of Company XXX.
- The company defines acceptable personal use on company time as reasonable and limited personal communication or recreation, such as reading or game playing.
- Employees are blocked from accessing certain websites during work hours/while connected to the corporate network at the discretion of the company. Such websites include, but are not limited to…

- Devices' camera and/or video capabilities are/are not disabled while on-site.

- Devices may not be used at any time to:

  o Store or transmit illicit materials

  o Store or transmit proprietary information belonging to another company

  o Harass others

  o Engage in outside business activities

  o Etc.

- The following apps are allowed: (include a detailed list of apps, such as weather, productivity apps, Facebook, etc., which will be permitted)

- The following apps are not allowed: (apps not downloaded through iTunes or Google Play, etc.)

- Employees may use their mobile device to access the following company-owned resources: email, calendars, contacts, documents, etc.

- Company XXX has a zero-tolerance policy for texting or emailing while driving and only hands-free talking while driving is permitted.

Devices and Support

- Smartphones including iPhone, Android, Blackberry and Windows phones are allowed (the list should be as detailed as necessary including models, operating systems, versions, etc.).

- Tablets including iPad and Android are allowed (the list should be as detailed as necessary including models, operating systems, versions, etc.).

- Connectivity issues are supported by IT; employees should/should not contact the device manufacturer or their carrier for operating system or hardware-related issues.

- Devices must be presented to IT for proper job provisioning and configuration of standard apps, such as browsers, office productivity software and security tools, before they can access the network.

Reimbursement

- The company will/will not reimburse the employee for a percentage of the cost of the device (include the amount of the company's contribution), or the company will contribute X amount of money toward the cost of the device.

- The company will a) pay the employee an allowance, b) cover the cost of the entire phone/data plan, c) pay half of the phone/data plan, etc.

- The company will/will not reimburse the employee for the following charges: roaming, plan overages, etc.

Security

- In order to prevent unauthorized access, devices must be password protected using the features of the device and a strong password is required to access the company network.

- The company's strong password policy is: Passwords must be at least twelve characters and a combination of upper- and lower-case letters, numbers and symbols. Passwords will be rotated every 90 days and the new password can't be one of 15 previous passwords.

- The device must lock itself with a password or PIN if it's idle for five minutes.

- After five failed login attempts, the device will lock. Contact IT to regain access.

- Rooted (Android) or jailbroken (iOS) devices are strictly forbidden from accessing the network.

- Employees are automatically prevented from downloading, installing and using any app that does not appear on the company's list of approved apps.

- Smartphones and tablets that are not on the company's list of supported devices are/are not allowed to connect to the network.

- Smartphones and tablets belonging to employees that are for personal use only are/are not allowed to connect to the network.

- Employees' access to company data is limited based on user profiles defined by IT and automatically enforced.

- The employee's device may be remotely wiped if 1) the device is lost, 2) the employee terminates his or her employment, 3) IT detects a data or policy breach, a virus or similar threat to the security of the company's data and technology infrastructure.

Risks/Liabilities/Disclaimers

- While IT will take every precaution to prevent the employee's personal data from being lost in the event it must remote wipe a device, it is the employee's responsibility to take additional precautions, such as backing up email, contacts, etc.

- The company reserves the right to disconnect devices or disable services without notification.

- Lost or stolen devices must be reported to the company within 24 hours. Employees are responsible for notifying their mobile carrier immediately upon loss of a device.

- The employee is expected to use his or her devices in an ethical manner at all times and adhere to the company's acceptable use policy as outlined above.
- The employee is personally liable for all costs associated with his or her device.
- The employee assumes full liability for risks including, but not limited to, the partial or complete loss of company and personal data due to an operating system crash, errors, bugs, viruses, malware, and/or other software or hardware failures, or programming errors that render the device unusable.
- Company XXX reserves the right to take appropriate disciplinary action up to and including termination for noncompliance with this policy.

Attached is also a sample Incident Response Plan as a template for the appropriate means to document the methods and procedures for the SIRT to follow during the course of their actions and activities.

SECURITY INCIDENT REPORT		
Report Classification:		
Report No.:	**Report Organization:**	
Report Date:	**Report Type** (initial, final, status):	
Report Generated By:	Date:	Time:
Title:	Telephone:	E-mail:
Signature:		
SECTION 1 – POC Information		
Incident Reported By:	Date:	Time:
Location:	Telephone:	E-mail:
Signature:		
ISSM Notified (Name):	Date:	Time:
Location:	Telephone:	E-mail:
Signature:		
CIO Notified (Name):	Date:	Time:
Location:	Telephone:	E-mail:
Method of Notification:		
Criminal Investigation Organization Notified (Name):		
Date:	Time:	
Office:	Telephone:	E-mail:
Method of Notification:		
SECTION 2 – Incident Information		
Date of Incident:	Time of Incident:	Ongoing?
Incident Facility Name:	Incident Facility Location:	
Affected Computer Systems (Hardware and/or Software):		

Classification of Affected Computer Systems:
Physical Location of Affected Systems:
Connections of Affected Systems to Other Systems:
Type of Incident (Data Destruction/Corruption, Data Spill, Malicious Code, Privileged User Misuse, Security Support Structure Configuration Modification, System Contamination, System Destruction/Corruption/Disabling, Unauthorized User Access, other – please identify):
Suspected Method of Intrusion/Attack:
Suspected Perpetrator(s) or Possible Motivation(s):
Apparent Source (e.g., IP address) of Intrusion/Attack:
Apparent Target/Goal of Intrusion/Attack:
Mission Impact: Success/Failure of Intrusion/Attack:
Attach technical details of incident thus far. Include as much as possible about the Detection and Identification, Containment, Eradication, and Recovery – steps taken (with date/time stamps), persons involved, files saved for analysis, etc.

<<INSERT YOUR COMPANY NAME AND/OR LOGO>>

Company Internet Access Policy

Disclaimer

The Internet is a constantly growing worldwide network of computers and servers that contain millions of pages of information. Users are cautioned that many of these pages include offensive, sexually explicit, and inappropriate material. Users are further cautioned that it is difficult to avoid at least some contact with this material while using the Internet. Even innocuous search requests may lead to sites with highly offensive content. Additionally, having an e-mail address on the Internet may lead to receipt of unsolicited e-mail containing offensive content. Employees and users (herein referred to as "Users," or "User") accessing the Internet do so at their own risk and understand and agree that <<company>> (herein referred to as "Company," or "The Company") is not responsible for material viewed or downloaded by users from the Internet. To minimize these risks, your use of the Internet at **The Company** is governed by the following policy:

Permitted Use of Internet and Company computer network

The computer network is the property of The Company and is to be used for legitimate business purposes. Users are provided access to the computer network to assist them in the performance of their jobs. Additionally, certain Users may also be provided with access to the Internet through the computer network. All Users have a responsibility to use The Company's computer resources and the Internet in a professional, lawful and ethical manner. Abuse of the computer network or the Internet, may result in disciplinary action, including possible termination, and civil and/or criminal liability.

Computer Network Use Limitations

PROHIBITED ACTIVITIES. Without prior written permission from The Company, The Company's computer network may not be used to disseminate, view or store commercial or personal advertisements, solicitations, promotions, destructive code (e.g., viruses, Trojan horse programs, etc.) or any other unauthorized materials. Occasional limited appropriate personal use of the computer is permitted if such use does not a) interfere with the User's or any other employee's job performance; b) have an undue effect on the computer or company network's performance; c) or violate any other policies, provisions, guidelines or standards of this agreement or any other of the Company. Further, at all times users are responsible for the professional, ethical and lawful use of the computer system. Personal use of the computer is a privilege that may be revoked at any time.

ILLEGAL COPYING. Users may not illegally copy material protected under copyright law or make that material available to others for copying. You are responsible for complying with copyright law and applicable licenses that may apply to software, files, graphics, documents, messages, and other material you wish to download or copy. You may not agree to a license or download any material for which a registration fee is charged without first obtaining the express written permission of the company.

COMMUNICATION OF TRADE SECRETS. Unless expressly authorized to do so, Users are prohibited from sending, transmitting, or otherwise distributing proprietary information, data, trade secrets or other confidential information belonging to The Company. Unauthorized dissemination of such material may result in severe disciplinary action as well as substantial civil and criminal penalties under State and Federal Economic Espionage laws.

Duty not to Waste or Damage Computer Resources

ACCESSING THE INTERNET. To ensure security, avoid the spread of viruses & malware, and to maintain The Company's Internet Usage Policies or Acceptable Use Policies, employees may only access the Internet through a computer attached to The Company's network and approved Internet firewall or other security device(s). Bypassing The Company's computer network security by accessing the Internet directly by personal connections such as (but not limited to) Cellular Networks, Wimax, modems, or proxy avoidance techniques or by any other means is strictly prohibited.

FRIVOLOUS USE. Computer resources are not unlimited. Network bandwidth and storage capacity have finite limits, and all Users connected to the network have a responsibility to conserve these resources. As such, Users must not deliberately perform acts that waste computer resources or unfairly monopolize resources to the exclusion of others. These acts include, but are not limited to, sending mass mailings or chain letters, spending excessive amounts of time on the Internet, playing games, engaging in online chat groups or other social media, uploading or downloading large files, accessing streaming audio and/or video files, or otherwise creating unnecessary loads on network traffic associated with non-business-related uses of the Internet.

VIRUS DETECTION. Files obtained from sources outside The Company, including disks brought from home, files downloaded from the Internet, newsgroups, bulletin boards, or other online services; files attached to e-mail, and files provided by customers or vendors, may contain dangerous computer viruses that may damage The Company's computer network. Users should never download files from the Internet, accept e-mail attachments from outsiders, or use disks from non-Company sources, without first scanning the material with Company-approved virus checking software. If you suspect that a virus has been introduced into The Company's network, notify The Company immediately.

No Expectation of Privacy

Employees are given computers and Internet access to assist them in the performance of their jobs. Employees should have no expectation of privacy in anything they create, store, post, send or receive using the company's computer equipment. The computer network is the property of The Company and may be used only for Company purposes.

Waiver of privacy rights. User expressly waives any right of privacy in anything they create, store, post, send or receive using the company's computer equipment or Internet access. User consents to allow company personnel access to and review of all materials created, stored, sent or received by User through any Company network or Internet connection.

Monitoring of computer and Internet usage. The Company has the right to monitor and log and archive any and all aspects of its Computer system including, but not limited to, monitoring Internet sites visited by Users, monitoring chat and newsgroups, monitoring file downloads, and all communications sent and received by users via Email, IM & Chat & Social Networking.

Blocking Sites With Inappropriate Content

The Company has the right to utilize hardware and software that makes it possible to identify and block access to Internet sites containing sexually explicit or other material deemed inappropriate in the workplace.

Blocking Sites With Non-productive Content

The Company has the right to utilize hardware and software that makes it possible to identify and block access to Internet sites containing non-work-related content such as (but not limited to) Drug Abuse; Hacking; Illegal or Unethical; Discrimination; Violence; Proxy Avoidance; Plagiarism; Child Abuse; Alternative Beliefs; Adult Materials; Advocacy Organizations; Gambling; Extremist Groups; Nudity and Risqué; Pornography; Tasteless; Weapons; Sexual Content; Sex Education; Alcohol; Tobacco; Lingerie and Swimsuit; Sports; Hunting; War Games; Online Gaming; Freeware and Software Downloads; File Sharing and Offsite Storage; Streaming Media; Peer-to-peer File Sharing; Internet Radio or TV; Internet Telephony; Online Shopping; Malicious Websites; Phishing; SPAM; Advertising; Brokerage and Trading; Web-Based Personal Email; Entertainment; Arts and Culture; Education; Health and Wellness; Job Search; Medicine; News and Media; Social Networking; Political Organizations; Reference; Religion; Travel; Personal Vehicles; Dynamic Content; Folklore; Web Chat; Instant Messaging or IM; Newsgroups and Message Boards; Digital Postcards; Education; Real Estate; Restaurant or Dining; Personal Websites or Blogs; Content Servers; Domain Parking; Personal Privacy; Finance and Banking; Search Engines and Portals; Government and Legal Organizations; Web Hosting; Secure Sites; or Web-based Applications.

Acknowledgement of Understanding

I have read and agree to comply with the terms of this policy governing the use of The Company's computer network. I understand that violation of this policy may result in disciplinary action, including possible termination and civil and criminal penalties.

Printed Name: _____

Signature: _____

Date: _____

<SYSTEM NAME> INCIDENT RESPONSE PLAN

INCIDENT RESPONSE PLAN (IRP)

VERSION 1.0.0

FOR

<SYSTEM NAME>

<INSERT CLIENT LOGO>

THIS PAGE INTENTIONALLY BLANK

CHANGE LOG

This record shall be maintained throughout the life of the document. Each published update shall be recorded. Revisions are a complete re-issue of entire document. A revision shall be made whenever the cumulative changes reaches ten percent (10%) of this document's content.

CHANGE / REVISION RECORD			
Date	Page/Paragraph	Description of Change	Made By:

TABLE OF CONTENTS

EXECUTIVE SUMMARY

The following table lists the <AGENCY> IA Controls that are satisfied through this artifact.

IA Control Number	IA Control Name
	Incident Response Planning

1.   OVERVIEW

<INSERT SYSTEM OVERVIEW>

The <SYSTEM NAME> Incident Response Plan (IRP) contains policies and guidelines necessary to identify and report system disruptions and security incidents. System disruptions are included since they are often the first indication of an incident.

1.1   Introduction

The <SYSTEM NAME> IRP documents the high-level procedures used to coordinate identification of system disruptions and security incidents and the steps for reporting them.

The <SYSTEM NAME> Incident Response Plan is predicated on the following processes:

- A process to protect information and information systems.

- A process of reporting incidents step-by-step.

- A process to detect attacks or intrusions.

- A restoration process to mitigate the effects of incidents and restoration of services.

- A closeout process for reporting and documenting lessons learned.

1.2   Objectives

The objective of the <SYSTEM NAME> IRP is to protect the <SYSTEM NAME> system, data stored and processed on the system, and to minimize loss or theft of information or disruption of critical computing services when incidents occur. Furthermore, this plan will include how to manage incident response according to the <AGENCY> policies.

To accomplish this objective, it is necessary to:

- Coordinate proactive activities to reduce the risk to <SYSTEM NAME> systems.

- Determine the size and trends of the security incident problem.

- Coordinate preparation for and response to disruptions and security incidents.

- Help the <SYSTEM NAME> site quickly and efficiently recover from security incidents and enable it to return to normal operation as soon as possible.

1.3   Applicability & Scope

Because every incident is different, the guidelines provided in this plan do not comprise an exhaustive set of incident handling procedures. These guidelines document basic information about responding to incidents that can be used regardless of hardware platform or operating system. This document describes the six stages of incident handling, with the focus on preparation and follow-up, including reporting guidelines and requirements.

1.4   Reporting Structure

Typically, the incident reporting community is organized into multiple levels: global, regional, and local. For the purposes of this plan, all incidents and reportable events (defined in the following "Reporting Guidelines") will be reported to the <SYSTEM NAME> Information Assurance Manager (IAM). <CLIENT NAME> personnel will not bypass the <SYSTEM NAME> structure and report to a higher authority.

2.   DEFINITIONS

2.1   Event

An event is an occurrence not yet assessed that may affect the performance of an information system and/or network. Examples of events include an unplanned system reboot, a system crash, and packet flooding within a network. Events sometimes provide indication that an incident is occurring.

2.2   Incident

An incident is an assessed occurrence having potential or actual adverse effects on the information system. A security incident is an incident or series of incidents that violate the security policy. Security incidents include penetration of computer systems, exploitation of technical or administrative vulnerabilities, and introduction of computer viruses or other forms of malicious code. Examples of security incidents include unauthorized use of another user's account, unauthorized use of system privileges, and execution of malicious code.

2.3   Security Incident Response

A security incident response outlines steps for reporting incidents and lists actions to be taken to resolve information systems security incidents and protect national security systems. Handling an incident entails forming a team with the necessary technical capabilities to resolve an incident, and contacting the appropriate sources to aid in the resolution when required, and report closeout after an incident has been resolved.

2.4   Technical Vulnerability

A technical vulnerability is a hardware, firmware, or software weakness or design deficiency that leaves a system open to potential exploitation, either externally or internally, thus increasing the risk of compromise, alteration of information, or denial of service.

2.5   Administrative Vulnerability

An administrative vulnerability is a security weakness caused by incorrect or inadequate implementation of a system's existing security features by the system administrator, security officer, or users. An administrative vulnerability is not the result of a design deficiency. It is characterized by the fact that the full correction of the vulnerability is possible through a change in the implementation of the system or the establishment of a special administrative or security procedure for the system administrators and users. Poor passwords and inadequately maintained systems are the leading causes of this type of vulnerability.

2.6   Causes of Incidents

There are at least four generic causes of computer security incidents:

- **Malicious Code.** Malicious code is software or firmware intentionally inserted into an information system for an unauthorized purpose.

- **System Failures, Procedures Failures or Improper Acts.** A secure operating environment depends upon proper operation and use of the <SYSTEM NAME>. Failure to comply with established procedures, or errors/limitations in the procedures or <SYSTEM NAME> system, can damage <SYSTEM NAME> or increase vulnerability/risk. While advances in computer technology enable the building of more security into <SYSTEM NAME>, much still depends upon the people operating and using the system. Improper acts may be differentiated from insider attack according to intent. With improper acts, someone may knowingly violate policy and procedures, but is not intending to damage the system or compromise the information it contains.

- **Intrusions or Break-Ins.** An intrusion or break-in is entry into and use of a system by an unauthorized individual.

- **Insider Attack.** Insider attacks can provide the greatest risk. In an insider attack, a trusted user or operator attempts to damage the system or compromise the information it contains.

2.7   Types of Incidents

The term "incident" encompasses the following general categories of adverse events:

- **Data Destruction or Corruption.** The loss of data integrity can take many forms including changing permissions on files so that they are writable by non-privileged users, deleting data files and or programs, changing audit files to cover-up an intrusion, changing configuration files that determine how and what data is stored and ingesting information from other sources that may be corrupt.

- **Data Compromise and Data Spills.** Data compromise is the exposure of information to a person not authorized to access that information either through clearance level or formal authorization. This could happen when a person accesses a system he is not authorized to access or through a data spill. Data spill is the release of information to another system or person not authorized to access that information, even though the person is authorized to access the system on which the data was released. This can occur through the loss of control, improper storage, improper classification, or improper escorting of media, computer equipment (with memory), and computer generated output.

- **Malicious Code.** Malicious code attacks include attacks by programs such as viruses, Trojan horse programs, worms, and scripts used by crackers/hackers to gain privileges, capture passwords, and/or modify audit logs to exclude unauthorized activity. Malicious code is particularly troublesome in that it is typically written to masquerade its presence and, thus, is often difficult to detect. Self-replicating malicious code such as viruses and worms can replicate rapidly, thereby making containment an especially difficult problem.

- **Virus Attack.** A virus is a variation of a Trojan horse. It is propagated via a triggering mechanism (e.g., event time) with a mission (e.g., delete files, corrupt data, send data). Often self-replicating, the malicious program segment may be stand-alone or may attach itself to an application program or other executable system component in an attempt to leave no obvious signs of its presence.

- **Worm Attack.** A computer worm is an unwanted, self-replicating autonomous process (or set of processes) that penetrates computers using automated hacking techniques. A worm spreads using communication channels between hosts. It is an independent program that replicates from machine to machine across network connections often clogging networks and computer systems.

- **Trojan Horse Attack.** A Trojan horse is a useful and innocent program containing additional hidden code that allows unauthorized computer network exploitation (CNE), falsification, or destruction of data.

- **System Contamination.** Contamination is defined as inappropriate introduction of data into a system not approved for the subject data (i.e., data of a higher classification or of an unauthorized formal category).

- **Privileged User Misuse.** Privileged user misuse occurs when a trusted user or operator attempts to damage the system or compromise the information it contains.

- **Security Support Structure Configuration Modification.** Software, hardware and system configurations contributing to the Security Support Structure (SSS) are controlled since they are essential to maintaining the security policies of the system. Unauthorized modifications to these configurations can increase the risk to the system.

Note: These categories of incidents are not necessarily mutually exclusive.

2.8   Avenues of Attack

Attacks originate through certain avenues or routes. If a system were locked in a vault with security personnel surrounding it, and if the system were not connected to any other system or network, there would be virtually no avenue of attack. More typically, however, there are numerous avenues of attack.

The following list outlines these avenues of attack:

- Local networks.

- Illegally-connected devices (including non-approved connections to a local network).

- Gateways to outside networks.

- Communications devices (e.g., modems).

- Shared disks.

- Downloaded software.

- Direct physical access.

2.9   Effects of an Attack

There are at least four effects of attacks that compromise computer security:

- **Denial of Service.** Any action that causes all or part of the network's service to be stopped entirely, interrupted, or degraded sufficiently to impact operations. Examples of denial of service include network jamming, introducing fraudulent packets, and system crashes and/or poor system performance, in which people are unable to effectively use computing resources.

- **Loss or Alteration of Data or Programs.** An example of loss or alteration of data or programs would be an attacker who penetrates a system, then modifies an Operating System-level program/configuration file (e.g., audit) so that the intrusion will not be detected.

- **Compromise of Protected Data.** One of the major dangers of a computer security incident is that information may be compromised. The release of classified information to people without the proper clearance or formal authorization jeopardizes our nation's security. Efficient incident handling minimizes this danger.

- **Loss of Trust in Computing Systems.** Users may lose trust in computing systems and become hesitant to use one that has a high frequency of incidents or even a high frequency of events that cause the user to distrust availability or integrity.

3.   ROLES AND RESPONSIBILITIES

<CLIENT NAME> is responsible for reporting any suspected intrusion to the <SYSTEM NAME> IAM. This ensures that appropriate <AGENCY> policies are followed, as they would if the system were hosted on an <AGENCY> network. Below are those responsibilities related specifically to the handling of an incident. In addition, this document outlines the responsibilities of the user, IAM and Auditor in handling an incident.

3.1   <SYSTEM NAME> Users

Computer users are nearly always most effective in discovering intrusions that occur. Despite the advances in automated intrusion detection systems, the end users detect most computer incidents. Users need to be vigilant for unusual system behavior that may indicate a security incident in progress.

Users are responsible for:

- Reporting all suspected <SYSTEM NAME> security violations immediately to the <SYSTEM NAME> IAM.

- Reporting any suspected compromise, component failure, abnormal system behavior, or vulnerability to the <SYSTEM NAME> system Administrator.

- Complying with the site's <SYSTEM NAME> security policies and procedures.

3.2   System Administrator & Network Administrators

SAs are responsible for the operational readiness and secure state of the computer systems, including:

- Reporting all suspected <SYSTEM NAME> security violations immediately to the <SYSTEM NAME> IAM.

- Advising the <SYSTEM NAME> IAM of security anomalies and vulnerabilities associated with the information system.

- Providing potential means of fixing identified vulnerabilities.

- Participating in the information system security incident reporting program.

- Coordinating with the <SYSTEM NAME> IAM to investigate and resolve security problems.

3.3   Information System Security Officer (ISSO)

<CLIENT NAME> has appointed an in-house ISSO that is responsible for information system security for the deployed <SYSTEM NAME> system. The <CLIENT NAME> ISSO is the first level of interaction for users experiencing security incidents. It is the <CLIENT NAME> ISSO's responsibility to coordinate incoming information, advise users on handling low-level security incidents, pass information up through the appropriate chain, and disseminate information downwards as appropriate.

The ISSO's responsibilities include:

- Reporting all security incidents to the IAM.

- Coordinating reporting with IAM to Approving Authority (AA) and notification to the AA of systems which may be affected.

- Reporting security incidents or deviation of security practices in accordance with site-specific requirements.

- Notifying the appropriate personnel and/or agencies of an incident, and requesting assistance when necessary.

- Reviewing and analyzing security-related events and security violations or failures.

- Investigating all actual security violations (with appropriate technical assistance) to determine the cause and the actions required to prevent recurrence.

- Generating an incident report for each security incident.

- Cooperating with and supporting the conduct of investigations of incidents conducted by authorized law enforcement authorities.

- Evaluating known vulnerabilities to determine whether additional safeguards are needed.

- Establishing definitions for types of incidents that should be reported by category and priority according to <AGENCY> policies.

- Coordinating with site security and following site Incident Reporting Procedures.

3.4   <SYSTEM NAME> Information Assurance Manager

The <SYSTEM NAME> IAM is responsible for the administration and management of the organization's computer security program, and is the focal point for all organizational information systems security concerns.

The <SYSTEM NAME> IAM:

- Passing incoming incident information from the ISSOs to network management and service/agency levels in a timely fashion.

- Advising the commanding officer in the event of a serious security incident, and coordinating the response with security personnel.

- Implementing the overall information system security program

- Ensuring that all information systems security related incidents and violations are immediately reported, properly investigated, and correctly resolved.

- Coordinating all targeted monitoring activity to include appropriate notification to the General Counsel and SSO for the system being monitored. During targeted monitoring activities, extreme care must be exercised in conducting targeted monitoring as a response to an incident or suspected incident to ensure that evidence is not destroyed, innocent personnel are not implicated, and the subject does not become aware of a planned monitoring activity.

- Gathering data, performing analysis and applying principles, procedures and methodologies to assist the investigating personnel in resolving problems.

- Collecting audit records from the local <SYSTEM NAME> components, and reviewing and retaining the local security audit trail.

- Appointing Security Incident Response Teams (SIRTs).

One of the most critical facets of responding to incidents is being prepared to respond *before* an incident occurs. Without adequate preparation, it is very likely that response efforts will be disorganized and that there will be considerable confusion among personnel. Preparation limits the potential for damage by ensuring responsible actions are known and coordinated. Planning for this preparation is an integral portion of setting the security policy.

3.5   Conducting Training

Training is an important part of protection. A workshop on responding to incidents can be one of the most valuable ways to help personnel at an organization learn how to handle incidents. Personnel should also be required to participate in periodic mock incidents in which written incident response procedures are followed for simulated incidents. For example, conduct "dry runs," in which, computer security personnel, system administrators, and managers simulate handling an incident. A major incident is not the time to discover that preparations and procedures are incomplete.

3.6   Reporting Responsibilities

3.6.1   <CLIENT NAME> ISSO/<SYSTEM NAME> IAM

- Report all known or suspected security weaknesses and incidents, including unauthorized disclosures of information.

- During the course of investigations, if targeted monitoring is required the <SYSTEM NAME> IAM must ensure caution and care are exercised in carrying these activities and proper logs and records are maintained.

- Ensure the proper review and integrity of audit trails

- Cooperate with the investigating forensic team.

4.   REPORTING GUIDELINES

Any user noticing anomalous or suspicious activity (incident or reportable event) will report the situation **immediately** to the <CLIENT NAME> ISSO, who will immediately notify the <SYSTEM NAME> IAM. The following table contains a list of Critical Items of Information (CII) that are a set of specific operational reporting criteria that enumerate unauthorized results, deemed by <AGENCY> to be the best indicators of an incident having strategic significance. CII are divided into priority 1 and 2 categories and will be periodically modified and updated to reflect, for example, a specific threat organization, vulnerability, virus, etc. The following table lists examples of reportable incident and event priorities for reporting the information to the <SYSTEM NAME> IAM.

Priority	Reportable Incident or Event
1	<ul><li>Any intrusion into a classified network with a perceived unauthorized result.</li><li>Any ongoing unauthorized privileged user, administrator, or root level access of a <AGENCY> System.</li><li>Any indications of Denial of Service or Distributed Denial of Service attacks.</li><li>Any new virus or worm for which no published countermeasure exists, any new virus whose propagation could likely outrun <AGENCY> containment capabilities, or any new virus that affects network services (e.g., E-mail and domain name system (DNS) services).</li><li>Any root level access on a system using new methods that exploit significant vulnerabilities shared by <AGENCY> systems.</li><li>Any incident involving a second level domain web server (e.g., www.<AGENCY>.com, etc.)</li><li>Any incident that negatively impacts ongoing <AGENCY> operations.</li></ul>
2	<ul><li>Any incident(s) that cross corporate boundaries.</li><li>Any intrusion of the corporate networks.</li><li>Any intrusion of a tactical or deployed operational network.</li></ul>

4.1 Incident Categories

Incidents reported to the <SYSTEM NAME> IAM shall be categorized according to the framework outlined in the following table:

Category	Description
0	**Exercise or Red Team Activity**
1	**Root Level Intrusion:** An unauthorized person completely controlled (root level) a <AGENCY> computer
2	**User Level Intrusion:** An unauthorized person gained user level privileges on a <AGENCY> computer
3	**Attempted Access:** An unauthorized person specifically targeting a service/ vulnerability on a <AGENCY> computer in order to gain unauthorized or increased access/privileges, but is denied access
4	**Denial of Service:** Use of a <AGENCY> computer or computer system is denied due to an overwhelming volume of unauthorized traffic
5	**Poor Security Practice:** A <AGENCY> computer was incorrectly configured or a user did not follow established policy
6	**Scan/Probe:** Open ports on a <AGENCY> computer were scanned with no DOS or mission impact
7	**Malicious Logic:** Hostile code successfully **infected** a <AGENCY> computer. Unless otherwise directed, only those computers that were infected will be reported as a Category 7 incident.
8	Unknown/ To Be Defined

4.2   Responding to an Incident

There are generally six stages of response:

- Preparation – one of the most important facilities to a response plan is to know how to use it once it is in place. Knowing how to respond to an incident BEFORE it occurs can save valuable time and effort in the long run.

- Identification – identify whether or not an incident has occurred. If one has occurred, the response team can take the appropriate actions.

- Containment – involves limiting the scope and magnitude of an incident. Because so many incidents observed currently involve malicious code, incidents can spread rapidly. This can cause massive destruction and loss of information. As soon as an incident is recognized, immediately begin working on containment.

- Eradication – removing the cause of the incident can be a difficult process. It can involve virus removal, conviction of perpetrators, or dismissing employees.

- Recovery – restoring a system to its normal business status is essential. Once a restore has been performed, it is also important to verify that the restore operation was successful and that the system is back to its normal condition.

- Follow-up – some incidents require considerable time and effort. It is little wonder, then, that once the incident appears to be terminated there is little interest in devoting any more effort to the incident. Performing follow-up activity is, however, one of the most critical activities in the response procedure. This follow- up can support any efforts to prosecute those who have broken the law. This includes changing any company policies that may need to be narrowed down or be changed altogether.

4.3   Organization

To adequately respond to an intrusion or incident, predetermined teams will participate depending on the incident characteristics. As the situation develops and the impact becomes more significant, the various teams will be called to contribute. The following figure depicts the <SYSTEM NAME> Incident Response organization.

<SYSTEM NAME> INCIDENT RESPONSE PLAN

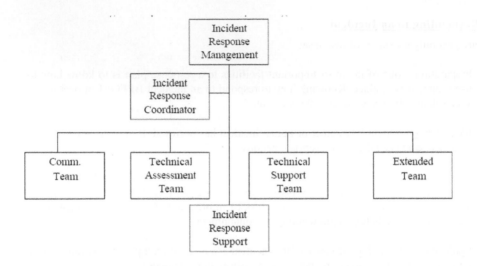

4.3.1   Escalation Levels

The escalation process will be invoked, as the severity level increases, to involve appropriate resources. Incidents will be handled at the lowest escalation level that is capable of responding to the incident with as few resources as possible in order to reduce the total impact, and to keep tight control. The following table defines the escalation levels with the associated team involvement.

Escalation Level	Affected Team (s)	Description
0	• Technical Assessment Team	Normal Operations. Engineering groups monitoring for alerts from various sources
1	• Technical Assessment Team • Incident Response Coordinator • Communication Team	A threat has been discovered, determine defensive action to take. Message employees of required actions if necessary.
2	• Incident Response Management • Incident Response Coordinator • Technical Assessment Team • Technical Support Team	A threat has manifested itself. Determine course of action for containment and eradication. Message employees of required

	• Communications Team	actions if necessary.
3	• Incident Response Management • Incident Response Coordinator • Extended Team • Technical Assessment Team • Technical Support Team • Communications Team • Incident Response Support Team	Threat is wide spread or impact is significant. Determine course of action for containment and eradication. Message employees. Prepare to take legal action for financial restitution etc.

4.4   Incident Response Process

The Incident Response Process is an escalation process where as the impact of the incident becomes more significant or wide spread, the escalation level increases bringing more resources to bear on the problem. At each escalation level, team members who will be needed at the next higher level of escalation are alerted to the incident so that they will be ready to respond if and when they are needed. The following figure depicts the over all process, while paragraph 4.4.1 outlines the roles and responsibilities of the individual teams.

<SYSTEM NAME> INCIDENT RESPONSE PLAN

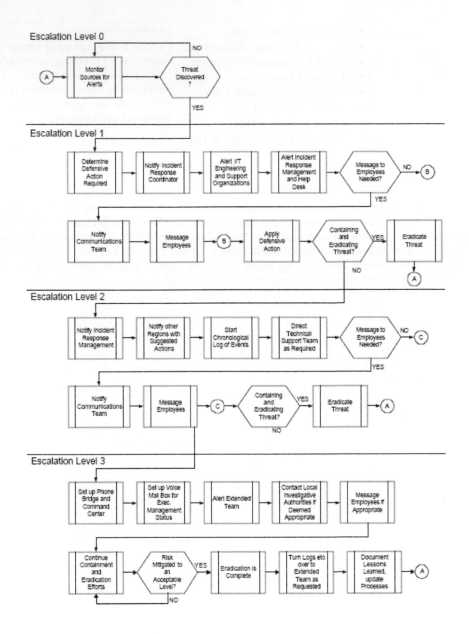

4.4.1   Incident Response Team Roles and Responsibilities

Escalation Level 0

- Technical Assessment Team
  1. Monitors all known sources for alerts or notification of a threat.

Escalation Level 1 -- A Possible threat has been discovered.

- Technical Assessment Team
  1. Determine initial defensive action required,
  2. Notify the Incident Coordinator,
  3. If employee action required such as updating anti- virus files, notify the Help Desk.

- Incident Coordinator
  1. Receive and track all reported potential threats,
  2. Escalate Incident Response to Level 2 if a report is received indicating that the threat has manifested itself,
  3. Determine relevant membership of the Technical Assessment and Technical Support teams,
  4. Alert I/T engineering organizations and applicable support organizations of the potential threat and any defensive action required,
  5. Alert Incident Response Management of the potential threat,
  6. Alert the Communication team.

- Communications Team
  1. If employee action required, message employees of required action.

Escalation Level 2 -- The threat has manifested itself.

- Incident Coordinator
  1. Notify Incident Response Management of the manifestation of the threat,
  2. Alert the Incident Response Support Team of the incident,
  3. Alert the Extended Team,
  4. Receive status from the Technical Assessment Team and report to Incident Response Management,
  5. Start a chronological log of events.

- Technical Assessment Team
  1. Determine best course of action for containment of the incident,
  2. Notify the Technical Support Team of any action that is required,
  3. Report actions taken and status to the Incident Response Coordinator.
- Incident Response Management
  1. Assume responsibility for directing activities in regards to the incident,

      2. Determine whether Escalation Level 2 is appropriate or escalate to level 3,

      3. Determine when the risk has been mitigated to an acceptable level.

- Technical Support Team
  1. Take what ever action as determined by the Technical Assessment Team
  2. Report actions taken, number of personnel involved etc. to Incident Coordinator for the chronological log

- Communications Team
  1. Message the <SYSTEM NAME> employee population informing them of the incident if deemed appropriate by Incident Response Management,
  2. Message the <SYSTEM NAME> employee population of any action they need to take as determined by the Technical assessment team and directed by Incident Response Management

Escalation Level 3 -- The threat has become widespread or has become a high severity level.

- Incident Response Management
  1. Direct the Incident Response Support team to:
     - i. Set up communications between all Incident Response Team Managers, and the Technical Support Team in the field,
     - ii. Assume occupancy of the command center.
     - iii. Initialize an incident voice mail box where status messages can be placed to keep <SYSTEM NAME> personnel statused.
  2. Alert the Extended Team of the incident notifying them of the Severity Level,
  3. Determine when the risk has been mitigated to an acceptable level,
  4. Status Executive Management as appropriate.

- Extended Team
  1. Contact local authorities if deemed appropriate,
  2. If local authorities are called in, make arrangements for them to be allowed into the command center
  3. Ensure that all needed information is being collected to support legal action or financial restitution.

- Incident Response Coordinator
  1. Continue maintaining the Chronological Log of Events,
  2. Post numbered status messages in the incident voice mail box for statusing <SYSTEM NAME> executive management.

- Communication Team

1. Message the <SYSTEM NAME> population as directed by Incident Response Management

- Technical Assessment Team
    1. Continue to monitor all know sources for alerts looking for further information or actions to take to eliminate the threat,
    2. Continue reporting status to the Incident Response Coordinator for the chronological log of events,
    3. Monitor effectiveness of actions taken and modify them as necessary,
    4. Status Incident Response Management on effectiveness of actions taken and progress in eliminating the threat,

- Technical Support Team
    1. Continue actions to eradicate the threat as directed by Incident Response Management and the Technical Assessment team,
    2. Continue to report actions taken, number of personnel etc. to the Incident Response Coordinator for the chronological log.

Post Incident
- Incident Response Management
    1. Prepare a report for <SYSTEM NAME> Executive Management to
    2. include:
        i. Estimate of damage/impact,
        ii. Action taken during the incident (not technical detail),
        iii. Follow on efforts needed to eliminate or mitigate the vulnerability,
        iv. Policies or procedures that require updating,
        v. Efforts taken to minimize liabilities or negative exposure.
    3. Provide the chronological log and any system audit logs requested by the
    4. Extended Team,
    5. Document lessons learned and modify the Incident Response Plan accordingly.

- Extended Team
    1. Legal and Finance work with the local authorities as appropriate in the case that the incident was from an external source,
    2. HR and Corp. Security work with [Company/Agency Name] management to determine disciplinary action in the case that the incident was from an internal source.

4.5 Response Timeline

After an incident has been identified, <SYSTEM NAME> personnel will utilize the following table as guidance for reporting the event.

Category	Reporting Timeline	Method of Reporting
1	Use reporting timelines outlined for Category 1-7 that exercise or red team activity is replicating	Telephone E-mail Approved methods
2	Ongoing: 1 hour from detection. Existing: 24 hours following validation by <SYSTEM NAME>.	Telephone E-mail Approved methods
3	48 hours following validation by <SYSTEM NAME>.	E-mail Approved methods
4	Ongoing: 10 minutes following start of activity. Event in Progress: Follow up report 1 hour after initial report. Additional reports shall be made on a schedule not to exceed 3 hours. Closeout Report: 48 hours after cessation of DOS.	Telephone E-mail Approved methods
5	48 hours following validation by <SYSTEM NAME>.	E-mail Approved methods
6	Major: 10 minutes from detection. Minor/Routine: 24 hours following validation by <SYSTEM NAME>.	Telephone E-mail Approved methods
7	Major (outbreak in progress): 10 minutes after detection. Minor (individual systems infected, no large	Telephone E-mail

	outbreak): 24 hours following validation by <SYSTEM NAME>.	Approved methods
8	Ongoing: 1 hour from detection. Existing: 24 hours following validation by <SYSTEM NAME>.	Telephone E-mail Approved methods

<SYSTEM NAME> INCIDENT RESPONSE PLAN

Appendix A

Incident Response Worksheet

SECURITY INCIDENT REPORT	
Report Classification:	
Report No.:	**Report Organization:**
Report Date:	**Report Type** (initial, final, status):
Report Generated By:	Date: Time:
Title: Telephone: E-mail:	
Signature:	
SECTION 1 – POC Information	
Incident Reported By: Date: Time:	
Location: Telephone: E-mail:	
Signature:	
ISSM Notified (Name): Date: Time:	
Location: Telephone: E-mail:	
Signature:	
CIO Notified (Name): Date: Time:	
Location: Telephone: E-mail:	
Method of Notification:	
Criminal Investigation Organization Notified (Name):	
Date: Time:	
Office: Telephone: E-mail:	
Method of Notification:	
SECTION 2 – Incident Information	

Date of Incident:	Time of Incident:	Ongoing?
Incident Facility Name:	Incident Facility Location:	
Affected Computer Systems (Hardware and/or Software):		
Classification of Affected Computer Systems:		
Physical Location of Affected Systems:		
Connections of Affected Systems to Other Systems:		
Type of Incident (Data Destruction/Corruption, Data Spill, Malicious Code, Privileged User Misuse, Security Support Structure Configuration Modification, System Contamination, System Destruction/Corruption/Disabling, Unauthorized User Access, other – please identify):		
Suspected Method of Intrusion/Attack:		
Suspected Perpetrator(s) or Possible Motivation(s):		
Apparent Source (e.g., IP address) of Intrusion/Attack:		
Apparent Target/Goal of Intrusion/Attack:		
Mission Impact:	Success/Failure of Intrusion/Attack:	
Attach technical details of incident thus far. Include as much as possible about the Detection and Identification, Containment, Eradication, and Recovery – steps taken (with date/time stamps), persons involved, files saved for analysis, etc.		

The following table lists possible questions that may need to be answered during an investigation.

SAMPLE INFORMATION THAT MAY BE NEEDED	
1.	What event(s) triggered suspicion of improper system use?
2.	Does the system have a warning banner? Is the banner displayed prior to the first keystroke?
3.	Where the hardware is physically located?
4.	What level of classified data is processed on the system?
5.	What organization/activity is supported by the system?
6.	What connectivity's are authorized to the system?
7.	What is the function of the system?
8.	What security software, if any, is used on the system?
9.	Are audit trails running normally and have they been reviewed regularly?
10.	Is a copy of the SSP available?

<SYSTEM NAME> INCIDENT RESPONSE PLAN

(U//)

Section 1

INCIDENT RESPONSE POLICY

VERSION 0.X

DOCUMENT CHANGE HISTORY

Date	Filename / Version #	Author	Revision Description

DOCUMENT REVIEW HISTORY

Date	Version #	Reviewers

TABLE OF CONTENTS

1 INTRODUCTION

1.1 BACKGROUND

The (AGENCY) requires agencies to adopt a minimum set of security controls to protect their information and information systems. The Federal Information Processing Standards (FIPS) 200, *Minimum Security Requirements for Federal Information and Information Systems*, specifies the minimum security requirements for federal information and information systems. The (AGENCY) is responsible for ensuring that all (AGENCY) information systems meet the minimum security requirements defined in FIPS 200 through the use of the security controls provided in the National Institute of Standards and Technology (NIST) Special Publication (SP) 800-53, *Recommended Security Controls for Federal Information Systems*. The Department developed the incident response policy and procedures to ensure controls are properly implemented and maintained. The incident response process is centered on the preparation, detection and analysis, containment, eradication, and recovery, and post incident activity. The incident response controls are listed and their implementation status specified in the System Security Plan (SSP).

1.2 PURPOSE

This policy establishes uniform policies, authorities, responsibilities, and compliance for incident response in (AGENCY). It also provides guidance for incident response in accordance with NIST SP 800-53 and 800-61.

1.3 SCOPE AND APPLICABILITY

The provisions of this policy pertain to all (AGENCY) information systems. Agency senior management shall ensure that information systems operated by or on behalf of the Department receive adequate security equivalent to the safeguards required of systems operated internally to the Department. Systems under development must meet the security planning requirements commensurate with the sensitivity of the information they house and the current life cycle phase in accordance with the *(AGENCY) System Development Life Cycle* (SDLC).

1.4 AUTHORITY

This policy is issued under the authority of the *(AGENCY)*. The most critical laws, regulations, Executive Orders, and directives pertaining to incident response and the protection of information system resources are indicated below. References to the full list of statutes, federal regulations, directives, and NIST publications applicable to IT security in (AGENCY) are located in the *{relevant documents}*.

- Federal Financial Management Improvement Act of 1996 (FFMIA)
- Federal Information Processing Standards (FIPS) 199, *Standards for Security Categorization of Federal Information and Information Systems*, December 2003
- Federal Information Processing Standards (FIPS) 200, *Minimum Security Requirements for Federal Information and Information Systems*, March 2006
- Federal Information Security Management Act of 2002 (FISMA)
- National Institute of Standards and Technology Special Publication 800-53, *Recommended Security Controls for Federal Information Systems*
- National Institute of Standards and Technology Special Publication 800-61, *Computer Security Incident Handling Guide*
- Office of Management and Budget (OMB) Circular A-130, *Management of Federal Information Resources*, Appendix III, *Security of Federal Information Resources*, November 2000
- Office of Management and Budget M-06-15, *Safeguarding Personally Identifiable Information*
- Office of Management and Budget M-06-16, *Protection of Sensitive Agency Information*
- Office of Management and Budget M-06-19, *Reporting Incidents Involving Personally Identifiable Information and Incorporating the Cost for Security in Agency Information Technology Investments*
- The Privacy Act of 1974

1.5 POLICY

1.5.1 INCIDENT RESPONSE

Incident response controls must be established and applied to all (AGENCY) information systems. The appropriate incident response capabilities, procedures, and mechanisms must be defined and developed during the Planning & Requirements Definition Phase of the system development life cycle, and updated and maintained throughout the remaining life cycle phases for the system in accordance with the SDLC. According to procedures and standards set forth by the Department, the information system must follow such established requirements on incident response training, testing, handling, monitoring, reporting, and response assistance. All (AGENCY) agencies shall review the incident response controls on an annual basis when the self-assessments are performed. Additionally, preventative measures must be taken to comply with OMB M-06-16 in regards to protecting personally identifiable information (PII).

1.6 ROLES AND RESPONSIBILITIES

Roles and responsibilities for incident response within (AGENCY) are identified below:

1.6.1 CHIEF INFORMATION OFFICER (CIO)

The Chief Information Officer has the following responsibilities with respect to incident response:

- Designates a Chief Information Security Officer (CISO) who shall carry out the CIO's responsibilities for incident response for the information system.

1.6.2 CHIEF INFORMATION SECURITY OFFICER (CISO)

The Chief Information Security Officer has the following responsibilities with respect to incident response:

- Carries out the CIO's responsibilities for incident response;
- Develops and maintains information security policies, procedures, and control techniques to address incident response;
- In coordination with (agency) Computer Security Incident Response Team (CSIRT), determine affective steps and resources in responding to incidents; and
- Through management of the Office of the Chief Information Officer (OCIO) Security, performs oversight of agency compliance with Departmental information incident response policy and procedures.

1.6.3 AUTHORIZING OFFICIAL (AO)

The Authorizing Official has the following responsibilities with respect to incident response:

- Approves the incident response controls contained within the SSPs as part of the certification and accreditation (C&A) process.

1.6.4 INFORMATION SECURITY OFFICER (ISO)

The Information Security Officer has the following responsibilities with respect to incident response:

- Plays an active role in coordinating the development and update of agency incident response plans and associated SSPs incident response controls; and
- Coordinate with the system owner any changes to the system and assessing the security impact of those changes.

1.6.5 SYSTEM OWNER

The System Owner serves as the overall responsible authority for the procurement, development, integration, modification, or operation and maintenance of the information system. The System Owner or System Owner Designee (designated in writing) has the following responsibilities with respect to incident response:

- Authorizes access to the information system and the types of privileges or access rights;
- Updates the incident response controls in the SSP whenever a significant change occurs or every three years at a minimum; and
- Implements the incident response controls.

1.6.6 SYSTEM USERS

(AGENCY) information system users are expected to review and comply with the policies, procedures, and standards for incident response.

1.7 COMPLIANCE

Compliance with this policy is mandatory. It is (AGENCY) policy that Department personnel and information systems abide by or exceed the requirements outlined in this policy and subsequent procedures. (AGENCY) Security will periodically assess agency adherence with this policy through various oversight and compliance measures.

In cases where an agency cannot comply with this policy for technical or financial reasons, or because it precludes an agency from supporting its mission or business function, justifications for non-compliance must be documented using the policy exemption process and submitted to the (AGENCY) for approval. Refer to the *{relevant documentation},* for template outline and instructions on the policy exemption process. Resulting risks from this deviation must be documented in the appropriate risk management and security planning documentation. Systems failing to meet minimum security planning requirements may be severely restricted in their operational readiness and availability.

APPENDIX A: ACRONYMS

C&A	Certification and Accreditation
CIO	Chief Information Officer
CISO	Chief Information Security Officer
DAA	Designated Approving Authority (Authorizing Official)
FFMIA	Federal Financial Management Improvement Act
FIPS	Federal Information Processing Standards
FISMA	Federal Information Security Management Act of 2002
ISO	Information Security Officer
NIST	National Institute of Standards and Technology
SDLCMM	System Development Life Cycle
SP	Special Publication
SSP	System Security Plan

Information Security

Incident Response Plan

Agency:

Date:

Contact:

TABLE OF CONTENTS

Introduction

Note to agencies – The purpose of an information security incident response program is to ensure the effective response and handling of security incidents that affect the availability, integrity, or confidentiality of agency information assets. In addition, an incident response program will ensure information security events, incidents and vulnerabilities associated with information assets and information systems are communicated in a manner enabling timely corrective action.

This template is intended to be a guide to assist in the development of an agency incident response plan, one component of an incident response program. Agencies may have various capacities and business needs affecting the implementation of these guidelines. This information security incident response plan template was created to align with the statewide Information Security Incident Response Policy 107-004-xxx.

ORS 182.122 requires agencies to develop the capacity to respond to incidents that involve the security of information. Agencies must implement forensic techniques and remedies, and consider lessons learned. The statute also requires reporting incidents and plans to the Enterprise Security Office. The Oregon Consumer Identity Theft Protection Act (ORS 646A.600) requires agencies to take specific actions in cases where compromise of personally identifiable information has occurred. This plan addresses these requirements.

The <agency> has developed this Information Security Incident Response Plan to implement its incident-response processes and procedures effectively, and to ensure that <agency> employees understand them. The intent of this document is to:

- o describe the process of responding to an incident,
- o educate employees, and
- o build awareness of security requirements.

An incident response plan brings together and organizes the resources for dealing with any event that harms or threatens the security of information assets. Such an event may be a malicious code attack, an unauthorized access to information or systems, the unauthorized use of services, a denial of service attack, or a hoax. The goal is to facilitate quick and efficient response to incidents, and to limit their impact while protecting the state's information assets. The plan defines roles and responsibilities, documents the steps necessary for effectively and efficiently managing an information security incident, and defines channels of communication. The plan also prescribes the education needed to achieve these objectives.

Authority

Statewide information security policies:

Policy Number	Policy Title	Effective Date
107-004-050	Information Asset Classification	1/31/2008
107-004-051	Controlling Portable and Removable Storage Devices	7/30/2007
107-004-052	Information Security	7/30/2007
107-004-053	Employee Security	7/30/2007
107-004-100	Transporting Information Assets	1/31/2008
107-004-110	Acceptable Use of State Information Assets	10/16/2007
107-004-xxx	Information Security Incident Response	draft

<agency> information security policies:

Policy Number	Policy Title	Effective Date

Terms and Definitions

Note to agencies –Agencies should adjust definitions as necessary to best meet their business environment.

Asset: Anything that has value to the agency

Control: Means of managing risk, including policies, procedures, guidelines, practices or organizational structures, which can be of administrative, technical, management, or legal nature

Incident: A single or a series of unwanted or unexpected information security events (see definition of "information security event") that result in harm, or pose a significant threat of harm to information assets and require non-routine preventative or corrective action.

Incident Response Plan: Written document that states the approach to addressing and managing incidents.

Incident Response Policy: Written document that defines organizational structure for incident response, defines roles and responsibilities, and lists the requirements for responding to and reporting incidents.

<agency> Information Security Incident Response Plan   <Date>

4

Incident Response Procedures: Written document(s) of the series of steps taken when responding to incidents.

Incident Response Program: Combination of incident response policy, plan, and procedures.

Information: Any knowledge that can be communicated or documentary material, regardless of its physical form or characteristics, including electronic, paper and verbal communication.

Information Security: Preservation of confidentiality, integrity and availability of information; in addition, other properties, such as authenticity, accountability, non-repudiation, and reliability can also be involved.

Information Security Event: An observable, measurable occurrence in respect to an information asset that is a deviation from normal operations.

Threat: A potential cause of an unwanted incident, which may result in harm to a system or the agency

Roles and Responsibilities

Note to agencies – These role descriptions come from the statewide information security policies and are presented here simply as an example. Agencies should adjust these descriptions as necessary to best meet their business environment and include any additional roles that have been identified in the agency that apply such as Security Officer, Privacy Officer, etc. Agencies need to identify roles, responsibilities and identify who is responsible for incident response preparation and planning, discovery, reporting, response, investigation, recovery, follow-up and lessons learned.

Staffing will be dependent on agency capabilities. The same person may fulfill one or more of these roles provided there is sufficient backup coverage. The following are suggested roles and responsibilities an agency should consider: incident response team members, incident commander, and agency point of contact to interface with the State Incident Response Team (required by statewide policy).

Agency Director	Responsible for information security in the agency, for reducing risk exposure, and for ensuring the agency's activities do not introduce undue risk to the enterprise. The director also is responsible for ensuring compliance with state enterprise security policies, standards, and security initiatives, and with state and federal regulations.
Incident Response Point of Contact	Responsible for communicating with State Incident Response Team (SIRT)and coordinating agency actions with SIRT in response to an information security incident.
Information Owner	Responsible for creating initial information classification, approving decisions regarding controls and access privileges, performing periodic reclassification, and ensuring regular reviews for value and updates to manage changes to risk.

| User | Responsible for complying with the provisions of policies, procedures and practices. |

Program

<detail on agency governance structure – identify who is responsible for managing information security incident response for the agency, who is responsible for developing policy, who is responsible for developing procedures, who is responsible for awareness, identification of any governing bodies such as management committees and work groups, etc. Include what information security incident response capabilities the agency has or identify outside resource and their capabilities. Include how agency will test plan and frequency. Include other related program areas such as business continuity planning, risk management, and privacy as they relate to incident response. >

Note to agencies –Procedures may in include Incident Reporting Procedures for staff, management, information technology, and Point of Contact.

The Incident Response Program is composed of this plan in conjunction with policy and procedures. The following documents should be reviewed for a complete understanding of the program:

1. <agency> Information Security Incident Response, Policy Number XXX-XX, located in Appendix <insert appendix number> at the end of this document.

2. <agency> Procedure: Information Security Incident Response, located in Appendix <insert appendix number> at the end of this document. The related flowchart for this procedure is found in Appendix <insert appendix number> at the end of this document.

Information security incidents will be communicated in a manner allowing timely corrective action to be taken. This plan shows how the <agency> will handle response to an incident, incident communication, incident response plan testing, training for response resources and awareness training

The Information Security Incident Response Policy, Plan, and procedures will be reviewed *<insert interval here, i.e. annually>* or if significant changes occur to ensure their continuing adequacy and effectiveness. Each will have an owner who has approved management responsibility for its development, review, and evaluation. Reviews will include assessing opportunities for improvement and approach to managing information security incident response in regards to integrating lessons learned, to changes to <agency's> environment, new threats and risks, business circumstances, legal and policy implications, and technical environment.

<u>Identification</u>

Identification of an incident is the process of analyzing an event and determining if that event is normal or if it is an incident. An incident is an adverse event and it usually implies either harm, or the attempt to harm the <agency>. Events occur routinely and will be examined for impact. Those showing either harm or intent to harm may be escalated to an incident.

<detail who is responsible for this step and the process that will be used>

The term "incident" refers to an adverse event impacting one or more <agency>'s information assets or to the threat of such an event Examples include but are not limited to the following:

- Unauthorized use
- Denial of Service

- Malicious code
- Network system failures (widespread)
- Application system failures (widespread)
- Unauthorized disclosure or loss of information
- Information Security Breach
- Other

Incidents can result from any of the following:

- Intentional and unintentional acts
- Actions of state employees
- Actions of vendors or constituents
- Actions of third parties
- External or internal acts
- Credit card fraud
- Potential violations of Statewide or <agency>'s Policies
- Natural disasters and power failures
- Acts related to violence, warfare or terrorism
- Serious wrongdoing
- Other

<u>Incident Classification</u>

Once an event is determined to be an incident, several methods exist for classifying incidents.

<detail who is responsible for this step and the process that will be used>

The following factors are considered when evaluating incidents:

- Criticality of systems that are (or could be) made unavailable
- Value of the information compromised (if any)
- Number of people or functions impacted
- Business considerations
- Public relations
- Enterprise impact
- Multi-agency scope

<u>Triage</u>

The objective of the triage process is to gather information, assess the nature of an incident and begin making decisions about how to respond to it. It is critical to ensure when an incident is discovered and assessed the situation does not become more severe.

<detail who is responsible for this step and the process that will be used>

- What type of incident has occurred
- Who is involved
- What is the scope
- What is the urgency
- What is the impact thus far
- What is the projected impact
- What can be done to contain the incident
- Are there other vulnerable or affected systems
- What are the effects of the incident
- What actions have been taken
- Recommendations for proceeding
- May perform analysis to identify the root cause of the incident

Evidence Preservation

Carefully balancing the need to restore operations against the need to preserve evidence is a critical part of incident response. Gathering evidence and preserving it are essential for proper identification of an incident, and for business recovery. Follow-up activities, such as personnel actions or criminal prosecution, also rely on gathering and preserving evidence.

<detail who is responsible for this step and the process that will be used>

Forensics

Note to agencies – in cases involving potential exposure of personally identifiable information it is recommended that technical analysis be performed.

In information security incidents involving computers, when necessary <agency> will technically analyze computing devices to identify the cause of an incident or to analyze and preserve evidence.

<agency> will practice the following general forensic guidelines:

- Keep good records of observations and actions taken.
- Make forensically-sound images of systems and retain them in a secure place.
- Establish chain of custody for evidence.
- Provide basic forensic training to incident response staff, especially in preservation of evidence

<detail who is responsible for this step and the process that will be used>

Threat/Vulnerability Eradication

After an incident, efforts will focus on identifying, removing and repairing the vulnerability that led to the incident and thoroughly clean the system. To do this, the vulnerability(s) needs to be clearly identified so the incident isn't repeated. The goal is to prepare for the resumption of normal operations with confidence that the initial problem has been fixed.

<detail who is responsible for this step and the process that will be used>

<u>Confirm that Threat/Vulnerability has been Eliminated</u>

After the cause of an incident has been removed or eradicated and data or related information is restored, it is critical to confirm all threats and vulnerabilities have been successfully mitigated and that new threats or vulnerabilities have not been introduced.

<detail who is responsible for this step and the process that will be used>

<u>Resumption of Operations</u>

Resuming operations is a business decision, but it is important to conduct the preceding steps to ensure it is safe to do so.

<detail who is responsible for this step and the process that will be used>

<u>Post-incident Activities</u>

An after-action analysis will be performed for all incidents. The analysis may consist of one or more meetings and/or reports. The purpose of the analysis is to give participants an opportunity to share and document details about the incident and to facilitate lessons learned. The meetings should be held within one week of closing the incident.

<detail who is responsible for this step and the process that will be used>

Education and Awareness

<agency> shall ensure that incident response is addressed in education and awareness programs. The programs shall address:

<Discuss training programs, cycle/schedule, etc. Identify incident response awareness and training elements – topics to be covered, who will be trained, how much training is required.>

<detail training for designated response resources>

Note to agencies – DAS has developed a suite of web-based user awareness modules. Additional modules are planned and currently Incident Response is targeted for early 2009. They are currently available to all state employees by accessing the state intranet and also are resident on the enterprise Learning Management System.

Communications

Note to agencies - Communication is vital to incident response. Therefore, it is important to control communication surrounding an incident so communications is appropriate and effective. Agencies should consider the following aspects of incident communication:
- ☐ *Define circumstances when employees, customers and partners may or may not be informed of the issue*
- ☐ *Disclosure of incident information should be limited to a need to know basis*
- ☐ *Establish procedures for controlling communication with the media*
- ☐ *Establish procedure for communicating securely during an incident*
- ☐ *Have contact information for the SIRT, vendors contracted to help during a security emergency, as well as relevant technology providers*

<agency> Information Security Incident Response Plan   <Date>

☐ *Have contact information for customers and clients in the event they are affected by an incident*

Because of the sensitive and confidential nature of information and communication surrounding an incident, all communication must be through secure channels.

<detail procedures for internal and external communications >

<detail how to securely communication, what is an acceptable method>

<detail who is responsible for communications and who is not authorized to discuss incidents>

Compliance

<agency> is responsible for implementing and ensuring compliance with all applicable laws, rules, policies, and regulations.

<detail agency compliance objectives and initiatives>

<list policies (statewide and agency, see authority section of plan), federal and state regulations), statutes, administrative rules that apply, etc.>

<All agencies are subject to the Identity Theft Prevention Act. Breaches as defined in the Identity Theft Prevention Act are only one type of an incident. If your agency is subject to the regulations list below for example, you should consider the following:

The Payment Card Industry-Data Security Standards requires entities to develop an Incident Response Plan, require organizations to be prepared to respond immediately to a breach by following a previously developed incident response plan that addresses business recovery and continuity procedures, data backup processes, and communication and contact strategies

HIPAA requires entities to implement policies and procedures to address security incidents, requires the creation of a security incident response team or another reasonable and appropriate response and reporting mechanism. Agencies subject to HIPAA should have both an incident response plan and an Incident response team, as well as a method to classify security incidents>

Specific to the Identity Theft Prevention Act agency plans should cover the following:

Consider potential communication channels for different circumstances, e.g., your plan may be different for an employee as opposed to a customer data breach.

* *Your human resources office*

* *Agency Public Information Officer (PIO)*

* *DAS Director's Office – 503-378-3104*

* *DAS Office Communication Manager – 503-378-2627*

* *State Chief Information Security Officer – 503-378-6557*

* *Department of Justice*

* *Oregon State Police – 503-378-3720 (ask for the Criminal Lieutenant)*

<agency> Information Security Incident Response Plan   <Date>

• *Other agencies that may be affected*

• *If security breach affects more than 1,000 consumers, contact all major consumer-reporting agencies that compile and maintain reports on consumers on a nationwide basis; inform them of the timing, distribution and content of the notification given to the consumers.*

• *Contact the credit monitoring bureaus in advance if directing potential victims to call them*
> *Equifax – 1-800-525-6285*
> *Experian – 1-888-397-3742*
> *TransUnion – 1-800-680-7289*

<agency> maintains personal information of consumers and will notify customers if personal information has been subject to a security breach in accordance with the Oregon Revised Statute 646A.600 - Identity Theft Protection Act. The notification will be done as soon as possible, in one of the following manners:

- Written notification
- Electronic, if this is the customary means of communication between you and your customer, or
- Telephone notice provided that you can directly contact your customer.

Notification may be delayed if a law enforcement agency determines that it will impede a criminal investigation.

If an investigation into the breach or consultation with a federal, state or local law enforcement agency determines there is no reasonable likelihood of harm to consumers, or if the personal information was encrypted or made unreadable, notification is not required.

Substitute notice
If the cost of notifying customers would exceed $250,000, that the number of those who need to be contacted is more than 350,000, or if there isn't means to sufficiently contact consumers, substitute notice will be given. Substitute notice consists of:

- Conspicuous posting of the notice or a link to the notice on your Web site if one is maintained, and
- Notification to major statewide Oregon television and newspaper media.

Notifying credit-reporting agencies
If the security breach affects more than 1,000 consumers <agency> will report to all nationwide credit-reporting agencies, without reasonable delay, the timing, distribution, and the content of the notice given to the affected consumers.

<The regulations listed above are provided as examples of compliance requirements and are not intended to be a complete listing.>

Implementation

<summary of initiatives, plans to develop tactical projects initiatives to meet plan components, including timelines, performance measures, auditing/monitoring requirements for compliance, etc.>

Approval

<approval sign off by agency decision makers, i.e. agency administrator, security officer, CIO, etc.>

By: _____

      Name, title   Date

By: _____

      Name, title   Date

APPENDIX E-4

Example of Agency Incident Response Plan

[Cover]

Agency

Incident Response Plan

EXAMPLE ONLY

Prepared by:

[Author Name]

[Title]

[Date]

Based on ISSA Model
Capitol of Texas Chapter

TABLE OF CONTENTS

FIGURES

TABLES

EXECUTIVE SUMMARY

The elements of a traditional agency computer security effort continue to be important and useful. Two trends necessitate the establishment of an incident response plan:

1) computers are widespread throughout the agency; the agency relies heavily on computers and cannot afford denial of service.

2) the agency computer systems and networks are at much higher risk to threats such as computer viruses, intrusions, and exposures.

The following examples of compute security incidents are now commonplace:

- A computer virus is copied to a LAN server; within minutes hundreds of other computers are infected; recovery takes several people and several days.

- Backups infected with viruses result in re-infected systems, requiring more time and expense.

- Vulnerabilities in software are discovered that permit unauthorized entry; explicit instructions on how to exploit the vulnerability become quickly known...

- System intruders copy password files and distribute them throughout large networks.

- Break-ins through international networks require cooperation of different government agencies.

- Outbreaks of viruses or system penetrations appear in the press, causing embarrassment and possible loss of public confidence.

These situations can cause the agency to face unnecessary expense in productivity, significant damage to systems, and damage to our reputation. Clearly, the need now exists to take action prior to suffering the consequences of a serious computer security problem.

[*AGENCY*] INCIDENT RESPONSE PLAN

1.0   Introduction

1.1 Purpose of the Incident Response Plan

An Incident Response Plan is required in order to bring needed resources together in an organized manner to deal with an adverse event related to the safety and security of an *Agency* Computer Resources. This adverse event may be malicious code attack, unauthorized access to *Agency* systems, unauthorized use of *Agency* services, denial of service attacks, general misuse of systems, or hoaxes.

1.2 Purpose of the Incident Response Team

The purpose of *Agency*'s Incident Response Team is to:
- Protect *Agency*'s Information assets,
- Provide a central organization to handle incidents
- Comply with requirements,
- Prevent the use of *Agency*'s systems in attacks against other systems (which could cause us to incur legal liability),
- Minimize the potential for negative exposure.

1.3 Objectives of the Incident Response Team

The objectives of *Agency*'s Incident Response Team are to:
- Limit immediate incident impact to customers and partners
- Recover from the incident,
- Determine how the incident occurred,
- Find out how to avoid further exploitation of the same vulnerability,
- Avoid escalation and further incidents,
- Assess the impact and damage in terms of financial impact, loss of image etc.
- Update policies and procedures as needed,
- Determine who initiated the incident.

2.0   Incidents

2.1 Incident Categories

An incident will be categorized as one of three severity levels. These severity levels are based on the impact to *Agency* and can be expressed in terms of financial impact, impact to services and/or performance of our mission functions, impact to *Agency*'s image or impact to trust by *Agency*'s customers, etc. Table 1 provides a listing of the severity levels and a definition/description of each severity level.

Severity Level	Description
Low	Incident where the impact is minimal. Examples are harmless e-mail SPAM, isolated Virus infections, etc.
Medium	Incident where the impact is significant. Examples are a delayed ability to provide services, meet agency's mission, delayed delivery of critical electronic mail or EDI transfers, etc.
High	Incident where the impact is severe. Examples are a disruption to the services, and/or performance of our mission functions. *Agency* proprietary of confidential information has been compromised, a virus or worm has become wide spread and is affecting over ____% of employees, or *Agency* Executive management has reported it.

Table 1: Severity Levels

3.0   Responding to an incident

There are generally six stages of response:

1. Preparation—one of the most important facilities to a response plan is to know how to use it once it is in place. Knowing how to respond to an incident BEFORE it occurs can save valuable time and effort in the long run.

2. Identification—identify whether or not an incident has occurred. If one has occurred, the response team can take the appropriate actions.

3. Containment—involves limiting the scope and magnitude of an incident. Because so many incidents observed currently involve malicious code, incidents can spread rapidly. This can cause massive destruction and loss of information. As soon as an incident is recognized, immediately begin working on containment.

4. Eradication—removing the cause of the incident can be a difficult process. It can involve virus removal, conviction of perpetrators, or dismissing employees.

5. Recovery—restoring a system to its normal business status is essential. Once a restore has been performed, it is also important to verify that the restore operation was successful and that the system is back to its normal condition.

6. Follow-up—some incidents require considerable time and effort. It is little wonder, then, that once the incident appears to be terminated there is little interest in devoting any more effort to the incident. Performing follow-up activity is, however, one of the most critical activities in the response procedure. This follow-up can support any efforts to prosecute those who have broken the law. This includes changing any company policies that may need to be narrowed down or be changed altogether.

3.1 Organization

To adequately respond to an intrusion or incident, predetermined teams will participate depending on the incident characteristics. As the situation develops and the impact becomes more significant, the various teams will be called to contribute. Figure 1 depicts the Incident Response organization.

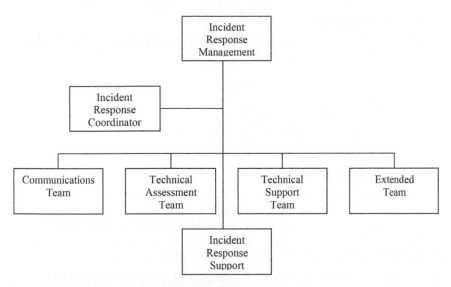

Figure 1: Incident Response Organization

3.2 Escalation Levels

As the incident has more impact (severity level increases), the escalation process will be invoked to involve appropriate resources. Incidents should be handled at the lowest escalation level that is capable of responding to the incident with as few resources as possible in order to reduce the total impact, and to keep tight control. Table 2 defines the escalation levels with the associated team involvement.

Escalation Level	Affected Team(s)	Description
0	■ Technical Assessment Team	Normal Operations. Engineering groups monitoring for alerts from various sources
1	■ Technical Assessment Team ■ Incident Response Coordinator ■ Communication Team	A threat has been discovered, determine defensive action to take. Message employees of required actions if necessary.
2	■ Incident Response Management ■ Incident Response Coordinator ■ Technical Assessment Team ■ Technical Support Team ■ Communications Team	A threat has manefested itself. Determine course of action for containment and erradication. Message employees of required actions if necessary.
3	■ Incident Response Management ■ Incident Response Coordinator ■ Extended Team ■ Technical Assessment Team ■ Technical Support Team ■ Communications Team ■ Incident Response Support Team	Threat is wide spread or impact is significant. Determine course of action for containment and erradication. Message employees. Prepare to take legal action.

Table 2: Escalation Levels

3.3 Escalation Considerations

Incident Response Management will consider several characteristics of the incident before escalating the response to a higher level. They are:

- How wide spread is the incident?
- What is the impact to business operations?
- How difficult is it to contain the incident?
- How fast is the incident propagating?
- What is the estimated financial impact to *Agency*?
- Will this affect *Agency*'s image negatively?

3.4 The Incident Response Process

The Incident Response Process is an escalation process where as the impact of the incident becomes more significant or wide spread, the escalation level increases bringing more resources to bear on the problem. At each escalation level, team members who will be needed at the next higher level of escalation are alerted to the incident so that they will be ready to respond if and when they are needed.

Figure 2 depicts the overall process, while paragraph 3.5 outlines the roles and responsibilities of individual teams. Team membership is contained in Appendix A.

3.5 Incident Response Team Roles and Responsibilities

3.5.1   Escalation Level 0

Technical Assessment Team

1. Monitors all known sources for alerts or notification of a threat. These sources are listed in Appendix B.

3.5.2   Escalation Level 1

A Possible threat has been discovered.

Technical Assessment Team

1. Determine initial defensive action required,
2. Notify the Incident Coordinator,
3. If employee action required such as updating aniti-virus files, notify the Help Desk.

Incident Coordinator

1. Receive and track all reported potential threats,
2. Escalate Incident Response to Level 2 if a report is received indicating that the threat has manefested itself,
3. Determine relevant membership of the Technical Assessment and Technical Support teams,
4. Alert I/T organizatons and applicable support organizations of the potential threat and any defensive action required,
5. Alert Incident Response Management of the potential threat,
6. Alert the Communication team.

Communications Team

1. If employee action required, message employees of required action.

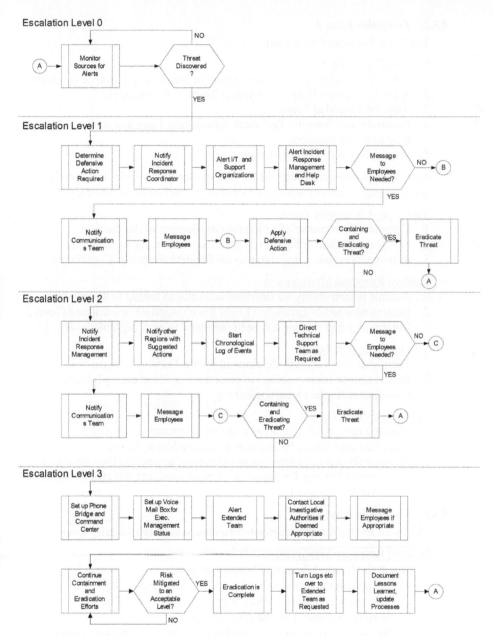

Figure 2: Incident Response Process

3.5.3 Escalation Level 2

The threat has manefested itself.

Incident Coordinator
1. Notify Incident Response Management of the manefestation of the threat,
2. Alert the Incident Response Support Team of the incident,
3. Alert the Extended Team,
4. Receive status from the Technical Assessment Team and report to Incident Response Management,
5. Start a chronological log of events.

Note: The chronological log will be used to support possible follow on legal action as determined by *Agency*'s General Counsel and Executive Director.

Technical Assessment Team
1. Determine best course of action for containment of the incident,
2. Notify the Technical Support Team of any action that is required,
3. Report actions taken and status to the Incident Response Coordinator.

Incident Response Management
1. Assume responsibility for directing activities in regard to the incident,
2. Determine whether Escalation Level 2 is appropriate or escalate to level 3,
3. Determine when the risk has been mitigated to an acceptable level.

Technical Support Team
1. Take what ever action as determined by the Technical Assessment Team
2. Report actions taken, number of personnel involved etc. to Incident Coordinator for the chronological log

Communications Team
1. Message the *Agency* employee population informing them of the incident if deemed appropriate by Incident Response Management,
2. Message the *Agency* employee population of any action they need to take as determined by the Technical assessment team and directed by Incident Response Management.

3.5.4 Escalation Level 3

The threat has become widespread or has become a high severity level.

Incident Response Management
1. Direct the Incident Response Support team to:
   - Set up communications between all Incident Response Team Managers, and the Techncal Support Team in the field,
   - Assume occupancy of the command center.
   - Initialize an incident voice mail box where status messages can be placed to keep *Agency* personnel statused.
2. Alert the Extended Team of the incident notifying them of the Severity Level,
3. Determine when the risk has been mitigated to an acceptable level,
4. Status Executive Management as appropriate.

Extented Team

1. Contact local authorities if deemed appropriate,
2. If local authorities are called in, make arrangements for them to be allowed into the command center
3. Ensure that all needed information is being collected to support legal action or financial restitution.

Incident Response Coordinator

1. Continue maintaining the Chronological Log of Event
2. Post numbered status messages in the incident voice mail box for statusing *Agency* executive management.

Communication Team

1. Message the *Agency* population as directed by Incident Response Management

Technical Assessment Team

1. Continue to monitor all know sources for alerts looking for further information or actions to take to eliminate the threat,
2. Continue reporting status to the Incident Response Coordinator for the chronological log of events,
3. Monitor effectiveness of actions taken and modify them as necessary,
4. Status Incident Response Management on effectiveness of actions taken and progress in eliminating the threat,

Technical Support Team

1. Continue actions to eradicate the threat as directed by Incident Response Management and the Technical Assessment team,
2. Continue to report actions taken, number of personnel etc. to the Incident Response Coordinator for the chronological log.

3.5.5   *Post Incident*

Incident Response Management

1. Prepare a report for *Agency* Executive Management to include:
    * Estimate of damage/impact,
    * Action taken during the incident (not technical detail),
    * Follow on efforts needed to eliminate or mitigate the vulnerability,
    * Policies or procedures that require updating,
    * Efforts taken to minimize liabilities or negative exposure.
2. Provide the chronological log and any system audit logs requested by the Extended Team,
3. Document lessons learned and modify the Incident Response Plan accordingly.

Extended Team

1. Legal and Finance work with the local authorities as appropriate in the case that the incident was from an external source,
2. HR and Security work with *Agency* management to determine disciplinary action in the case that the incident was from an internal source.

APPENDIX A. CONTACT LISTS

Incident Response Teams

Incident Response Management

Organization	Contact Name	Phone Numbers

Incident Response Coordinator

Organization	Contact Name	Phone Numbers

Technical Assessment Team

Organization	Contact Name	Phone Numbers

Technical Support Team

Organization	Contact Name	Phone Numbers

Incident Response Support Team

Organization	Contact Name	Phone Numbers

Communications Team

Organization	Contact Name	Phone Numbers

Extended Team

Organization	Contact Name	Phone Numbers

Business Functions Contacts

Organization	Contact Name	Phone Numbers

Regional Contacts

IBU	Contact Name	Phone Numbers

External Support Contacts

Organization	Contact Name	Phone Numbers
Department of Public Safety (for Capitol Complex)	Sergent James Jordon	512-463-3478
Special Crime Services, Department of Public Safety (all other areas of State)	Commander Enrique Garcia	512-424-2200, Ext. 3030
Austin FBI Office	Supervisory Resident Agent Rick Copeland	(512) 345-1111
San Antonio FBI Computer Crime Squad	Senior Agent Robert Nino	(210) 225-6741
Austin High Tech Crime Unit	Senior Police Officer Harlan Scales	(512) 458-0405

APPENDIX B. LIST OF SOURCES FOR ALERTS OR NOTIFICATION OF A THREAT

Source	Responsibility to Monitor
ASSIST—Automated Systems Security Incident Support Team ftp://ciac.llnl.gov.pub/ciac/secdocs/assist	
BUGTRAQ—A mailing list designed for the detailed and open discussion of security vulnerabilities in UNIX systems. http://www.eecs.nwu.edu/~jmyers/bugtraq/index.html	
CERT—In response to computer security threats, the Advanced Research Projects Agency (ARPA) established the Computer Emergency Response Team (CERT) Coordination Center to support users of the Internet. http://www.cert.org	
CERT-NL—CERT-NL is the SURFnet Computer Emergency Response Team which deals with computer and network security incidents related to hacking, vulnerabilities and viruses. ftp://ftp.nic.surfnet.nl/surfnet/net-security/cert-nl/docs/bulletin/	
CIAC—The U.S. Department of Energy's Computer Incident Advisory Capability. Established in 1989, CIAC provides computer security services to employees and contractors of the Department of Energy. http://ciac.llnl.gov/cgi-bin/index/bulletins	
Sun Microsystems Security Advisories for Sun Workstations gopher://fas-gopher.harvard.edu/11/.abcd/.security/.sun	
8LGM—An organization that provides security advisories about weakness in various Unix Operation Systems. 8LGM provides detailed explanations about how security holes can be exploited. http://www.8lgm.org/advisories.html	
NT BugTraq—NTBugtraq is a mailing list for the discussion of security exploits and security bugs in Windows NT and its related applications. NTBUGTRAQ@LISTSERV.NTBUGTRAQ.COM	
Microsoft Security Advisory—Discusses Security vulnerabilities in all Microsoft products and has patches available. http://www.microsoft.com/security/default.asp	
ANSIR Advisory—National Infrastructure Protection Center (NIPC) Information System Advisory	
ZDNet http://www.zdnet.com/	
ISS Xforce http://xforce.iss.net/	
Symantic Anti-Virus Support	

Alert—The Alert will be covering the following topics: • Security Product Announcements • Updates to Security Products • New Vulnerabilities found • New Security Frequently Asked Question files. • New Intruder Techniques and Awareness majordomo@iss.net	
Bugtraq • Information on Unix related security holes/backdoors (past and present) • Exploit programs, scripts or detailed processes about the above • Patches, workarounds, fixes • Announcements, advisories or warnings • Ideas, future plans or current works dealing with Unix security • Information material regarding vendor contacts and procedures • Individual experiences in dealing with above vendors or security organizations • Incident advisories or informational reporting LISTSERV@NETSPACE.ORG	
Computer Underground Digest—Covers many issues of the computer underground CU-DIGEST-REQUEST@WEBER.UCSD.EDU	
Firewalls—This list is for discussions of Internet "firewall security" systems and related issues. majordomo@lists.gnac.net	
INFSEC-L Information Systems Security Forum—Discussions of information systems security and related issues listserv@etsuadmn.etsu.edu	
Intrusion Detection Systems—The list is a forum for discussions on topics related to development of intrusion detection systems. Topics include: • techniques used to detect intruders in computer systems and computer networks • audit collection/filtering • subject profiling • knowledge based expert systems • fuzzy logic systems • neural networks • methods used by intruders (known intrusion scenarios) • cert advisories • scripts and tools used by hackers • computer system policies • universal intrusion detection system majordomo@uow.edu.au	
NT Security—Mailing list discussing Windows NT security as well as the Windows 95/98 and Windows For Work Group security issues. The issues discussed will be everything at the host and application level security as well as at the network level.	

NETWORK DDOS INCIDENT RESPONSE CHEAT SHEET

Tips for responding to a network distributed denial-of-service (DDoS) incident.

General Considerations

DDoS attacks often take the form of flooding the network with unwanted traffic; some attacks focus on overwhelming resources of a specific system.

It will be very difficult to defend against the attack without specialized equipment or your ISP's help.

Often, too many people participate during incident response; limit the number of people on the team.

DDoS incidents may span days. Consider how your team will handle a prolonged attack. Humans get tired.

Understand your equipment's capabilities in mitigating a DDoS attack. Many under-appreciate the capabilities of their devices, or overestimate their performance.

Prepare for a Future Incident

If you do not prepare for a DDoS incident in advance, you will waste precious time during the attack.

Contact your ISP to understand the paid and free DDoS mitigation it offers and what process you should follow.

Create a whitelist of the source IPs and protocols you must allow if prioritizing traffic during an attack. Include your big customers, critical partners, etc.

Confirm DNS time-to-live (TTL) settings for the systems that might be attacked. Lower the TTLs, if necessary, to facilitate DNS redirection if the original IPs get attacked.

Establish contacts for your ISP, law enforcement, IDS, firewall, systems, and network teams.

Document your IT infrastructure details, including business owners, IP addresses and circuit IDs; prepare a network topology diagram and an asset inventory.

Understand business implications (e.g., money lost) of likely DDoS attack scenarios.

If the risk of a DDoS attack is high, consider purchasing specialized DDoS mitigation products or services.

Collaborate with your BCP/DR planning team, to understand their perspective on DDoS incidents.

Harden the configuration of network, OS, and application components that may be targeted by DDoS.

Baseline your current infrastructure's performance, so you can identify the attack faster and more accurately.

Analyze the Attack

Understand the logical flow of the DDoS attack and identify the infrastructure components affected by it.

Review the load and logs of servers, routers, firewalls, applications, and other affected infrastructure.

Identify what aspects of the DDoS traffic differentiate it from benign traffic (e.g., specific source IPs, destination ports, URLs, TCP flags, etc.).

If possible, use a network analyzer (e.g. tcpdump, ntop, Aguri, MRTG, a NetFlow tool) to review the traffic.

Contact your ISP and internal teams to learn about their visibility into the attack, and to ask for help.

If contacting the ISP, be specific about the traffic you'd like to control (e.g., blackhole what networks blocks? rate-limit what source IPs?)

Find out whether the company received an extortion demand as a precursor to the attack.

If possible, create a NIDS signature to focus to differentiate between benign and malicious traffic.

Notify your company's executive and legal teams; upon their direction, consider involving law enforcement.

Mitigate the Attack's Effects

While it is very difficult to fully block DDoS attacks, you may be able to mitigate their effects.

Attempt to throttle or block DDoS traffic as close to the network's "cloud" as possible via a router, firewall, load balancer, specialized device, etc.

Terminate unwanted connections or processes on servers and routers and tune their TCP/IP settings.

If possible, switch to alternate sites or networks using DNS or another mechanism. Blackhole DDoS traffic targeting the original IPs.

If the bottle neck is a particular a feature of an application, temporarily disable that feature.

If possible, add servers or network bandwidth to ha... the DDoS load. (This is an arms race, though.)

If possible, route traffic through a traffic-scrubbing service or product via DNS or routing changes.

If adjusting defenses, make one change at a time, so you know the cause of the changes you may observ...

Configure egress filters to block the traffic your syst... may send in response to DDoS traffic, to avoid addi... unnecessary packets to the network.

Wrap-Up the Incident and Adjust

Consider what preparation steps you could have tak... to respond to the incident faster or more effectivel...

If necessary, adjust assumptions that affected the decisions made during DDoS incident preparation.

Assess the effectiveness of your DDoS response process, involving people and communications.

Consider what relationships inside and outside you... organizations could help you with future incidents.

Key DDoS Incident Response Steps

1. Preparation: Establish contacts, define proced... and gather tools to save time during an attack.

2. Analysis: Detect the incident, determine its sc... and involve the appropriate parties.

3. Mitigation: Mitigate the attack's effects on the targeted environment.

4. Wrap-up: Document the incident's details, dis... lessons learned, and adjust plans and defense...

Additional DDoS Response References

Denial-of-Service Attack-Detection Techniques
http://www.computer.org/portal/site/dsonline...

A Summary of DoS/DDoS Prevention, etc. Techniq...
http://sans.org/reading_room/whitepapers/intrusion/121...

Network Protocols and Tools Cheat Sheets
http://packetlife.net/cheatsheets/

ITICAL LOG REVIEW CHECKLIST FOR
URITY INCIDENTS

heat sheet presents a checklist for reviewing
l logs when responding to a security incident. It
so be used for routine log review.

ral Approach

entify which log sources and automated tools
u can use during the analysis.

py log records to a single location where you
ill be able to review them.

inimize "noise" by removing routine, repetitive
g entries from view after confirming that they
e benign.

termine whether you can rely on logs' time
amps; consider time zone differences.

cus on recent changes, failures, errors, status
anges, access and administration events, and
her events unusual for your environment.

backwards in time from now to reconstruct
tions after and before the incident.

rrelate activities across different logs to get a
mprehensive picture.

velop theories about what occurred; explore
s to confirm or disprove them.

tial Security Log Sources

and workstation operating system logs

tion logs (e.g., web server, database server)

y tool logs (e.g., anti-virus, change detection,
n detection/prevention system)

nd proxy logs and end-user application logs

ber to consider other, non-log sources for
events.

l Log Locations

S and core applications: /var/log

s OS and core applications: Windows Event
curity, System, Application)

Network devices: usually logged via Syslog; some use
proprietary locations and formats

What to Look for on Linux

Successful user login	"Accepted password", "Accepted publickey", "session opened"
Failed user login	"authentication failure", "failed password"
User log-off	"session closed"
User account change or deletion	"password changed", "new user", "delete user"
Sudo actions	"sudo: … COMMAND=…" "FAILED su"
Service failure	"failed" or "failure"

What to Look for on Windows

Event IDs are listed below for Windows 2000/XP. For
Vista/7 security event ID, add 4096 to the event ID.

Most of the events below are in the Security log;
many are only logged on the domain controller.

User logon/logoff events	Successful logon 528, 540; failed logon 529-537, 539; logoff 538, 551, etc
User account changes	Created 624; enabled 626; changed 642; disabled 629; deleted 630
Password changes	To self: 628; to others: 627
Service started or stopped	7035, 7036, etc.
Object access denied (if auditing enabled)	560, 567, etc

What to Look for on Network Devices

Look at both inbound and outbound activities.

Examples below show log excerpts from Cisco ASA
logs; other devices have similar functionality.

Traffic allowed on firewall	"Built … connection", "access-list … permitted"

Traffic blocked on firewall	"access-list … denied", "deny inbound"; "Deny … by"
Bytes transferred (large files?)	"Teardown TCP connection … duration … bytes …"
Bandwidth and protocol usage	"limit … exceeded", "CPU utilization"
Detected attack activity	"attack from"
User account changes	"user added", "user deleted", "User priv level changed"
Administrator access	"AAA user …", "User … locked out", "login failed"

What to Look for on Web Servers

Excessive access attempts to non-existent files

Code (SQL, HTML) seen as part of the URL

Access to extensions you have not implemented

Web service stopped/started/failed messages

Access to "risky" pages that accept user input

Look at logs on all servers in the load balancer pool

Error code 200 on files that are not yours

Failed user authentication	Error code 401, 403
Invalid request	Error code 400
Internal server error	Error code 500

Other Resources

Windows event ID lookup: www.eventid.net

A listing of many Windows Security Log events:
ultimatewindowssecurity.com/…/Default.aspx

Log analysis references: www.loganalysis.org

A list of open-source log analysis tools:
securitywarriorconsulting.com/logtools

Anton Chuvakin's log management blog:
securitywarriorconsulting.com/logmanagementblog

Other security incident response-related cheat
sheets: zeltser.com/cheat-sheets

INITIAL SECURITY INCIDENT QUESTIONNAIRE FOR RESPONDERS

Tips for assisting incident handlers in assessing the situation when responding to a qualified incident.

Understand the Incident's Background

What is the nature of the problem, as it has been observed so far?

How was the problem initially detected? When was it detected and by whom?

What security infrastructure components exist in the affected environment? (e.g., firewall, anti-virus, etc.)

What is the security posture of the affected IT infrastructure components? How recently, if ever, was it assessed for vulnerabilities?

What groups or organizations were affected by the incident? Are they aware of the incident?

Were other security incidents observed on the affected environment or the organization recently?

Define Communication Parameters

Which individuals are aware of the incident? What are their names and group or company affiliations?

Who is designated as the primary incident response coordinator?

Who is authorized to make business decisions regarding the affected operations? (This is often an executive.)

What mechanisms will the team to communicate when handling the incident? (e.g., email, phone conference, etc.) What encryption capabilities should be used?

What is the schedule of internal regular progress updates? Who is responsible for them?

What is the schedule of external regular progress updates? Who is responsible for leading them?

Who will conduct "in the field" examination of the affected IT infrastructure? Note their name, title, phone (mobile and office), and email details.

Who will interface with legal, executive, public relations, and other relevant internal teams?

Assess the Incident's Scope

What IT infrastructure components (servers, websites, networks, etc.) are directly affected by the incident?

What applications and data processes make use of the affected IT infrastructure components?

Are we aware of compliance or legal obligations tied to the incident? (e.g., PCI, breach notification laws, etc.)

What are the possible ingress and egress points for the affected environment?

What theories exist for how the initial compromise occurred?

Does the affected IT infrastructure pose any risk to other organizations?

Review the Initial Incident Survey's Results

What analysis actions were taken to during the initial survey when qualifying the incident?

What commands or tools were executed on the affected systems as part of the initial survey?

What measures were taken to contain the scope of the incident? (e.g., disconnected from the network)

What alerts were generated by the existing security infrastructure components? (e.g., IDS, anti-virus, etc.)

If logs were reviewed, what suspicious entries were found? What additional suspicious events or state information, was observed?

Prepare for Next Incident Response Steps

Does the affected group or organization have specific incident response instructions or guidelines?

Does the affected group or organization wish to proceed with live analysis, or does it wish to start formal forensic examination?

What tools are available to us for monitoring network or host-based activities in the affected environment?

What mechanisms exist to transfer files to and from affected IT infrastructure components during the analysis? (e.g., network, USB, CD-ROM, etc.)

Where are the affected IT infrastructure components physically located?

What backup-restore capabilities are in place to as in recovering from the incident?

What are the next steps for responding to this inci (Who will do what and when?)

Key Incident Response Steps

1. Preparation: Gather and learn the necessary t become familiar with your environment.

2. Identification: Detect the incident, determine scope, and involve the appropriate parties.

3. Containment: Contain the incident to minimi effect on neighboring IT resources.

4. Eradication: Eliminate compromise artifacts, necessary, on the path to recovery.

5. Recovery: Restore the system to normal operations, possibly via reinstall or backup.

6. Wrap-up: Document the incident's details, re collected data, and discuss lessons learned.

Additional Incident Response Reference

Incident Survey Cheat Sheet for Server Administra
http://zeltser.com/network-os-security/security-incident-survey-cheat-sheet.html

Windows Intrusion Discovery Cheat Sheet
http://sans.org/resources/winsacheatsheet.pdf

Checking Windows for Signs of Compromise
http://www.ucl.ac.uk/cert/win_intrusion.pdf

Linux Intrusion Discovery Cheat Sheet
http://sans.org/resources/linsacheatsheet.pdf

Checking Unix/Linux for Signs of Compromise
http://www.ucl.ac.uk/cert/nix_intrusion.pdf

CURITY INCIDENT SURVEY CHEAT SHEET
R SERVER ADMINISTRATORS

for examining a suspect system to decide
ther to escalate for formal incident response.

essing the Suspicious Situation

etain attacker's footprints, avoid taking actions that
ss many files or installing tools.

at system, security, and application logs for
sual events.

at network configuration details and connections;
anomalous settings, sessions or ports.

at the list of users for accounts that do not belong
ould have been disabled.

at a listing of running processes or scheduled jobs
nose that do not belong there.

for unusual programs configured to run
matically at system's start time.

k ARP and DNS settings; look at contents of the
 file for entries that do not belong there.

for unusual files and verify integrity of OS and
cation files.

network sniffer, if present on the system or
able externally, to observe for unusual activity.

tkit might conceal the compromise from tools;
your instincts if the system just doesn't feel right.

ine recently-reported problems, intrusion
tion and related alerts for the system.

u Believe a Compromise is Likely...

e an incident response specialist for next steps,
otify your manager.

t panic or let others rush you; concentrate to
making careless mistakes.

ping an on-going attack, unplug the system from
etwork; do not reboot or power down.

horough notes to track what you observed, when,
nder what circumstances.

ows Initial System Examination

t event logs   eventvwr

Examine network configuration	arp -a, netstat -nr
List network connections and related details	netstat -nao, netstat -vb, net session, net use
List users and groups	lusrmgr, net users, net localgroup administrators, net group administrators
Look at scheduled jobs	schtasks
Look at auto-start programs	msconfig
List processes	taskmgr, wmic process list full
List services	net start, tasklist /svc
Check DNS settings and the hosts file	ipconfig /all, ipconfig /displaydns, more %SystemRoot%\ System32\Drivers\etc\hosts
Verify integrity of OS files (affects lots of files!)	sigverif
Research recently-modified files (affects lots of files!)	dir /a/o-d/p %SystemRoot%\ System32

Avoid using Windows Explorer, as it modifies useful file
system details; use command-line.

Unix Initial System Examination

Look at event log files in directories (locations vary)	/var/log, /var/adm, /var/spool
List recent security events	wtmp, who, last, lastlog
Examine network configuration	arp -an, route print
List network connections and related details	netstat -nap (Linux), netstat -na (Solaris), lsof -i
List users	more /etc/passwd
Look at scheduled jobs	more /etc/crontab, ls /etc/cron.*, ls /var/at/jobs
Check DNS settings and the hosts file	more /etc/resolv.conf, more /etc/hosts

Verify integrity of installed packages (affects lots of files!)	rpm -Va (Linux), pkgchk (Solaris)
Look at auto-start services	chkconfig --list (Linux), ls /etc/rc*.d (Solaris), smf (Solaris 10+)
List processes	ps aux (Linux, BSD), ps -ef (Solaris), lsof +L1
Find recently-modified files (affects lots of files!)	ls -lat, find / -mtime -2d -ls

Incident Response Communications

Do not share incident details with people outside the
team responding to the incident.

Avoid sending sensitive data over email or instant
messenger without encryption.

If you suspect the network was compromised,
communicate out-of-band, e.g. non-VoIP phones.

Key Incident Response Steps

1. Preparation: Gather and learn the necessary tools, become familiar with your environment.

2. Identification: Detect the incident, determine its scope, and involve the appropriate parties.

3. Containment: Contain the incident to minimize its effect on neighboring IT resources.

4. Eradication: Eliminate compromise artifacts, if necessary, on the path to recovery.

5. Recovery: Restore the system to normal operations, possibly via reinstall or backup.

6. Wrap-up: Document the incident's details, retail collected data, and discuss lessons learned.

Other Incident Response Resources

Windows Intrusion Discovery Cheat Sheet
http://sans.org/resources/winsacheatsheet.pdf

Checking Windows for Signs of Compromise
http://www.ucl.ac.uk/cert/win_intrusion.pdf

Linux Intrusion Discovery Cheat Sheet
http://sans.org/resources/linsacheatsheet.pdf

Checking Unix/Linux for Signs of Compromise
http://www.ucl.ac.uk/cert/nix_intrusion.pdf

ored by Lenny Zeltser, who leads a security consulting team at SAVVIS, and teaches malware analysis at SANS Institute. Special thanks for feedback to Lorna Hutcheson, Patrick Nolan, Raul Siles, oudis, Donald Smith, Koon Yaw Tan, Gerard White, and Bojan Zdrnja. Creative Commons v3 "Attribution" License for this cheat sheet v. 1.7. More cheat sheets?

Index

329

Printed and bound by CPI Group (UK) Ltd, Croydon, CR0 4YY

03/10/2024

01040341-0010